AF257387

# Looking for Elizabeth

# Looking for Elizabeth

The Life of
Elizabeth Harrower

## Helen Trinca

LA TROBE
UNIVERSITY PRESS

IN CONJUNCTION WITH BLACK INC.

Published by La Trobe University Press in conjunction with Black Inc.
Wurundjeri Country
22–24 Northumberland Street
Collingwood VIC 3066, Australia
enquiries@blackincbooks.com
www.blackincbooks.com
www.latrobeuniversitypress.com.au

La Trobe University plays an integral role in Australia's public intellectual life, and is recognised globally for its research excellence and commitment to ideas and debate. La Trobe University Press publishes books of high intellectual quality, aimed at general readers. Titles range across the humanities and sciences, and are written by distinguished and innovative scholars. La Trobe University Press books are produced in conjunction with Black Inc., an independent Australian publishing house. The members of the LTUP Editorial Board are Vice-Chancellor's Fellows Emeritus Professor Robert Manne and Dr Elizabeth Finkel, and Morry Schwartz and Chris Feik of Black Inc.

Copyright © Helen Trinca, 2025
Helen Trinca asserts her right to be known as the author of this work.

ALL RIGHTS RESERVED.
No part of this publication may be reproduced, stored in a retrieval system, or transmitted in any form by any means electronic, mechanical, photocopying, recording or otherwise without the prior consent of the publishers.

9781760645755 (paperback)
9781743824153 (ebook)

 A catalogue record for this book is available from the National Library of Australia

Cover design by Beau Lowenstern
Text design and typesetting by Aira Pimping
Cover image by Ferdinand H. Nolte, courtesy of Linda Nolte
Index by Garry Cousins

*To Jo Trinca, 1925–2020*

# Contents

# Introduction

THE CARRIAGEWORKS CREATIVE HUB IN THE INNER SYDney suburb of Eveleigh is a cavernous space housed in an old railway workshop. Art, theatre and music events and festivals compete with harsh industrial architecture. It's a difficult space for relatively intimate events and on 14 December 2015 it proved a poor choice for the annual presentation of the Prime Minister's Literary Awards. It was a particularly hot and sticky evening for the writers, publishers and journalists gathered for drinks and the announcement by Prime Minister Malcolm Turnbull.

The stand-up event was noisy and crowded and 87-year-old Elizabeth Harrower was struggling. Someone had found the writer a seat, but she was not happy. It was difficult to hear, and the heat was enervating. But as she waited for the prime minister to arrive, Harrower was excited. Her fifth novel, *In Certain Circles*, was shortlisted in the fiction category and many thought she had a good chance of taking out the $80,000 prize. It was a fine book, and it came with a compelling backstory: Harrower had completed it forty-five years earlier but had refused publication and stashed the manuscript away in her archive at the National Library of Australia. The belated publication of this 'lost' Australian novel had been a minor literary sensation that year and Harrower's profile had risen. She had never quite recovered from missing out on another prestigious literary prize, the Miles Franklin, for her 1966 novel,

*The Watch Tower.* A win now, half a century later, would go a long way to healing that wound.

But it was not to be: Turnbull announced as the winner the West Australian novelist Joan London, for *The Golden Age.* Harrower knew London and rated her highly but was a little disappointed. The award would have capped a remarkable late-age renaissance for a writer who had turned her back on her typewriter and her talent in the 1970s.

As the formalities ended, Harrower was impatient to leave; she caught a cab alone back to her flat in Cremorne on the other side of Sydney Harbour. She was tired and slept fitfully, but by morning she had recovered her equilibrium. She was not about to let this rejection dent her delight at the second act she was experiencing. 'I'm tough,' she told her publisher, Text's Michael Heyward, when he telephoned her a few hours later.

Indeed, she was. Elizabeth Harrower had had a long and challenging life, but she had never lost faith in her books – and the messages they held for the world.

1

—

## A Divorced Child

WHAT A DIFFERENCE A NAME MAKES. ELIZABETH Harrower's 1928 birth certificate recorded the baby born to parents Francis and Margaret as 'Betty'. That's how she was known to her family for all her ninety-two years – a good, old-fashioned name; one might even say a working-class one. No pretension. Not even a second name. Indeed, Betty seemed a half-hearted effort from young parents who had married a scant nine months before her birth. A plain name for a baby who may have been conceived out of wedlock, a short name for an addition to two families building their futures in the New South Wales industrial city of Newcastle.

It would be decades before Betty became Elizabeth and more years still before her birth certificate was officially changed. That she bothered with the paperwork in 2012 at the age of eighty-four underlines how serious she was about the presentation of her story as she moved from the Newcastle of coal and steel and brickworks to the intellectual milieu of Sydney and beyond.[1]

It is easy to portray that journey to the elite literary circles of twentieth-century Australia as a scramble out of the working class. Both sides of her family had Scottish heritage. Elizabeth's mother, Margaret Burns Hughes, born on 15 July 1909 and known as Daisy, had immigrated as a child with her mother, Helen, and two younger brothers in 1920 at the age of eleven. Daisy's father, Robert, had arrived a few months earlier and worked in Queensland before finding a job at BHP in Newcastle, where the family joined him. Elizabeth's father, Francis Sharp Hastings Harrower, was born in Australia on 14 August 1906, to Scots migrant David Harrower and Catherine, who had also been born in Australia and was therefore known as a 'colonial'.

In the early years of the twentieth century in suburbs close to the BHP steelworks, these two, largely immigrant, families were surrounded by people with the same Scots accents and customs. Elizabeth's grandfathers were ironworkers but hers was not a strictly working-class childhood. Her maternal grandmother, Helen, ran small private women's hospitals and boarding houses; her paternal grandmother, Catherine, taught Elizabeth the piano and urged her to get an education. In 1928, when Elizabeth was born, her mother's people were still finding their way around the class divisions in a country closely connected to Britain, but the Harrowers were more established in their solid brick-and-tile home in Church Street, Mayfield. Australia was in the grip of the Great Depression and faced the possibility of another war, but Frank Harrower had steady work. He spent time in the merchant navy before getting a post with good job security on the railways. Elizabeth would understand early in her life that she was different from the children who walked shoeless to school. Elizabeth's mother, Daisy, spent her teenage years with her parents and two younger brothers, James and Robert, in their somewhat chaotic Newcastle household. Daisy's father was a hard worker but also an alcoholic, and it was her mother who kept the show on the road with her 'residentials' and the hospitals she at times ran, which may well have offered abortions for women otherwise driven to dangerous backyard operators.

It's not clear where Frank and Daisy met, but by the time they married – on 14 May 1927, at the Presbyterian Manse in Mayfield – she was living in Bellbird, 50 kilometres from Newcastle, carrying out domestic duties. Frank was not yet twenty-one, Daisy still only seventeen, and they needed their fathers' permission to wed. Elizabeth was born on 8 February the following year, by which time it is likely the couple was living in the Hughes household. The new family was happy enough until 1935, when Frank was transferred to a station called Tamban Loop, 300 kilometres from Newcastle. He was ambitious and diligent, an upright man who was keen to get ahead on the railways, but promotion meant doing time at often isolated hamlets. However, his young wife refused to move with him to Tamban Loop.

Frank was desperate to keep his family together but could not convince Daisy to join him in the bush, and in November 1936 he began divorce proceedings on the grounds of her desertion. In turn, she accused him of adultery. Back then, long before no-fault divorce was introduced in the 1970s, the state supreme court cross-examined the parties to apportion blame and decide whether a couple would be permitted to divorce. The system was saturated with religious and moral expectations, and the damage done to individuals forced into lengthy court actions was profound. In March 1937, a young woman alleged to have slept with Frank in a hotel in Tamban Loop was named in public notices in *The Daily Telegraph* and *The Sun*. The ads were designed to flush her out and force her to give evidence so a judge could decide if Frank was an adulterer.

The divorce proceedings were delayed, but Daisy was ambitious and determined to build a bigger life. In 1937, she moved to Sydney to train as a nurse at the Royal Hospital for Women in Paddington. Nine-year-old Elizabeth was parked in Newcastle with her maternal grandparents and her two young adult uncles, one of whom was a successful amateur boxer and the other a sweet-natured lad who played the mouth organ and taught her to whistle. With both parents missing, Elizabeth also spent time with the Harrowers, including Frank's younger sister, Adell, an accomplished competition pianist. She grew fond of Aunty Dell, who was just sixteen years older than her.

As a little girl, Elizabeth had hazel eyes and long brown plaits and was tall for her age and generation – she would reach 5′8″ as an adult. She had mixed feelings about school, but spent most of her time writing letters, including to her absent parents. She liked to learn and was a born writer. 'I did it terrifically and I was dimly aware too that I took the opportunity to write letters to girlfriends or anyone who seemed to be willing to have a letter and dimly aware that they would look at me in some surprise,' Elizabeth recalled in 2012. 'I was really writing and practising. Wrote reams of diaries.'[2] She was brought up as a 'word child'.[3]

Her parents' divorce case was still unresolved in 1938 when Frank, working at Casino, 500 kilometres north of Newcastle, again tried to save the marriage. He convinced Daisy and Elizabeth to join him for a fortnight in the January holidays. But Casino was hot and distant, and reconciliation proved impossible. Frank tried again the following year when he was stationed at Murrurundi in the Upper Hunter, closer to Newcastle. Daisy was set to join him, and had hopes of setting up a private hospital there, but on the way to the town heard Frank had been unfaithful and pulled the plug. So, in 1939, three years after their initial separation, Frank launched a fresh action, asking for the restoration of conjugal rights as the first step to a divorce based on his wife's refusal to cohabit.

Daisy was working at St Luke's Hospital in Sydney as an obstetrics nurse and was not about to return to the marriage. In 1940, she enrolled Elizabeth as a boarder at Manly Grammar School for Girls so she could see more of the twelve-year-old. The young girl hated the school, high on the cliffs above the ocean, and missed her mother living across the harbor. Finally, in October 1940, Frank Harrower was granted a decree nisi – the first step in the divorce proceedings. The decree absolute was granted on 21 August 1941. Elizabeth would record that event in her calendar diary every year for decades, a reminder of a trauma that had marked her childhood. Years later she said that 'youth, hard times, separations and families at odds with each other' all contributed to her parents' failed marriage, yet she found it hard to accept.[4]

Elizabeth recalled: 'All I can say is that I was a divorced child ... and I was the only divorced child, really. I think it is very sad for children, especially when there are no other divorced children. It was just unheard of really and children can be very, very mean to other children if they are not identical, very mean.'[5] She struggled for years with the stigma of absent parents and newspaper reports of the divorce. She never forgot the shame she endured as a child.

Frank was now all but physically absent from his daughter's life, although he continued to write to her and to pay alimony to Daisy and maintenance for Elizabeth until she turned sixteen in 1944. That alone marked him as an honourable man at a time when women were often left penniless because their ex-husbands refused payments.

Elizabeth's childhood was filled with conflicting emotions. 'Everything was irregular because I was moving about,' she recalled.[6]

Her maternal grandparents, with whom she lived for several years, moved house several times. It was an unhappy household. Her grandfather Robert was drunk almost every weekend and accused his wife of 'playing up' or 'carrying on' with various men. Despite the chaos, Elizabeth displayed an 'enthusiastic disposition', which she put down to genetics: 'If anyone ever discusses nature over nurture, I think nature, nature, nature. As the Dickens character says, cheerfulness kept breaking through, which to me is a bit mysterious.'[7]

She may have inherited that optimism from her maternal grandmother, whom she called MumMum – the larger-than-life, energetic Scot who built businesses, liked men and married three times. Helen was a canny operator, known to many as 'Nurse' (although it's not clear what training she had), who was successful enough to employ maids in her boarding houses. She was a diligent migrant, saving to buy a house and moving up in her new country.

Her drunken husband was a liability, and she threw him out just after Easter in 1939, when Elizabeth was still living with them, and sued for divorce. The child had already suffered through years of her parents' divorce proceedings and in 1940 the two divorces overlapped. Grandparents Helen and Robert Hughes were in court in Newcastle on 3 October; parents Margaret and Frank Harrower were in the same court on 22 October. Elizabeth had had a front-row seat for these humiliating legal processes – although in 1940, at boarding school in Manly, she was quarantined from local gossip.

In court that October, Helen alleged her husband was a drunk and that the household was at the mercy of his moods. She testified that on one occasion her husband 'seemed to lose control of his reason altogether. He went into the bathroom, took off his clothes, and came out with only a sheet on, without having a wash … He was always making these allegations [of adultery] and making my life a hell. Family members told the court that even when he was not 'under the influence' the situation at home was one of 'armed neutrality'. Cut and dried one would think, but the judge refused a divorce. Instead, Helen was charged with perjury over a white lie, placed on a good behaviour bond and forced to begin new proceedings, finally winning a divorce in 1943 on the grounds of desertion'.[8]

Warring parents and grandparents, two very public divorces, alcoholism, adultery, boarders and patients; it's not surprising that in later life Elizabeth did not want to talk about her childhood. She was not exaggerating when she told me in 2012 that she had seen 'an awful lot of unhappy marriages when I was quite young'. From an early age she understood the tragedies played out behind the front doors of Australian homes. The power games of marriage became a core theme of her fiction, along with the emotional neglect of children. When her parents 'deserted' her in Newcastle, the little girl was devastated. One night when she was about nine, she lay on the road waiting for a car to run her over.[9]

Was her childhood really so wretched? Towards the end of her life, Elizabeth offered a mixed commentary. Sometimes she painted herself as the abandoned child who lived in 'many different houses, with different sets of relatives, and attended many different schools, including boarding school, which I hated'.[10] At other times she was part of a warm Newcastle unit: 'From the time I was a baby, my grandmother filled me with tales of the Old Country. The snow, wee witches, Hallowe'en, Robbie Burns, folksongs, and magic.'[11] Uncle Robert, her mother's brother, who was seventeen, was 'very good to me'; he bought her Easter eggs and joined her in board games. She had limited contact with her father after he went to Tamban Loop in 1935 when she was seven, but her mother was present till she went to Sydney in 1937 to work as a trainee nurse. It's not clear how much time her mother spent in Newcastle in the next couple of years although in April 1939 she gave her address as Newcastle. But by the start of the school year in 1940, Elizabeth, about to turn twelve, had left the industrial city for her Manly boarding school. Her mother was living at Roslyn Gardens, in Kings Cross. Neither she nor Elizabeth would live permanently in Newcastle again.

The Hughes clan was strongly connected to their Scottish family. Elizabeth recalled: 'From early on in the war when I was twelve or thirteen, I wrote to Steph [a second cousin], and we sent parcels to Britain. There was some sort of campaign to send food that wasn't perishable to relatives in Britain. So, this whole family belonged to my grandmother, my mother and me, and I was very pleased about it.'[12]

In contrast, Harrower rarely spoke of her father's relatives, yet it seems she saw them when she lived in Newcastle. She visited her grandmother Catherine's house in Mayfield, where she had a warm relationship with Aunty Dell, who had won eisteddfods and achieved honours in piano exams. In many ways Elizabeth had a conventional Australian childhood:

I was a suburban child, I suppose, although the [Newcastle] suburb was close to the Hunter River and the bush was round about and we used to go down there sometimes and look about, but I think I felt more at home in suburban streets, probably. We used to go to the beach, and I liked swimming, I could always swim, and I had holidays in the country, and I loved the country when I got there, liked the fresh air. I seem to remember always being outside and roaming around. I was cheerful and liked company, liked people, people were always very important to me.[13]

The young Elizabeth loved words and her mother read to her from *Alice in Wonderland*, *Grimm's Fairy Tales*, Peter Pan and Wendy. There were lots of stories, but never Australian ones. Ethel Turner's classic, *Seven Little Australians*, had been very popular since its publication in 1894 and there was a burgeoning nationalism around Australian culture, but many parents were still more attached to Britain.

*Elizabeth as a child in Newcastle.*

'I can't remember learning to read,' Elizabeth told Hazel de Berg in an oral history recording in 1967. 'It seems I could always read, really, and then I read newspapers and labels, anything that was printed I read, and still do.' Indeed, print was everywhere, making sense of the world. No one writer, but all writers, had messages, and Elizabeth was eager to hear them. She was convinced she had messages of her own to relay. At the age of eight she submitted her first piece to a children's paper. The editors told her to keep trying. 'And so, I kept trying. But when I think that nobody encouraged me to do it, and there was always a lot of turmoil going on around, I'm surprised that I had that much initiative.'[14]

From her earliest years Elizabeth had a strong sense of the value of her mind and her work. People might let her down, but words would always save her. 'I can't think who I would be if I hadn't read so much when I was very, very young,' she told ABC broadcaster Ramona Koval in a radio interview in 2013.

> I … felt very clever with words even as a child. Pencils, writing letters: at a very early age, I just felt that it was my thing that I could do, I suppose … I wanted everyone to know my deepest feelings and I can only imagine what they might have been when I was ten or so. I always took to the pen and paper when, say, school friends went to hospital with appendicitis, or somebody won the lottery. Any opportunity for me to write a letter, I took it.[15]

During World War II, Elizabeth watched soldiers leaning from the carriages of troop trains drop scraps of paper bearing their names in the hope someone would write to them. Elizabeth did, often stuffing letters into bottles that she released into the ocean, believing that someone, somewhere, would respond. The child also sent countless letters of complaint to her separated parents. 'I wanted them to know exactly what was going on and what I thought about it,' she told writer Giulia Giuffrè in a 1985 interview. Letter writing became an obsession. It was second nature for writers to put things on paper, she said, almost 'like doing daily physical jerks'.[16] As an adult, she acknowledged that a lonely childhood was a prerequisite for a novelist and that an unhappy childhood was a great help to a writer. 'Most of them, most that I know, were either lonely or misunderstood … and they were often great readers, they tended always to like books and to have been read to as children.'

But her childhood dogged her. Jinx Nolan, whose parents, artist Sidney Nolan and Cynthia Nolan, were close friends of Elizabeth's, recalled her as 'very protective of her past … the older she gets, the less she is interested in talking about it'. Elizabeth's friend, the journalist and photographer, Sally McInerney, told me: 'I don't remember Elizabeth ever talking about her personal past – there was always a feeling that although her life was like a very welcoming house with many rooms, there were some rooms which visitors should not try to enter.'

Elizabeth certainly did not want to talk about her father. After her parents' divorce, she saw Frank rarely, in part because he worked in the bush. But he never stopped attempting to contact her. It was not easy. His new wife, Elma, was not keen for him to see his daughter. Elma was eighteen years younger than Frank and it was a difficult partnership. Their daughter, Yvonne, Elizabeth's half-sister, recalled the secret correspondence: 'Letters would come from Betty and he would take them and read them but they would never be shared. I never knew who they were from.'

There was more disruption for Elizabeth in 1941, when her mother re-partnered with a man seventeen years her senior: Richard Herbert Kempley. He had been married previously in the UK and had two adult sons – Richard, born in 1912, and Jack, born in 1918. Richard senior, who was born in 1892, had spent several years in the British navy before arriving in Australia.[17]

When Daisy Harrower, now known by her birth name of Margaret, met Kempley he was a man on the way up but he came with baggage. Mystery surrounds Kempley's early years in Australia. It was an era when people could assume new identities, leave spouses behind and move to another town to set up a new life. It appears he was operating as an accountant when he met Daisy, but it's likely he had a more colourful backstory. There is no record of a Kempley marriage at that time and it is likely Richard never divorced his first wife. He and Margaret may have begun living together in Sydney in 1940 once the Harrower decree nisi was granted. Whatever their legal status, the Kempleys presented as a respectable family and Richard delivered financially as he set up a new life for his wife and stepdaughter in Sydney.[18]

# 2

# Sydney: The War Years

ELIZABETH HARROWER WAS TWELVE WHEN SHE MOVED to Sydney and left behind the difficult years as the 'divorced child' who had faced careless, sometimes neglectful, adults. In the city she had her mother back, even if she had to share her with her stepfather. It was a fresh start, one that allowed the family to move into a middle-class world of white-collar jobs, suburban lawns and respectability.

Elizabeth was enchanted by the physical beauty of the city – its beaches, its inner-city flats where singles and young marrieds pursued a slightly bohemian lifestyle, its wealthy, lush suburbs sweeping along both sides of the harbour. Sydney, with its population of 1.5 million, offered a level of privacy, anonymity even, which had been impossible in Newcastle, and the Kempleys gradually shed their old lives. Over the next few years they lived in Manly, Balgowlah and Cammeray. Along the way, Elizabeth gained first-hand experience of the gritty world of Kings Cross when the family rented apartments there when they were between houses.

The city, even in war time, was much more interesting than Newcastle, and the household was calmer than her grandmother's 'residentials' even if Elizabeth had to navigate dangerous emotional terrain and witness a less-than-ideal marriage. Since childhood, Kempley, whom Elizabeth called Uncle Dick, had been a difficult person. Whipped by his father and sent off to the Greenwich Naval Academy as a schoolboy in 1906, he carried emotional scars. Elizabeth and her mother forged an alliance to counter his moods and dominance. Grandmother Helen noted that her daughter 'had a terrible time with R'.[1]

As a teenager, Elizabeth buried herself in books and developed a passion for the public library in the Queen Victoria Building. It was built over an old brewery and the smell of hops and malt lingered. She told me she read in an 'enthusiastic and greedy way' and worked her way through the collection, looking for the key to life: 'One great book led to another great book. I read hugely. There was nothing anyone could mention that I hadn't read, it was food and drink to me.' She marvelled at the stories of people such as dancer Isadora Duncan and actor Ellen Terry, at their strength and eccentricity, and wondered how they had broken out of the rigid roles imposed on them by society.

In many ways, Elizabeth was cocooned from the world, protected by a stepfather who was building his accountancy business and selling real estate. He does not seem to have been in a hurry for Elizabeth to join the workforce: he could afford to support her.

When Elizabeth was about sixteen, there was money for her first domestic airflight and in December the family holidayed in Hobart. On Christmas Day, they threw snowballs on Mount Wellington, drove all over the mountains and dined in a spot where the waitresses wore gloves and headdresses.[2] There was money too for specialised attention for her teenage acne; Elizabeth consulted a dermatologist for x-ray treatment, a common cure for adolescent spots in the late 1940s and early 1950s but not one every family could afford. She visited her relatives in Newcastle, on one occasion being photographed in the garden of the Harrower family home in Church Street, her long plaits tied neatly with ribbons.

Elizabeth made friends in Sydney but felt slighted when others did not value her insights. As a teenager she was naive and socially awkward, yet certain that she understood human behaviour more than most. She continued the habit of reading that would remain throughout her life, finding wisdom in writers such as Karen Blixen, the Russian novelists, Ibsen and Shakespeare: 'I think we could sit down with Shakespeare and the ancients and not read another book and we'd be much wiser at the end. Because they knew everything, really, and we just have to find it out all over again – probably not as well. But they knew first.'[3]

In her teenage years, Elizabeth had to cope with a challenge to the respectable life the Kempleys had created. She never spoke of it, but in 1944 a Richard Herbert Kempley was convicted, along with three others, of buying and selling liquor above the prices that had been legislated during the war, sentenced to three years and sent to Long Bay Gaol.[4] Was Margaret Kempley referring to this scandal when she told Elizabeth twenty years later that while 'silly things may have been done in the past', Richard had, in effect, gone straight since then?[5]

On Elizabeth's seventeenth birthday in February 1945, as the Yalta conference prepared for an end to the war in Europe, Margaret presented her daughter with a copy of a small book called *The White Cliffs*, by Alice Duer Miller, inscribing it: 'To Betty, with love from Mum.' It was a long poem which, according to the dust jacket, expressed 'completely and beautifully what many Americans feel about England in this dark hour'. The book had been a huge hit in the United States, and many people heard it read on radio by actor Lynn Fontanne. Elizabeth treasured her copy.

The teenager wondered about her future. 'I had a good opinion of my IQ,' she told broadcaster Ramona Koval in 2013. 'So, I was often taking myself off to places in Sydney where they could test you on this, that or the next thing, and it always seemed to be a good result, except in manual tasks. I wasn't so good at ... those ... I'd come away feeling quite pleased but not quite knowing what to do with myself, and these people who took money neverthe-less didn't have any good ideas for you about what you might do.' She did, however, learn to touch type, and that skill would prove useful for a life of writing.

While Elizabeth was well read, she did not go to university. Later in life she suggested to me this was because university was only open to girls 'whose fathers were judges or specialists'. In the 1940s only a fraction of Australians – 0.2 per cent – were at univer-sity and women comprised about 20 per cent of that group.[6] It was indeed not open to all, but Elizabeth's comment, made when she was in her eighties, revealed a sensitivity towards class and privilege: something she would explore in her novels. Instead of university she took night courses in semantics and history (the reading list included Philip Boswood Ballard's *Thought and Language* and Bertrand Russell's *An Inquiry into Meaning and Truth*), comparative philology and linguistics. She studied for three years from 1947 while working at a fashion factory, McGinley & Carpenter, in Pitt Street, Sydney. At nineteen, it was her first real job, and her duties included opening and closing the workroom each day; helping customers who sought advice on fashion; and pricing, invoicing and dispatching goods. The hours were long, but it was a 'very jolly, pleasant' atmosphere, and the tall, slender youngster often modelled dresses for clients.[7]

*Elizabeth during her trip to Mount George*

About this time, Elizabeth visited her father and his new wife and baby sons at Mount George, about 200 kilometres from Newcastle, where Frank was the relief stationmaster and later ran the small local store. But by now her father was almost a stranger.

Back in Sydney, she was thrilled by a city so in love with life:

The war-time brown-out ended, and all the lights came on. The city was full of returning troops, new ideas, new people, and hope. There was a feeling in the air, to quote D.H. Lawrence inappropriately: Look! We have come through! In my memory, later, everything about the city was ravishing – the light, the glorious day. The harbour … had hospital ships, troop ships and working ships, and it was all highly significant, and the streets even after the war were crammed with soldiers, people coming back from the war. The city was filled with life and people were discovering things. After the war inventions came and it was quite exciting … There were small numbers of European migrants, and they brought little interesting things to the arcades, the Imperial, His Majesty's, the Hotel Australia. You surged in there and everything was available to everyone.[8]

There were other changes: her grandmother Helen remarried and Uncle Rob, who had taught her to whistle, was killed in Sandakan, Borneo, in 1945. Her father's second family expanded but Elizabeth did not meet her half-siblings – Yvonne, Francis and David. Aunty Dell married and had two children – Verity and Thurza – but Elizabeth did not get to know her cousins till later.

By 1951 Richard Kempley was wealthy enough to plan a grand tour of Scotland and England, departing in March. The family would visit Margaret's Aunty Minnie and other Scottish relatives, as well as Richard's family in England. Europe was also on the itinerary for this year-long trip. For Richard and Margaret, both migrants, the journey home was proof of their financial success in Australia.

Travel to the UK had been restricted during the war, but now Australians headed to the old country to see family and visit a place many knew only from films or postcards. Flights were expensive and most chose to make the six-and-a-half-week trip by ship, booking passages for about $2000 in today's value. The journey served also as a holiday and a chance to visit exotic ports. The 23-year-old Elizabeth travelled with her parents, unlike many young women who made the trip with friends or alone, keen for a working holiday in London.

Elizabeth was excited: the last few years had been 'rather a dull, tedious, horrible period, over which we'll draw a veil, before I was lucky enough to leave the country when I was 23'.[9] She was curious about her Scottish heritage, although she had no intention of remaining in the UK.

On 5 January, about three months before sailing, Elizabeth had a day off work from the fashion factory. She told her diary: 'Most welcome. Work has been too fraught with emotion for me. Talked to Mum for ages & dressed very slowly to go to town. Read a couple of very nice letters from Aunty Minnie. Went to town – paid Drs bill – changed some gloves … Mum & I read this afternoon. After dinner I wrote to Steph and Aunty Minnie. All excited about the trip. 12 weeks to go. Will we get there? I wonder.'

Although she had grown up thinking of Scotland as her second home, Elizabeth had mixed feelings about leaving Sydney. She had developed a deep fondness for her boss, the slightly older

Miss Maclean, and the idea of leaving her behind was too much to bear. She was jealous when Miss Maclean spent time talking to her immediate manager, Mr Carpenter. 'Every second day I seem to have a grievance about something,' Elizabeth wrote in her diary. She felt deserted, ate lunch alone, grew 'as mad as a hatter' and admitted she was too fond of Miss Maclean 'for my own good'. The women shopped for shoes at Farmers department store. When Miss Maclean revealed her fiancé had been offered a new job, Elizabeth was devastated: 'Anything may happen next. Guess she'll leave work soon – may even go abroad anytime. I hate change – I always do … Hate the thought of Miss Maclean leaving or going away … I feel shut out and hate it … I feel so sad tonight.' Elizabeth was in her early twenties, yet almost childish in her desperation. She had had a miserable time in her early years and her need for affection and approval was obvious.

The Kempleys were now living in Cowdroy Avenue, Cammeray, just across the harbour from the Sydney CBD. Sometimes Elizabeth and her mother drove with Richard and sat in the car while he showed a property to his real estate clients. Sometimes the women headed to town to select fabric for a beach coat or a sundress. Elizabeth bought gloves, read books, saw films with her mother: *Summer Stock*, *Annie Get Your Gun* and *Flamingo Road*. One day the women went to a friend's home while Richard listened to the horse races on the radio. 'We tried on our frocks and talked and played poker of all things in the evening,' Elizabeth reported in her diary. Mother and daughter were almost like older and younger sister.

Elizabeth was emotionally dependent on her mother and when Margaret went to hospital for an operation on her leg, she was sure 'something awful' would happen. She wrote in her diary that 'It's no fun without Mumma'. But the big drama was taking place at her workplace, where her affection for Miss Maclean played havoc with her emotions. On 29 March, her last day at work, she stood in the office and cried so hard she was almost ill: 'When you don't have many people it's hard to leave someone you are so fond of.'

In the 1950s, the departure of cruise vessels was celebrated in style, with friends and relatives allowed on board to sip bubbly in the cabins before farewelling the travellers. Elizabeth wondered if she would survive the ordeal. 'Loads of people came to see us off – but I only saw Miss Maclean,' she wrote in her diary. 'I felt I just couldn't bear to leave her – the moment when everyone had to go to shore was ghastly. The streamers, the music playing, the tears & the heartbreak. I held onto Miss Maclean – I felt I might never see her again. I'm afraid I might change – or she might. Anything could happen & I really can hardly bear to think that when I come back everything will be different.'

These words sound like those used for a lover. Elizabeth wrote them twelve days into the journey from Sydney. She had had time to settle her emotions but also time for disappointment. In an era when people exchanged letters as easily as we send email and when snail mail was delivered quickly across the continent, Elizabeth hoped for letters from her old boss. When the ship reached Adelaide, there were no fewer than three 'beautiful' letters from Miss Maclean waiting for her. But at Fremantle there was no mail: 'The thing that stands out in my mind about today is the hurtful & surprising fact that I didn't hear from Miss Maclean at all – I absolutely counted on her & feel really sick with disappointment tonight. I wonder why she didn't write … The bottom seemed to have fallen out of the world – my whole inside feels flattened.'

What are we to make of these emotions? Crushing on slightly older women like Miss Maclean is not unusual for teenage girls, but at twenty-three Elizabeth's passion was intense. There is no suggestion she saw this as anything other than a platonic friendship, but her feelings were raw. Perhaps it was not surprising: throughout her life Elizabeth displayed strong emotions. Her mother told her 'You are so intense' and Elizabeth noted: 'I do understand life, and generally, with intensity ... Even now, everything impinges.'[10] In a 1980 interview with Jim Davidson, editor of the literary journal *Meanjin*, she agreed there was a 'concentration and intensity' in her work: 'But I think it's natural, it's my only natural way of writing. And if I sometimes launch into something that doesn't demand it, things don't work out well. It's simply the wrong voice.'

The ship ploughed on and the passengers grew bored. Sun frocks, big hats and bathing suggested glamour, but the onboard routine was a relentless round of meals, quoits, darts and table tennis. Everyone changed for dinner, where salads were suddenly on the menu. But later there was little to do except march around the deck to stave off the tedium before flopping back into deck chairs. There was tension as Richard and Margaret quarrelled, and Elizabeth noted: '[Richard] was in a bad way and wanted to argue about anything. So, he did. Then he marched off to have a drink. Mum nearly had a stroke – I've never seen her so annoyed.' Margaret had had enough and decided she and Elizabeth would disembark at Colombo and take a ship back to Australia. Interestingly, she had the financial independence to do so, which suggests Richard had transferred funds to his wife. The women had 'quite a bit of money in our own names'. They arranged their exit with the purser, but when Richard realised, he had the 'biggest fright of his career' and apologised. The women dropped their plan and the voyage proceeded smoothly.[11]

This cycle of marital rupture followed by reconciliation made a deep impression on Elizabeth. Richard's capacity for what we now call coercive control was startling. It added to Elizabeth's childhood memories of the shame of her parents' divorce and the chaos of her grandparents' marriage. Her stepfather was financially dominant and emotionally manipulative – a dreadful combination – and Elizabeth wondered if she would ever escape to a more peaceful world.

As the voyage continued, she made friends with other single women on board and joined them for drinks in the assistant surgeon's cabin. She was still crushing on Miss Maclean and hanging out for a letter as the ship neared Colombo. Her happiness depended 'wholly & solely on a letter from Miss Maclean which I hope to heavens I'll receive'. With its perfume of cinnamon flowers Colombo proved exotic, but the travellers were exhausted by the 'number of natives following us, begging or coaxing us into shops. They were horrible ... I felt ill at night.' There was no word from her former boss. Elizabeth fired off a telegram and told her diary: 'I'll go into a decline if I don't hear from her soon.'

Then Lady Bedingfeld joined the ship in Bombay. She was a great traveller, an independent woman who was 'fair, pretty & very English', and Elizabeth was smitten. She told her diary:

> She adores travelling, has just spent weeks in Karachi – has been
> to America three times since the war – also to the West Indies.
> France for dress shows & the Grand Prix & a chalet there last

Xmas. I have been completely fascinated listening to her. I heard about Monte Carlo … I heard about the Taj Mahal & the Canadian Rockies – about deep sea fishing in the West Indies & trout fishing in Kashmir … We talked about Russia & Communism & the East & about religion … Lady Bedingfeld is very interested in writing & has written a couple of books – but didn't enlarge on the subject … She is very sweet & has such a girlish enthusiastic way of saying things.

So, another small crush on an exotic, older woman? Elizabeth's excitement at meeting this liberated Englishwoman was palpable. She sensed her life opening up. For years she had read about a world outside Australia, but she had been hesitant and unworldly and lacked the natural confidence of girls from a more privileged, moneyed class. Now Australia felt 'like another planet, like the moon, so separate from the rest of the world'. Elizabeth had been diffident about leaving Sydney, but by the time the ship left Bombay she had decided 'never to return to Australia'.[12] As the sea journey drew to a close, the young woman confided to her diary: 'I don't feel a bit like going home after the holiday is over – I may stay in London and work there and travel around.' It was a decision that would define much of her adult life.

# 3

# Scotland: A New World

IN THE 1950S, GREAT BRITAIN EXERTED A SIGNIFICANT pull upon Elizabeth Harrower, as it did on many of her contemporaries. Elizabeth had grown up with stories from her mother and grandmother about Kelty and Paisley in Scotland and the family they had left behind there. On 12 May 1951, when she saw the English coast, Elizabeth felt like waving flags and breaking into tears at the same time. It was 'a tremendously touching moment', she wrote in her diary. The ship docked at Tilbury, and within a couple of days the Kempley trio were with their relatives at Alloa on the north bank of the Forth in the Central Lowlands. There was much talk and a host of gatherings and outings. Elizabeth found a book of ballads, picked the tunes out on the piano and sang throughout the house – 'My Heart's in the Highlands' and 'Blue Bonnets Over the Border'.[1] Her Scots ancestry was important to her – all grandparents and great-grandparents, bar one, came from Scotland and 'news of ancient relatives was told to me as a child'.[2] She had been surrounded by Scottish accents in Newcastle and now felt at home in Scotland.

The visitors revelled in scenery that was very different from that of Australia, and in the sense of history. They trooped to Edinburgh to see Judy Garland perform live, but when the three Australians took a trip up the Clyde it was a fiasco. They were badly organised and caught the wrong steamer. Richard, displaying familiar tetchiness, was 'in no mood to help', Elizabeth complained to her diary. More successful was a visit to Peebles to see the 'glorious country' near the Tweed River. There were more trips to Edinburgh for concerts and theatres and days spent at Inverness and Lairg.

Through it all Elizabeth was in awe of, if not slightly in love with, her second cousin, Margaret Dick, who was twelve years older, single and a civil servant in Glasgow. Margaret was a bright woman who may have worked at the code-busting base at Bletchley Park during the war. She spoke excellent French and had close connections in France and, during the war, with the Free French movement based in London. Elizabeth was drawn to this relative who 'doesn't talk down to me' and conversed about books and writing with aplomb. In her diary she wrote: 'I wish I could speak to her on more equal terms. I just don't know enough to hold up my end of the conversation.'

On a trip with the extended family to Loch Alsh in the Highlands, the others were 'a bit miserable' but Elizabeth was happy just talking to Margaret, whom she saw as a kindred spirit: 'What fun to find another human being! … We talked for ages – & it's the nicest possible feeling to find you are related to someone who is uncannily like yourself.' Conversation with Margaret was exhilarating and Elizabeth sensed that a life of the mind was within her grasp. 'All week I've been reading Plato's *Republic* – and it has opened up new worlds for me!' she reported to her diary. 'It's so beautifully logical and reasonable – it was like listening to a dear friend lecturing on a subject that I'd known and loved once & forgotten.'

The crush on her Sydney boss, Miss Maclean, was fading, and Elizabeth wrote to her to say she probably would not go back to Australia, although she was not yet certain. She told her diary:

I want, in my inner heart, to stay very much, if I discover the right job & have means of studying. I would like to matriculate & take a degree in psychology. But whether such things are possible or not – I can't say. I'd like to talk it over with Margaret when she comes home on Saturday. Of course, I don't like the idea of being so far from Mum – I hate to think how I'll feel the day she goes back. [But]I feel that this is my only hope of a life of my own – if I make mistakes in it – at least they'll be my own. I was so completely in the wrong element at home & I would be again if I went back. Ruts are almost impossible to escape & I can see the old life stretching out like an octopus to engulf and drag me down. To have seen freedom & go back to that life would be madness.

Her parents planned a trip to London, but Elizabeth resisted: 'Don't feel like going to London with Mum and UD [Uncle Dick].' On the way south with her stepfather and mother she was gloomy. England was 'not half as nice' as Scotland, she told her diary, and the car journey was marked by 'appalling seaside and industrial towns' on the way to York. 'It was dull, tiring & depressing. Mum seemed exhausted.' Richard was 'in a very bad temper – wouldn't ever stop for morning or afternoon tea & hardly for lunch without an argument'. In London her mother was 'acting like Hamlet – maybe because I'm staying [in the UK] – maybe she's ill – I don't know'. The idea of parting was tough for both women who were just eighteen years apart in age. Her stepfather, however, was on Elizabeth's side, telling her to stay in the UK. Perhaps he could sense mother and daughter were too close, and that Elizabeth needed to break away in order to mature; perhaps he wanted his wife to focus on him alone.

In September, Elizabeth was at the family home in Alloa and was determined to remain in the UK. Margaret Dick was relocating to Edinburgh for work, and Elizabeth wrote in her diary: 'When I went to see her off in the train I felt completely deserted & most unhappy. There's no doubt that I am more like Margaret than anyone else I've ever known & seem to understand her because our minds work in the same way. Though she knows a terrific amount more than I do. It's such a comforting feeling to be like someone else for a change.' She helped Margaret move to a new room in Edinburgh and hoped she could get a room there herself. 'Will miss Margaret very much,' she told her diary.

Six months earlier, Elizabeth had been devastated when she left Miss Maclean. Now she was enthralled by another older woman. There was a pattern here and she would later use her novels to interrogate the relationships between older and younger sisters and older and younger women. She was interested in exploring friendships that gave the younger woman the courage to break free of coercive behaviour or limiting environments. But in 1951 she had no thought of being a novelist. Instead, she headed to the continent with her parents, to tour France, Switzerland, Germany and Italy, including a fortnight in Capri. She longed for letters from Margaret, and when her cousin wrote on 16 September noted: 'Thank heavens!'

What was it about Margaret Dick at thirty-five that so captivated Elizabeth? One attraction was surely her ability to be in the world, to hold seriously important jobs and yet to reserve a part of herself from the daily grind. Another was that Margaret was a huge reader.

Elizabeth's affection was reciprocated. Margaret was the more powerful person at this time, but years later she would say it was Elizabeth who gave her the courage to begin writing novels.

Elizabeth was looking for models for how to live, searching for an identity, and Margaret was someone who loved life yet had 'the disposition of a scholar'. Words and language mattered to Margaret, just as they were central to Elizabeth's efforts to make sense of the world. Elizabeth bore the scars of the 'divorced child' and had faced the unpredictability of her mother's remarriage. Now she was ready to break with her parents. Margaret Dick promised the independence Elizabeth was beginning to covet. This was more than a crush, and the mutual affection and intellectual respect the women found in Scotland would persist throughout their lives. They would share houses in Edinburgh, London and Sydney, and a conversation that began at Alloa would continue across decades marked by success, disappointments, work and countless dinner parties, lunches, movies and concerts. Over the years, some would wonder whether the cousins were a lesbian couple, they were so close, but these two were family, not lovers. 'Elizabeth', her friend Stephanie Claire recalled, 'regarded Margaret Dick as being absolutely part of the furniture of her life.'

Like Elizabeth, Margaret had had a disrupted childhood: she had grown up between the wars in a peripatetic family, living in fourteen different places and attending many schools. And like her younger cousin, she had found solace in books. In an oral history interview for the National Library of Australia, Margaret recalled: 'I suppose I was a terrible person, really, I had such a one-sided interest in the intellectual, in reading. And I had brought myself up in contact with – oh Socrates and all the great people of all the ages, so that ordinary people were not interesting to me.'[3]

Margaret Dick was ten when tanks, sent to break up the General Strike of 1926, arrived in her Scottish village, an event she saw as key to her politicisation. Her family was conservative but the sight of tanks in her quiet village street turned her into a believer in social justice. It was the start of a lifelong commitment to left-wing politics. At eighteen she joined the civil service in Glasgow and spent several years in the department of internal revenue. Transferred to Edinburgh, she took on a role in her union. 'A brilliant public speaker', according to Elizabeth, she campaigned for equal rights for women and improved conditions for workers. For many years Margaret was part of the union's executive committee, whose members included a later prime minister of Britain, James Callaghan. During the war Margaret studied linguistics at night school and began writing fiction. Increasingly she thought of her day job as a 'completely misspent life', but it was only after Elizabeth arrived and she discovered her second cousin too had 'done a fair amount of writing' that Margaret left the security of her civil service job and focused on fiction while taking smaller typing positions.

Margaret had always written but had 'never seriously tried to publish anything'. She recalled: 'Because of this tremendously wide reading that I had done, I felt that nothing I could say could possibly be of the slightest interest because I compared myself naturally only with genius, and it took me a long time to realise that this wasn't necessary, to be a genius, it was only necessary to have something to say and to say it.' Elizabeth, so inexperienced in life, yet so sure about words, had no such misgivings about life as a novelist. Margaret recalled her cousin saying that if you had something to say, 'you must say it as well as you could, and you didn't have to compare yourself with Dostoevsky'.

Elizabeth's parents left the UK for Australia on 1 January 1952. Soon the cousins were together in Edinburgh, with Elizabeth working at T. Wall & Sons Ltd, at The Creameries, as a temporary shorthand typist. She was, her employer said, 'most conscientious and willing'.[4] Margaret was writing seriously and supporting herself with temporary jobs, but Elizabeth wanted to be a psychologist and began to study Greek so she could sit the entrance exam for the University of London. She spent two years preparing for exams in advanced English literature, advanced ancient history and Greek, living at times with the Dick family at Alloa and at Kelso, a market town on the Tweed in the Scottish Borders. Elizabeth recalled: 'I sat in my little Scottish village earnestly learning Greek, and this I enjoyed tremendously and I'm always very pleased with myself when I think that I actually read *The Republic* and various other things in Greek.'[5]

She sat the entrance exams, passed brilliantly and by autumn 1954 had won a place to study psychology at the university. It had been her dream for years, but now she had second thoughts. 'After I'd got the confounded thing [entry] I'd strained my eyes, you know, and I felt I'd done a great deal of work by this time, and I had started to write, so I never did go to London University and I never did become a psychologist,' she recalled. 'That was about the time that I decided I wanted to write novels instead. I think that I decided to do this because I looked at the London University syllabus and I looked at the texts for psychology, and they looked very mechanistic, and I realised that none of the people I admired were — I liked Jung at that time, I was interested in his ideas, and he wasn't even mentioned on the list, and I thought this was rather poor, and I realised that I would be having to learn about statistics when I didn't think of human beings in that way.'[6] She had always had 'an alarming and dangerous interest in human nature' and 'wanted to tell people things'.[7] Now she wanted to deliver those messages to the world, not as a therapist but as A Writer.

Elizabeth had read her way from A to Z in the public library in Sydney and had absorbed the lessons well. She now had a crack at writing a short story, 'Absent Friends'. It was a scant 1375 words, and she sent it off under a pseudonym, Claire Harwell, to a publisher, with 'all communication to Miss B. Harrower'. It centred on a conversation between three women in an office as they discussed a former employee who had married a German and left Australia with him. It's not clear why Harrower opted to hide behind a fake name. Her family still called her Betty and perhaps she considered Claire more suitable for a novelist; perhaps she did not want to be revealed as the author. In any event, she was not successful, and the manuscript was returned. The young author told herself: 'Well, I'm written out, I have nothing else to say.'[8]

In fact, she had a lot to say. In Scotland, she had begun a novel, *Down in the City*, but had put it aside when studying for the entrance exam. In London, her plans to study psychology on hold, Elizabeth Harrower settled down to write.

4

The London Years

FOR MORE THAN FIVE YEARS IN LONDON IN THE 1950S, Elizabeth Harrower lived in rundown flats and bedsits in once-grand mansion houses, where office girls washed their smalls in handbasins and lined up to cook their omelettes in the communal kitchen. 'You would go to look for rented places and there would be these alarming landladies and they would say "spotless, clean" and oh my God, unbelievable, just astonishing, sharing a bathroom and a shilling in the slot for hot water, and mice in the kitchen,' she recalled. 'A cream bun once a week was a treat.'[1] There were freezing winters and smog, yet it was a happy time. Elizabeth had the support of extended family in Scotland, and Margaret Dick was close at hand. For most of the London years, the cousins lived together in digs in Bayswater, Chelsea, Kensington, Wandsworth and Clapham. Both worked at typing or clerical jobs – Elizabeth did a stint with an undertaker – but the main game was to write. They went to Sunday afternoon films, caught buses all over London, took in plays at the Royal Court theatre in Sloane Square and struck up new friendships. Elizabeth learnt to live on a small budget and even took a trip to Greece. Later she managed holidays in France, Italy and Spain.

London was a perfect writing environment. Years later she told fellow novelist Christina Stead that the fact her London bedsits were often serviced removed a lot of distractions. She had been very productive because 'in one room with a typewriter and no cleaning and no other room to wander into, I had to work'.[2]

She took time off for politics, influenced perhaps by Margaret Dick's interest. British Labour was out of office, but Clement Attlee, who had led the country immediately after the war, was still the party's charismatic leader. Elizabeth had shown no interest in politics in Australia, but in Britain politics was unmissable as old class structures were challenged and some people worked to build a more equal society. 'I was converted, so to speak, in England, in London, no, in Bath, in a hotel, with a radio going behind me,' Elizabeth recalled. 'I heard Attlee give a speech for the Labour Party and it seemed to me to make such extraordinarily good sense … I was very enthusiastic about the Labour Party. Because, of course, England was so shattered by the war: food was still rationed when I got there and people were very, very poor.'[3]

She was at the centre of events:

The world was on the brink of a nuclear event with the Cold War and the Berlin airlift, and you had to be there to know how electrifying it was. In London we were very much more conscious of Cold War danger than people were here [in Australia] I think. You felt then that you were a sitting target. At one meeting I heard Bertrand Russell and Linus Pauling say that we could all be flattened next week, and in those days, there was always some crisis going on, so that it seemed quite possible.[4]

In 1958 when the nuclear disarmament movement organised a march from London to the atomic weapons research establishment, 75 kilometres away at Aldermaston, Elizabeth joined the protesters. She didn't walk the entire distance, breaking off about 4 kilometres from Trafalgar Square and rushing back to her typewriter and the draft of her next novel.[5] Elizabeth was proud of those radical days. Her enthusiasm for politics was linked closely to her love of Greek and Roman history: she cried when she read about the fall of Athens. And she developed another habit that would last a lifetime. She was a print junkie, devouring *The Guardian*, *The Observer* and *The Sunday Times* as well as the leftist *New Statesman*. When the Suez Canal crisis erupted in 1956 with Egypt's decision to nationalise the canal, Elizabeth wrote to *The Sunday Times*, protesting Britain's intervention.[6] She was a sponge for ideas and the culture that London offered, tuning into BBC3 programs such as Max Beerbohm's music hall show, and scraping together enough to see the radical John Osborne drama *Look Back in Anger* at the Royal Court. She counted herself lucky to have seen 'the finest actors in the UK many times, in London, in Stratford'. She told Jim Davidson in 1980: 'In London for years I lived on an incredibly tight budget to be able to write, so I took advantage of all that was free – all the galleries and museums. I hadn't really looked at paintings till then but made up for that a bit. I saw quantities of plays, no matter what else was forgone. I used to hope for tickets to concerts and operas, and occasionally they did turn up.'[7]

There were plenty of jobs if you could type and Elizabeth juggled paid work with her writing. She loved London but was horrified by the British class system, which was still deeply embedded even as post-war politics challenged the old structures with innovations such as the National Health Scheme. 'I couldn't stand the way they treated each other, horrible,' Elizabeth recalled. 'To see some people humbled and some people overbearing.'[8]

There was so much to think about, to write about: 'I was sep-arated from my parents by letters, and I was just inclined to write down everything I thought, in diaries, letters, everything. I decided I was going to start writing a novel, so I started … People think the fifties weren't interesting, but they were wonderful years. So much was changing and there was so much at risk, [in] the Cold War. Even the fogs in London were sort of mysterious and glamorous.'[9] She struggled financially but one year bought an expensive coat (which she would wear for more than twenty years) then lay awake all night worrying 'in a fever with the thing shining at me like *Hamlet*'s father's ghost'.[10] Her ambition to move up the class ladder, she confessed, had encouraged her to spend beyond her means.

She and Margaret had fun, but they kept clear of Australians and Elizabeth was proud to say she knew no other expats and was not part of the Kangaroo Valley set – the Aussies who gravitated to Earl's Court, which had long been a meeting place for young travellers from Australia and New Zealand. It was the suburb of shared rooms and minivan sales but it held no appeal for Elizabeth. She had not dismissed Australia completely, but she was no longer very interested in her home country. Despite her huge appetite for books, she had still not read an Australian novel. She was an Australian writing about Australians, but Australian writers would have no influence on her work in these years.

She knew the book she wanted to write – the one about the abandoned, neglected child who lived with her grandmother in a sprawling, careless household. This story, arguably *her* story, would emerge later as *The Long Prospect*, but Harrower believed a writer must practise the craft. She pulled out the foolscap pages she had typed years ago in Scotland and then set aside for her studies and started to work on *Down in the City*. Harrower was 'teaching' herself to write, convinced it would be a pity to waste her Newcastle origin story when she had not yet proved she could construct a novel. She 'wrote and rewrote and rewrote and rewrote [*Down in the City*] really working terrifically hard just to work up some … experience'.[11] And while she avoided being a typical Australian abroad, she turned to her home country as the setting for the novel.

A typing whiz, she worked directly on the keyboard then rewrote four or five times. It was freezing in her Lancaster Gate digs, so she would pull on a woolly hat, nurse a hot water bottle, put a shilling in the slot and bang away on her new Oliver. So began the routine she would follow for years, writing six days a week and aiming for four foolscap pages, double-spaced, every day. She wrote several drafts, making handwritten corrections at night, reading it over and over. The next day she would take in corrections and begin her next four pages.

Harrower was a natural storyteller: 'I never did anything deliberately,' she told Ramona Koval in 2013.

I know some writers study people, look at them, take notes. With me, anything that I have ever written that has been any good has had to be accidental and intuitive and nothing done on purpose is any good – for me. So, I didn't take little notes, and, just, things occur to you, you might see something in a bus, or a stranger might tell you something at a gathering, a few significant words that they might say to you because they will never see you again. It's intuitive and unconscious. It's not deliberate because that kills things for me.

The story of *Down in the City* came easily enough, but she was keen to finesse her writing and worked 'terribly hard on it'. She claimed later that she was not very fond of the novel although it was 'sincere in its way and, as I say, a tremendous effort. It was mainly an exercise. I was working myself up so that when I did want to say something, I would have more command of technique.'[12] In the novel, a rough, working-class man, Stan Peterson, 'marries up'. His bride, Esther Prescott, is from a well-heeled family living in Sydney's eastern suburbs. Sheltered by her father and stepmother and brothers from the rawness of the city, Esther is in some ways like a lamb to the slaughter when it comes to Stan's aggressive charm. Yet she is not a passive victim; Esther makes a choice at some level between the boredom of her safe home and the dangers of life with Stan. 'Not being bored is quite important,' Harrower told Giulia Giuffrè in 1985.

Esther is eager to explore the world, but what she discovers is her weakness in the face of male power. Harrower had begun writing about the issues that would intrigue her throughout her life: 'The power of people over each other, the power we have over ourselves and the power we give other people over us … the power we have over them at all … Really strong stuff, stuff of life, is what the novels I like are all about.'[13]

Harrower completed *Down in the City* in early 1956 and sent it to a British publisher. But the manuscript was returned. She rewrote it and sent it off to another local publisher. There was another rejection and another rewrite before Cassell finally accepted the work. The company had been established a century earlier with an educational focus and a mission to bring literature to a mass audience. It had begun as a magazine publisher and later specialised in the serialisation of classics, as well as reference books and military works. Its authors included G.K. Chesterton, Winston Churchill, Ayn Rand and Dashiell Hammett. In August 1956, Elizabeth received a letter from Cassell director Bryan Gentry saying, 'We are most enthusiastic about your first novel … we would like to undertake publication.'

Harrower had submitted the novel under the nom de plume Antonia Reid. Once again she was reluctant to reveal herself as the author of a book that drew on her personal history. Her impulse to conceal her identity suggests she saw the book as autobiographical. But somewhere along the way, she reverted to her own name. Antonia Reid became Elizabeth Harrower and by September 1956 she had a contract with Cassell. In June 1957, advance copies of *Down in the City* arrived on her doorstep at 34 Sloane Gardens, Chelsea. Not bad for an Aussie expat with no contacts in London's literary or publishing circles who, at Margaret's suggestion, had consulted a catalogue, the *Writers and Artists Yearbook*, for names and addresses of publishers. The post-war period had seen the rise of the 'angry young man' novelist and playwright and there was a masculine bias in publishing, which made Harrower's success in gaining a publisher as an outsider even more remarkable.

When *Down in the City* was published, critics marvelled at Harrower's skill in evoking Sydney from the bedsits of London. But like other expats, such as Madeleine St John, who wrote the Sydney-based novel *The Women in Black* while living in London council housing, Elizabeth found distance helped her distil the essence of Australia. 'I was thinking of Sydney with a lot of affection and picturing the city itself, the sky, the light, everything about it. I was just feeling the breezes, the southerly buster, so I was enjoying that …

I'd read hugely all my life, but absolutely nothing about Sydney. So, I wrote about it and claimed it,' Elizabeth told me in 2012. It sounds arrogant. Was Harrower suggesting that other writers' portraits of Sydney were inferior to her own rendering? Perhaps, but it is more that she made sense of the city through her writing. Since childhood, words had mattered and putting her ideas and thoughts on paper – whether in books, letters or her diaries – was central to the way she confronted life. Her world was filtered, created and controlled through the lens of her writing.

The book begins with a prologue, a vivid description of Sydney's harbour and its beaches which sits slightly oddly with the narrative and, as academic Elizabeth Webby suggests, may well have been written at the request of Cassell in an effort to explain urban Australia to British readers.[14] The city radiates a powerful light in the novel, but *Down in the City* is about darkness: the darkness that descends on an 'intelligent, watchful young woman of good family who became involved with a man a few notches down the social scale'.[15] Harrower was toying with ideas that would dominate her work – the coercion, control and compromise of marriage and male–female relationships. Not for her 'the well-adjusted, the snugly married, the smart and successful, the fashionable'.[16] Esther Prescott is destined for precisely that world until she is swept (like the mother in D.H.Lawrence's 1913 novel, *Sons and Lovers*, who falls passionately in love with a rough miner from a lower class) into an unpredictable, dangerous relationship with Stan. Like Elizabeth's stepfather, Richard Kempley, Stan is a self-made man who sails close to the wind in his business operations. Esther is forced to anticipate her husband's moods and navigate his petty cruelties. Like Elizabeth and her mother, the young bride in *Down in the City* walks on eggshells around an unpredictable husband. Since her childhood, Harrower had never trusted the 'glossy surface' of life. There was not necessarily horror beneath, but 'you should never take anything too much for granted, you just have to think a lot more about everything', she told Giuffrè in 1985. 'It often seems to me … that we're directed to think about a few things at a time, few things rise up in public life, in newspapers and radio and so on and a few topics are thrashed to death while underneath life is going on.'

*Down in the City* attracted more attention from critics back home than in the UK. Poet and playwright Ray Mathew wrote in *The Sydney Morning Herald*: 'Simple, unaffected observation is the keynote of Miss Harrower's style.'[17] He was not entirely convinced by the male characters and highlighted instead Harrower's skill in describing the charms of the city. Almost twenty years later, when the academic D.R. Burns revisited Harrower's work, he applauded her focus on Sydney, arguing that unlike earlier Australian novelists she tended 'to go where the air is polluted and look closely rather than breathing deeply'. At a time when other writers were wedded to the 'myth of an egalitarian society', she interrogated the 'areas of personal abrasion caused by class differences'. Elizabeth had been repelled by the British class system, but in *Down in the City* she offers an unvarnished portrait of the social and economic stratification in her own country.

From the distance of London, Harrower's 'hymn to Sydney' signalled the writer's interest in a new kind of Australian fiction, according to critic Susan Sheridan, one set in contemporary urban society that was quite different from the nation's tradition of 'masculine social realism and the emerging metaphysical modernism practised by Patrick White and the young Randolph Stow'.[18]

*Down in the City* had been Harrower's training novel. Now she turned to the book she hungered to write, the story of her Newcastle childhood.

5

A Writing Life

E LIZABETH HARROWER OFTEN DISMISSED SUGGESTIONS that her novels were based on her life and discouraged interviewers from searching for correlations. 'The emotional truth is there in all of the books, but none of the facts,' she said. 'It's like putting real electricity into a dream palace. None of the books are actual accounts by any means. They're less extreme than reality because reality is so unbelievable. Besides which, people can only take so much. You don't want to frighten them, do you? Or do you?'[1]

She told Giulia Giuffrè in 1985 that 'there's probably no fact in any of my novels that corresponds with anything in my life'. But Harrower was being disingenuous: there is no missing the autobiographical basis of *The Long Prospect*, a story of adult moral corruption seen through the eyes of a twelve-year-old child, Emily. Harrower argued that the setting in an industrial town was incidental to this tale about 'men and women trapped by circumstances, and just, generally, struggling to know their own natures'. She said it would be going much too far to suggest she was Emily, but she drew heavily on the people and the places she knew as a child. The parallels with her years in Newcastle when her parents divorced and she lived with her feisty grandmother, Helen Hughes, are obvious. In the novel, Emily's mother, Paula, is absent in Sydney, where she runs a dress shop, and her father, Harry, works in an outback bank. They have abandoned Emily to her grandmother Lilian, who

43

runs a boarding house, likes men and enjoys a drink. Emily develops a close friendship with a boarder, Max, who encourages her to learn, but the suspicious grandmother and her small-minded hangers-on accuse him of being 'horribly intimate' with her. Their friendship is destroyed, and Emily is delivered a dramatic life lesson. Lilian is the female equivalent of Stan Peterson in *Down in the City* – narcissistic and lacking the ethical framework needed to live with honour in the world. She destroys the relationship between Emily and Max not so much because she deems it inappropriate but because she can.

Harrower had moved away from the parochialism of Newcastle and in London wrote with subtlety and psychological insight about the people she had observed there as a child. Her portraits of Lilian and her cronies are devastating, but the central male character is almost the direct opposite of Stan Peterson – cerebral, honourable and kind. Critic Ivor Indyk noted that male readers were more comfortable with Max – 'a man who could be kind to a child without having evil intentions'.[2] However, Max is flawed and lacks self-control. He is 'kind and confused, rather than brutal and confused', according to the American critic Nicholas Birns: 'As a sensitive, non-controlling man, he is a harbinger of a new, less conventional and domineering kind of man. But not only is he there before his time, he also cannot divest himself of the male privilege he has always assumed with regard to Emily. Max abuses his authority, not out of an excess of insurgent charisma but out of an excess of benevolence.'[3]

In May 1957, just before *Down in the City* was published, Harrower sent *The Long Prospect* to Cassell. The novel had to get past a critical reader's report to the publisher. Over three foolscap pages, the reader, D.L.B., was half-hearted: 'This is a study of a singularly unhappy adolescence: the years from about 12–13 in the life of an Australian schoolgirl, living with her young grandmother in a very dreary factory suburb. It is written with considerable insight and sensitivity, and the book has a lot of good things in it; but the result is loose and unsatisfactory … Characters are never described, some never properly set … The opening is particularly bad …' The reader suggested *The Long Prospect* would not work for Cassell, given it was focused on publishing novels in serial form.

Harrower also faced the barrier, as she put it later, of it being a time 'when things Australian were (to the rest of the world) still lost in primaeval mists and slime'.[4] But Cassell picked up the novel all the same, sending an advance of 100 pounds through her newly acquired agents Pearn, Pollinger & Higham (in 1958 renamed David Higham Associates) in Soho.

It took a year to get the novel into print: Cassell was initially unhappy with the title because it had been used previously and suggested instead *Life and Emily Lawrence*. But the novelist Paul Scott, who worked at her agency, declared that title a 'stinker'. Elizabeth half-heartedly suggested *The Narrow Look*. In the end, Cassell stuck with the original.[5]

Meanwhile, Margaret Dick had been just as productive as Elizabeth. She had approached Heinemann about her first novel, *Rhyme or Reason*, but the publishers wanted proof she was not a one-trick pony and asked her to write a second novel. Margaret, working two days a week to support herself, produced *Point of Return*, published in 1958, with *Rhyme or Reason* released the following year.

Elizabeth had been renting her Sloane Gardens flat for about a year but was tiring of her landlady, Mrs Jensen, who 'was appalling, watching everyone coming and going like a concierge, and generally dispensing negative charm around her unfortunate guests'.[6] It was time to move and by April 1958 Elizabeth and Margaret were sharing digs at 3 Dents Road, Clapham. It was there that Elizabeth received her first copies of *The Long Prospect*.

The novel was greeted enthusiastically by Australian reviewers. On 28 April, *The Sydney Morning Herald*'s Sidney J. Baker wrote: 'Here is a book so different in motif and presentation from what we are accustomed to that there are few local standards of comparison. For that matter, there are not many overseas writers who can be compared with Elizabeth Harrower – D.H. Lawrence perhaps, and Katherine Mansfield, but not a great number of others. For here is one of those rare novels which become immediately memorable for their delicacy and understanding, and for their author's enviable ability to trace tender filaments of feeling and mood to their ultimate emotional sources.' Harrower, Baker noted, was something of an expert on lonely people; *Down in the City* was 'full of action, full of characters, full of vivid pictures of Sydney' while *The Long Prospect* had 'a much narrower canvas'. Grandmother Lilian was a 'sadistic sensualist who has buried two husbands and has had assorted lovers'. The child Emily suffers 'moods of desolation and perplexity, the same confused anxiety to win approval, the same desire to avoid emotional disaster'.[7]

Like other contemporary critics, Baker, who became friends with Harrower when she returned to Sydney, knew nothing of her childhood and made no connections with her life. He had some criticisms of *The Long Prospect* but concluded: 'To condemn the novel [for these occasional issues] would be comparable to condemning Patrick White for the poetic symbolism of his books: the cumulative rewards are much more important than the obstacles.' It was heady stuff for Harrower to be mentioned in the same breath as Lawrence and Mansfield and White, who was already known for *The Aunt's Story*, *The Tree of Man* and *Voss*, which had just won the inaugural Miles Franklin Literary Award. Harrower's novels had been identified by Australian critics as serious literary work. The following year, *The Long Prospect* made the long list of seventeen novels vying for the Miles Franklin, but the judges chose Randolph Stow's first novel, *To the Islands*.[8]

No matter, Elizabeth was on a roll. Almost immediately she began her third novel, *The Catherine Wheel*, writing at a table at Dents Road. After two books set in Australia, Harrower was ready to write about the London bedsits and flats where she had lived in a city smothered in a dense fog so different from the penetrating sunlight of Sydney. By May 1958, she had written a short outline, and was playing around with various titles, including *Tightrope* and *With Love and Ambiguity*. She placed expatriate Australian law student Clemency James at the centre of the story. Clemency begins a disastrous romantic and sexual relationship with the wild, and wildly attractive, former actor Christian Roland. Nothing much happens in the novel, which focuses on Clem's interior battles as she struggles to separate fantasy from reality, passion from logic, and to navigate love and intimacy. At one level, it's a realist novel about an impossible passion for an unstable, unpredictable man; at another it's a searing psychological case study.

Written in the first person, *The Catherine Wheel* revealed Harrower's range and willingness to experiment with style. The point of view shifts as we are asked to see Clemency as alternately victim and agent. The charismatic but flawed Christian is more sympathetically drawn than the aggressive Stan Peterson in *Down in the City*, but his impact on those around him is no less damaging. The conundrum for the reader, however, is that while Stan is described by an 'objective' narrator, we see Christian – and his de facto wife, Olive – through the eyes of the passionate Clemency, an unreliable witness. Indeed, one of the challenges of this book is getting a clear take on the protagonists as they engage in intense, repetitive exchanges about their feelings. Scholar Nola Adams, researching her master's thesis in the 1980s, considered the novel a parody of romantic, obsessive love. It was melodramatic and gothic – 'a subtle psychological study of a female character's approach to and evasion of inner awareness'.[9]

By the time she wrote *The Catherine Wheel*, Harrower had become disillusioned with the idea that formal psychological study could explain motive and behaviour. For her, Christian's behaviour defied easy categorisation. She told Giuffrè in 1985 that there would be no reason to write a novel if behaviour could be easily defined as neurotic: 'It takes a novel to show and then [it's] up to other people to make up their minds. It's not for a novelist to label. You hope that people will be interested.'

Harrower was intrigued by these characters and later wrote two plays based on the novel. In her stage directions for one, she described Clemency as 'an Australian, almost twenty-six, living in London for some years and studying law by correspondence. She is intelligent, natural, without guile. When she meets Olive and Christian Roland, she is mentally tired, bored. They are new creatures to her. At first, she is only mildly interested in them. Later, in her efforts to "redeem" Christian, she achieves a high degree of selflessness.' Christian, Harrower wrote, was 'an ex-actor of thirty, a dissolute and dangerous man who has suffered and caused much damage in the past. He is youthful, forceful, volatile, gay and genuinely charming. Not quite on the rails and sometimes aware of it, he is basically a tragic figure. He is a near alcoholic and very good-looking.'[10]

Harrower had created two malevolent characters in her early novels – the hyper-male Stan of *Down in the City* and the carelessly evil Lilian of *The Long Prospect*. In her third novel she once again explored emotional destruction, but Christian is no cardboard copy of either Stan or Lilian. Rather, he is a fully realised character with his own brand of toxicity. Once again, there are pointers to Harrower's life in this book, and it is tempting to wonder if *The Catherine Wheel* was based on an affair she might have had in her twenties. Decades later, Elizabeth told her Sydney hairdresser, Ulrik Funch, that she had had a couple of relationships in London, but there are few clues to this in the thousands of words she wrote to friends throughout her life. When Giuffrè asked Harrower in 1985 whether a writer needed to have been in love to write about love, she said: 'Well, I think you do. Obviously, if I had never been in love or had any experience of love I could not have written about it but also I don't think you have to be so specific as to say that if you haven't been married for fifteen years you can't have characters that have been married for fifteen years, any more than you have to have died to have somebody die in a book. I consider that in my way I've lived dangerously, and I haven't lived a self-protective sort of life.'

It was not the first time that Harrower claimed to have lived dangerously. Indeed, it was almost her personal slogan, repeated at various times during her life. She used the phrase to explain how many financial risks she had taken; she had not pursued a career in an office but had saved money and funded her writing life. She had gone without, had lived on a shoestring. She also talked to me of 'living dangerously in the sense of finding out more and more about human nature'. And her comment to Giuffrè suggested she had taken risks in her emotional and sexual life.

*Elizabeth on board the* Southern Cross, *1959*

By 1959 *The Catherine Wheel* was ready for publication, and Harrower was ready to go home. She had not missed Australia; in fact, her absence from her home had begun a highly productive period in her life. She had transformed from Betty to Elizabeth in her own 'coming of age' story and had believed she would never go back to Australia. She was close to her mother, but it's likely she was relieved to be away from her difficult stepfather. But now friends in Sydney reported her mother was missing her. Elizabeth was nostalgic, too, after seeing images of kookaburras and sheep at one of the 24-hour Movietone News cinemas popular in the 1950s. There was also the matter of money. She had supported herself with short-term typing jobs and had likely received money from her mother, but her books were not selling. She wondered whether Australia might provide more support for novelists than was available in London. As a published writer with good reviews, she decided it would be interesting to 'come back as this new person'.[11]

At forty-three, Margaret Dick, also struggling to make a career from writing, was ready to try Australia and decided to travel with Elizabeth. The cousins booked their tickets and packed up their lives, leaving their shelves of books and their cocoa mugs with their landlady in Dents Road. They were looking forward to the trip, but they told each other they would return to the UK. These London years had been good for Elizabeth. She had mined her life for her writing. Now she delivered *The Catherine Wheel* to Cassell and boarded the *Southern Cross* for the six-and-a-half-week journey home. To have produced three novels in less than five years was impressive. Harrower would never again experience the isolation and anonymity she had enjoyed in London, nor the solitude that allowed such concentration on her work.

6

# Home Again

N JULY 1959, READERS OF *THE BULLETIN* LEARNT THAT two young women writers had arrived in Sydney on the *Southern Cross* from England and would be welcomed home by Mr and Mrs R.H. Kempley of Mosman. Elizabeth Harrower and Margaret Dick, described as friends rather than cousins, had made the social pages, albeit in a somewhat muddled report. Margaret was described as a writer with 'several books' published in her eight years in London,[1] even though Elizabeth had also published two novels and it was she who had been overseas for eight years. Whatever. The women were returning in style and Margaret, who had paid her own fare rather than seek an assisted migration passage, would quickly fall in love with Australia. Elizabeth was not so sure. She was shocked by the complacency: 'People were trailing through the street, trail, trail, trail, plonkety, plonk. And, I thought, my God, this is not a serious country.'[2]

At the time newspaper reporters scanned the manifests of ships arriving from overseas in search of passengers with a story to tell, and *The Bulletin* report was not the only press coverage the cousins received. *The Sydney Morning Herald* published a photograph of the pair and noted that the 'Australian novelist' and 'Scottish novelist' were in Sydney for a year. It reported they had been surprised when they boarded the ship in the UK to discover copies of their own novels – *The Long Prospect* and *Point of Return* – in the library. They didn't borrow them during the six-week-long voyage, stating, somewhat grandly: 'You never read your books again, once they've been published.'[3]

*The literary cousins (Elizabeth on the left) featured in*
The Sydney Morning Herald, *1959.*

The press attention was a fillip for the women, who were identified by Sydney's small literary circle as promising new blood. *The Sydney Morning Herald*'s literary editor, Sid Baker, who had reviewed *The Long Prospect*, made contact, and the English Association also reached out. Over time the cousins would become stalwarts of the local branch of the international writers' association PEN. At meetings they rubbed shoulders with Gwen Meredith, the playwright and radio writer already famous for her long-running serial *Blue Hills*, the short-story writer and novelist Margaret Trist and the writer Olaf Ruhen.[4] Both Margaret and Elizabeth reviewed books for *The Sydney Morning Herald* and established a profile in the city's tiny creative community.

Not long after they arrived, they travelled to Bogan Gate, near Parkes, in western New South Wales, to visit Frank Harrower, who was working as a fitter and turner. It was a difficult visit. Frank's second wife, Elma, had never welcomed his daughter and he had been forced into an almost secret correspondence with Elizabeth.

Back in Sydney the cousins committed to their writing, although both worked, at least part-time. Now even Elizabeth was in love with Australia: 'I took to the place all over again and liked it so much, I felt the level of goodwill was much higher here than in most other places and people were very pleasant to me.'[5] Margaret's novel *Rhyme or Reason*, completed a couple of years earlier, was published by Heinemann. It is the story of a young woman, Lisa, who starts a new job in a UK town as an efficient civil servant and falls hopelessly in love with the fiancé of one of her flatmates, leading to a 'dual life'. Meanwhile, Cassell was preparing *The Catherine Wheel* for publication. There is some symmetry between the two novels dealing with the struggles of two young 'outsiders' – one an Australian expat, the other living away from her home city – as they contend with their impossible love objects. There is no evidence the cousins discussed their work, but they appear to have mined similar emotional terrain.

In Australia they worked on short stories, hoping for publication in overseas journals and magazines. Margaret was a devotee of the form; Elizabeth was less convinced and preferred the longer format of the novel. The cousins sent their work off to editors but faced the slog of typing and retyping copies and then coping with the rejection slips. Elizabeth was relentless in efforts to market her work, trying to interest American publishers and develop local contacts. She was practised at this. In London, she had not known any writers, publishers or agents yet had three novels accepted: 'All submissions, negotiations, conducted by post.'[6]

Even with her contacts in Australia, it was a hard market to crack, especially for women: 'No-one ever talked books or had read anything you'd written: that side of your life was like a guilty secret ... Eventually a few women writers crept out of hiding into the surrounding silence. It was SO different, that only very hardy souls, impelled to write, did write and, no question, it was harder for women.'[7] Elizabeth was desperate to build a writer's life, but she needed a job. Armed with a reference from the Sydney city librarian (who had known this keen reader for ten years before she went to the UK) and with help from Sid Baker, she found work in the ABC's program department. Margaret also took a job at the national broadcaster, working on radio programs based around poetry and music.[8]

When *The Catherine Wheel* was released in October 1960, it generated limited interest in the UK. In October, *The Times Literary Supplement* said it failed 'to touch the heart', although the reviewer conceded Harrower had captured the bedsit squalor of London.[9] In Australia, however, critic Barbara Jefferis raved. The setting was London, but the book was 'entirely Australian in ethos' and a 'remarkably good novel'. Like a small handful of Australian writers, Harrower had the 'imaginative vision' to write of what she had discovered about life 'instead of following a shallow "selling" formula'. The book showed patience, integrity and perception, and there were no 'second hand emotions ... no faked solutions, none of the emotional clichés most writers use to spare themselves the trouble of profound thought'.

Jefferis noted Harrower's interest in 'the mechanics of loneliness' and her 'outsider' heroines, as well as her understanding of human psychology. 'What she has understood herself and made strikingly clear to her readers in *The Catherine Wheel* is the basic human truth that, on the emotional level at least, what happens to a person is what he or she wants to happen – that emotional suffering is only possible where it in some sense and to some degree serves the sufferer.' Harrower's writing failed her at times, Jefferis said, and the 'discipline of the prose' did not match 'the tremendous discipline of thought'. It was a minor quibble, and the review continued: 'Few Australian novels have equalled *The Catherine Wheel* in understanding the way in which anguish leads to the gradual getting of wisdom.'[10]

In contrast, Nancy Keesing, writing in *The Bulletin*, was unimpressed: 'Halfway through reading the book one wonders, what is the matter with it?'[11] Hers was a tough review and Olaf Ruhen jumped to Harrower's defence, writing to *Age* journalist John Hetherington to suggest he read the book. Hetherington did so and early in 1961 travelled from Melbourne to interview this new 'find' of Australian literature for a series on writers.

Elizabeth had just left her ABC job after a year of earning a regular wage. She was determined to write rather than make a career at the broadcaster: 'I did not want to rise up [the ranks at the ABC] because I would stay there, and I would not write … I lived dangerously, I did without things, I was actually hungry. It was hard but enjoyable.'[12] She applied for a Commonwealth Literary Fellowship to allow her to write full-time but was not successful. Instead, she was 'writing and starving and still enjoying myself'.[13] She and Margaret shared a bedsit – with the use of a shared bathroom – in Neutral Bay, and that is where Hetherington interviewed her.

In a profile published in *The Age* in April and *The West Australian* in May, Hetherington reported that the women lived 'in complete amicability' even though they were both professional writers working on their novels – set in Sydney – from nine to five, six days a week. Harrower sat at a table in the kitchenette, typing on her faithful Oliver, while Dick worked in the bed-sitting room. Hetherington wrote that Harrower at thirty-three was a slim brunette of about 5′10″ in medium heels, with 'responsive, hazel eyes under strong brows, a high-bridged nose, and a sensitive, though slightly ironic mouth'.[14]

She told him one reason she had come back from London in 1959 was to 'refresh her local knowledge; she felt she was falling out of touch with the way Australians think, talk and live'. She had moved out of her mother's house overlooking Balmoral Beach because it was too comfortable and she had feared losing interest in writing: 'It was so beautiful, it was gorgeous. I thought if everyone in Europe knew how gorgeous it was, they would all want to come.' Interestingly, she did not mention her stepfather; Harrower was already erasing Richard Kempley from her biography.

She told Hetherington she had worked the passion for Sydney out of her system in *Down in the City* and that her new novel, *The Watch Tower*, was 'more about people and less about Sydney … Perhaps that will make it a better novel.' She had always been interested in people for their motives, their secret impulses, the working of their minds and in 'trying to discover what went on behind their masks'. She planned to return to London because she feared becoming a 'mental beachcomber' in Sydney, even though the cousins were enjoying the city's theatre and ballet and opera. Harrower rattled off her favourite authors – Stendhal, Tolstoy, Mauriac, Colette, Saul Bellow, Truman Capote, Elizabeth Bowen and Nadine Gordimer. Hetherington noted that Harrower saw herself as a ruthless truth-teller, capable of upsetting people. She told him she did not want to write only of beautiful things, because that would be dishonest, unintelligent and boring. The newspaper feature established her as a writer, just as her passport said. There was plenty of 'colour' in these two novelists writing their hearts out in a tiny bedsit overlooking one of the loveliest sections of the harbour. Bohemian but orderly. Elizabeth emerged as friendly but a little reticent, composed but unaffected. She revealed, for example, that her mother was always on the lookout for nice shoes for her tall daughter with big feet.

Harrower continued her efforts to build a career as a professional writer. She tried to have her backlist published in Australia and the United States. She pushed for her short stories to be published in the US and tried to interest theatre companies in a couple of plays. It was tough. In 1962, for example, she received a scalding letter from *Good Housekeeping* via her American agent. Rejecting her short story, associate editor Lonnie Coleman said: 'The people in "The Beautiful Climate" seem to us odd to the point of unreality. I'm sorry to say and we don't quite know what the author is trying to say.'[15] That same year, *The New Yorker* rejected a short story called 'The Last Days', which was clearly based on Elizabeth's departure from London with Margaret Dick.[16] Harrower also pushed the two plays based on *The Catherine Wheel*, sending *Beginner's Class* (set in Sydney) to the Elizabethan Theatre Trust, and *The Catherine Wheel* (set in London) to her London agency, David Higham Associates. In June, there was bad news: Margery Vosper, a London screenwriter, had read the script and reported that it worked as a novel but not on the stage.

Harrower also sent *Beginner's Class* to an agent in New York, and after a rejection letter wrote to him to say she thought it the 'least original and least feeling piece of work I had ever written' but wondered if it might have worked on television. She sent him a copy of the stage version of *The Catherine Wheel* and told him it was 'considerably better' than *Beginner's Class*, which was her first play. But she considered Australian acting standards so poor she didn't really want it produced in her own country. 'You may think it wordy, or more like movie script' but she believed it could be a good play.[17]

Harrower may not have thought much of *Beginner's Class* but it was a finalist in the Journalists' Club play competition and the Melbourne Little Theatre and the University of NSW's Department of Dramatic Art were interested in it. She told the Australian poet and editor Max Harris that it was a 'limbering up exercise, not a very inspired piece of work'.[18] In this period she also wrote another play, *The Bosom of the Family*. Meanwhile, US publishers rejected her novels *The Catherine Wheel* and *The Long Prospect*. An agent had sent the latter book to nine publishers without success.

Harrower was determined to see *The Catherine Wheel* published in Australia and on 5 July 1961 forwarded a copy to Sir Allen Lane at Penguin in London, with the hope of Penguin publishing it here. She told him she had been disappointed by Cassell's failure to promote the book. 'In Australia for the past two or three years a number of critics have linked my name as a writer with Patrick White's,' she wrote. 'This is excessive praise as I well realise; but in London, going to the other extreme, my novels have been issued with no publicity, no indication on the blurb even, that in Australia at least they have been well thought of. Nevertheless, with one exception, the UK critics who have happened to come across *The Catherine Wheel* have reviewed it favourably, and here, where it has been more widely seen, its reception has been generous and enthusiastic.'

Harrower was feeling the lack of a network; other writers had university friends and 'careers launched by best friends writing passionate reviews'. She maintained she was pleased 'no one did me any favours',[19] but in the early 1960s the effort of turning a promising start into a career took its toll.

In Adelaide, Max Harris was working with Geoffrey Dutton and Brian Stonier to establish a local list at Penguin Australia, so Harrower wrote to Harris and forwarded copies of *The Long Prospect* and *The Catherine Wheel*.[20] Harris was editing a new journal called *Australian Letters* and replied: 'I must confess, shamefully for a literary editor, that I hadn't come across your work before. However, I immediately tackled "The Long Prospect" and was quite inordinately delighted with it … [it is] one of the major achievements in the post-war Australian novel. I think I'll send a copy to Patrick White … I'd be most curious to hear his response.'[21]

It is hard to overstate the influence of Max Harris on Australian literature in the twentieth century – not only as a creator, but as an editor, an enabler, a promoter. Born in 1921, Max was a scholarship boy who, unlike Elizabeth, attained a university education and youthful notoriety. Harris was confidence writ large. At nineteen he co-founded the literary journal *Angry Penguins*, with Dutton among others; soon he was embraced by the set at the Heide arts enclave outside Melbourne. Harris was mixing with the cream of Australian culture – Sidney Nolan, Arthur Boyd, John and Sunday Reed. The journal marked out new territory for poetry and the modernists and angered more traditional writers, some of whom in 1943 submitted poems under the fake name Ern Malley – an incident which remains Australia's most famous literary hoax. The poems were published, the hoax was exposed and Harris was charged with obscenity, found guilty and fined five pounds. Undaunted, he continued to play a key role in Australian culture, running the Mary Martin Bookshop in Adelaide and forcing down book prices in an industry still dominated by London publishers. He and Dutton co-edited *Australian Book Review*, along with *Australian Letters*, and were involved in the establishment in 1965 of the paperback publishers Sun Books. When the national daily *The Australian* launched in 1964, Harris was one of its most powerful commentators, highly critical yet highly nurturing of the national culture.

Geoffrey Dutton was equally influential. Born just a year after Harris, Dutton was the son of graziers at Kapunda, South Australia, but also enjoyed the privileges of a metropolitan life, living at times in a grand family home on the edge of the Adelaide parklands. He went to Geelong Grammar School and Adelaide University, where he and Harris connected. Like other sons of Australia's grazier class, Dutton studied at Oxford. After serving in the RAAF during the war, he wrote, edited and farmed. Like Harris, he had an enduring impact on Australian culture.

Harrower's background was very different: her gender worked against her, and she was also of the generation of women who unconsciously assumed the greater power and talent of men. The 'divorced child' lacked the natural confidence of Dutton and Harris, but she had grit and a belief in her work. Her approach to Harris paid off. He wrote to say that he and Dutton would 'enthusiastically' recommend publication of *The Long Prospect* as a UK Penguin but with special Australian promotion and distribution. Harris told Harrower that her books had been 'inexplicably neglected' by Australian critics and suggested that Cassell, as a publisher of periodical and reference books, was perhaps a poor choice for a literary work. The publisher's brand tended to 'conceal the advanced style and sensibility of your writing', he said.

Harris was keen to publish an extract from her new novel in *Australian Letters*. She wrote back to say that she had done 'all these odd bits of writing' and had begun the first draft of a novel [*The Watch Tower*] only a few weeks earlier so could not provide a useful extract. A month later she had second thoughts, and suggested Harris could use a section of the new book. She had some short stories but opened fire on her London agent who 'thinks only of women's magazines, and the New York agent [who] wants material specially tailored for his market. As writing to formula is either against the grain or beyond me, and in spite of knowing that it is a case of "export or perish" I have reached the point where, if I do write a short story I keep it. Even so, though I much prefer the 80,000 words of a novel to move round in, it sometimes seems a sensible idea to try another short story, so I do, and then, as I say, file it!' She agreed the Cassell brand was a hurdle for some UK critics and admitted the lack of attention to her work had been discouraging at times.

In the end, Harris decided on an essay in the December 1961 edition of *Australian Letters* to introduce her work, along with a short story, 'Lance Harper – His Story', and an extract from *The*

*Long Prospect*. Harrower was thrilled: 'After decades (it seems) of traditional struggles, it is encouraging to be done "moderately proud"', she told him. The essay was an important effort to situate Harrower in the first rank of Australian novelists. It did not carry Harris's byline but has always been accepted as his work. He noted Cassell was seen as publishing 'library' rather than 'literary' novels and this was one reason why Harrower's books had received 'only perfunctory critical attention on the one hand, and an almost non-existent market demand in Australia on the other'.[22]

Like critic Sid Baker, Harris ranked Harrower alongside 'Australia's dominating literary genius' Patrick White, but noted she had a 'slighter range and power'. She was, however, 'head and shoulders above the current pack of sociological realists in the national novel. Way below her, Randolph Stow and Christopher Koch are groping for the kind of penetrating humanism that she has realised fully and beautifully.' That must have been especially sweet praise for Harrower given that Stow had won the Miles Franklin in 1958 ahead of *The Long Prospect*. Harris was arguing Harrower's novel was second only to White's *Voss* in post-war Australian writing. He also praised *The Catherine Wheel* and said that despite the London setting, the 'pervading ethos of the writing [was] still mutedly Australian'.

Harris then analysed *The Long Prospect* at length. He found some difficulties with its 'complex, intellectually loaded style which, while lacking the convolutions of Patrick White, required careful sympathetic reading'. However, the author had a 'breathtaking talent for precise and beautiful observation' and she had written 'something far beyond the novel of manners and mores ... she interprets every incident and detail in terms of experiential meanings'. There was more about her technique, including allusions to Proust, Faulkner and White, before Harris addressed the story. 'It is an anti-Lolita theme,' he wrote, 'the passionate and helpless affection of a 12-year-old girl for a middle-aged man, expressing itself in a relationship of great innocence and yet intensity … The relationship is destroyed casually and capriciously by the girl's piss-ant grandmother.'

The theme of sub-adolescent love had rarely been observed so profoundly, Harris wrote, but he suggested that if *The Long Prospect* became an Australian classic, it would be because of its description of Australian society. The novel offered a 'devastating insight into the grass-roots philistinism, the non, rather than anti-humanism, which represents some kind of spiritual norm in "average" Australian living … Elizabeth Harrower has drawn the Australian manifestation, the minds that go with the Saturday bets, the prawn suppers at the pubs, the cheesy egotisms that crack a few bottles of beer Sunday mornings in the kitchen.'

There was a good slice of snobbery in Harris's words, but his analysis positioned *The Long Prospect* as far more than a 'coming of age' story. He praised Harrower's ability to see Australia through a fresh lens. Australian literature, he wrote, was 'peopled with great hearts in the outback, urban eccentrics, the mannered and civilised people of Martin Boyd's world, corrupt unionists, the Richard Mahoneys [sic] disintegrating from within, the Jimmy Crocketts rotted from outside. But the evil of the ordinary, the destructive seeds within the average mind, are rarely described in detail. Barry Humphery [sic] may satirise the surface absurdities of the Australian norm: but Elizabeth Harrower has seen deep into the destructive core.' Harris went on to make a big call: 'The talent of Patrick White is too vast and hydra-headed to be either interpreted or placed within any Australian tradition of the novel. It may well be that we will be more inclined in the future to think of Elizabeth Harrower's work as providing some kind of historical watershed in the twentieth century Australian Novel.'

It was a remarkable essay. Harris had created a place in the canon for Harrower's work in a way that would have been impossible in London. Her decision to return to the smaller pool of Sydney had paid off: she was now recognised as a serious writer in her home country. The following March, she met Harris at the Adelaide Festival Writers' Week and felt that while he was 'very nice' he had her pegged as 'a Henry Jamesian girl'. Harris, it seems, had seen the influence of James and the similarities to his childlike, 'unaware' heroines who lost their innocence in the new American world where they were 'forced to recognise that the world is ambiguous, divided'.[23]

Harrower had driven from Sydney with her new friend Olaf Ruhen, theirs a rollicking journey as he belted out Australian ballads. In Adelaide the writers were billeted with families and Elizabeth got to grips with literary politics. The festival, she found, was 'virtually owned by poets' and she had felt generally patronised by those who questioned her pedigree. And then: 'Back in Sydney, novel writer? Who is she? What school did she go to? What did she do at Uni?' She told Harris: 'I hadn't realised before that you not only will make enemies, but ought to, if you go out into the literary world.' Her suspicion of writers' cliques continued through her life. A decade later she declared she did not want to be part of any literary society, anywhere: 'Even here, I haven't much taste for it. It's a small literary world anywhere, I suppose and (even here) nice people do each other over too much.'[24]

Harrower was working hard on *The Watch Tower*. It was taking longer than expected and two and a half years after returning from London she was worried about money. The Harris essay had rescued her from literary obscurity, but could she afford to go on writing? She had lived dangerously, using up money saved from her ABC job, but she was running out. She told Harris in August 1962 that she had finished a draft of *The Watch Tower* but 'must shelve it for a few months or a year and take a job'. Soon, financial relief would come from another key figure in Australian literature, a fellow writer who would nurture her career but also dominate a relationship that would push Elizabeth to the edge.

# 7

# The Kylie Question

IT WAS AT A LAUNCH PARTY FOR NANCY PHELAN'S NOVEL *The River and the Brook*, early in 1962, that Elizabeth Harrower met Kylie Tennant, the writer and editor with whom she had her most intense adult relationship.[1] Tennant had orchestrated the meeting. She was working as a reader for the British-based Macmillan publishing company and had heard about the young writer who had appeared relatively recently on the Sydney literary scene with three novels to her credit.

Tennant was one of Australia's most popular writers, able to influence careers through her work as an editor and mentor and her membership of the advisory board of the Commonwealth Literary Fund, which dispensed grants to writers. Tennant had likely read John Hetherington's positive feature about Harrower published a few months earlier and knew Harrower was working on her fourth novel. Tennant's goal that night was to convince Harrower to leave Cassell and come across to Macmillan. The publisher was keen to back Australian work at a time when overseas houses were starting to pay attention to the local market. It would be four years before Macmillan set up an Australian arm here, but it had a showroom in the city and a powerful presence in Tennant.

The fifty-year-old had published a swag of books since her first novel, *Tiburon*, was released in serial form in *The Bulletin* in 1935. Like her later bestsellers *The Battlers*, *Time Enough Later* and *Ride on Stranger*, the book documented the poverty and struggles of the working class. Her commitment to politics and social causes had made Tennant an influential book reviewer and newspaper commentator with a big following. As a young woman in the 1930s she had gathered material by making trips on foot – a 450-kilometre trek from Sydney to Coonabarabran, and a similar trek from Coonabarabran to Brisbane. She had rented rooms in the poorest areas of inner Sydney that made her physically ill. She even spent a week in jail in the pursuit of 'copy'. Late that decade she made another trip to western New South Wales, travelling to Goulburn, Yass, Young, Cootamundra and Leeton with a horse and cart and a female companion to gather material for *The Battlers*.

Tennant was among a group of authors committed to writing in their fiction about the social and political issues of the time – determined to tell Australian stories and influenced by turn-of-the-century storytellers and poets such as Henry Lawson and Joseph Furphy. She was a charismatic woman, still handsome in middle age, and her reputation preceded her. Harrower must have been flattered by the attention of this older writer whose somewhat careless approach to her appearance only added to her appeal. It is not clear if Elizabeth had read any of Tennant's books; after all, she proudly claimed not to have read a single Australian novel before she came back to Australia from London in 1959. Had she caught up with Tennant's backlist by the time they met? As writers they were chalk and cheese – Harrower's stories were fundamentally psychological; Tennant's work verged on journalism and was influenced by Russian social realism. Their life circumstances were also very different. Elizabeth was single, a somewhat unusual situation in an era when it was taken for granted women would marry early, while Tennant was married with two children. Elizabeth had found her way out of industrial Newcastle; Tennant was from a middle-class family based in the suburbs of Sydney's north. Unlike Elizabeth, Tennant had gone to university – although she did not complete her degree. Unlike Elizabeth, she had not travelled outside Australia. Her focus was national while Harrower took a more global stance. Yet, despite these differences and their age gap, the two were drawn to each other, perhaps in part because they had both suffered chaotic childhoods. Elizabeth of course had a history of forming deep connections with women older than herself and had already explored the relationship between older and younger women in her fiction.

Harrower, friendly but guarded, was attracted to the extrovert Tennant, who was fond of holding court at social events. Tennant's gregarious demeanour, described as a carapace by her biographer, Jane Grant, hid a complicated personal life. She was married to the Christian socialist schoolteacher, writer and editor Lewis Rodd, known as Roddy. He was several years older than her and had long adopted the role of mentor and facilitator of his wife's career. They had been together for more than thirty years by the time of the Phelan party, but their marriage was troubled. Some years before, Tennant had had a brief sexual affair with another man and confessed all to her husband. Prone to depression, he had previously threatened suicide and Kylie's confession pushed him over the edge. He made repeated attempts to kill himself and in 1961 threw himself under a train at Sydney's Circular Quay. He survived but lost an arm and a foot. The marriage continued but the couple never again slept together.[2] When Kylie met Elizabeth in 1962, she was struggling with guilt about her husband and with the domestic demands of raising two children: her sixteen-year-old daughter, Benison, and John, known as Bim, who was five years younger than his sister. In her diary on 12 January 1961, she had written: 'I have a husband who is insane, two children, a house, a very old truck, five hens, two cats (one with four kittens) and about a thousand pounds in the bank.'[3] Elizabeth was a breath of fresh air; she was suitably impressed by the older writer, but she was Tennant's intellectual equal and shared her left-wing political views.

Soon Elizabeth agreed that Macmillan would publish her fourth novel. Kylie began to understand that her new friend's financial situation was parlous. By the end of the year, she had helped Elizabeth into a job managing the Macmillan showroom in Pitt Street – a base for the publisher's sales staff and a place where booksellers could browse new work. The regular wage was welcome but now Elizabeth had only nights and weekends to work on *The Watch Tower*. Even so, she and Margaret Dick were regular visitors to the Rodd bungalow in Hunters Hill. The household was rowdy, but the 'divorced child' found a ready-made family in Kylie and Roddy and their children.

Tennant had always loved the bush, seeing it is as an escape from domestic pressures and as the two women grew closer, she determined to buy a weekend shack in the Blue Mountains, a space for writing where they would be together while Roddy remained behind at Hunters Hill. By November 1964, the women had agreed to jointly purchase a cottage on a former plant nursery at Blackheath. Elizabeth's share was funded by her mother, who had access to her own money.

At the time the Kempleys were on an extended stay in the UK and Europe; they spent months in Scotland and Spain before renting a cottage in the Cornish village of St Mawes. Richard had not been well, and the couple chose the area for its sunny climate. Margaret wrote to her daughter to say she was delighted with the Blackheath plan and that 'you & Kylie have found this little house & that everyone is pleased with it and happy about it'. She explained to Elizabeth, who had been anxious about what questions the bank or the tax department might have, that 'no one asks awkward questions … no need for explanations re the name signed for the house'. She asked Elizabeth, whom she still called Betty or Bet, if the cottage had electric light, whether it was sewered or had a septic tank, warned her against white ants and dry rot and wrote: 'Having all the trees & shrubs should make it look very pretty & apple trees. It altogether sounds a very pleasant investment.' The letter – one of only two from her mother which survive – shows the extent to which Elizabeth relied on her.[4]

Elizabeth took driving lessons, presumably to make it easier to get to the mountains. She was a little anxious about her bank balance, but in January 1965 she and Kylie spent their first days as co-owners, cleaning a 'very dirty' Hillside Farm. Elizabeth wrote to Margaret Dick: 'There was nothing for it but work. Kylie whacked in, in spite of being really half-crippled with arthritis … It's rather large, fragile and filthy … But we are trying to keep our hearts high … I wish to heavens Kylie at least felt physically better.'

Were they in love, these two writers joining finances to buy this retreat in the mountains? Were they lovers or just good friends? Did they acknowledge the depth of their connection to themselves, let alone each other? There is no evidence of a physical relationship but based on a batch of Elizabeth's letters to Margaret Dick in 1972, it is clear her emotional involvement with Kylie was intense. Most of Elizabeth's letters to Kylie, however, appear to have been retrieved by Elizabeth and destroyed, and only a handful of Kylie's letters to other people mention Elizabeth. Kylie speaks as an older, almost motherly, friend in these letters, and her letters to Elizabeth are similarly no-nonsense missives which dodge any emotional terrain.

*Kylie Tennant with her daughter, Benison, in Sydney, 1960.*

Looking back sixty years, Kylie's daughter, Benison Rodd, believed Elizabeth was probably in love but that Kylie wanted a friendship, not a love affair. In the 1960s, Benison was an art student at Sydney Technical College and often walked to the Macmillan showroom to see Elizabeth after class or to meet her mother, Kylie. The teenager had mixed feelings about Elizabeth: 'I think she was trying to get Mum away from Dad, but Mum wouldn't leave Dad because Dad was an invalid,' Benison told me in 2024. Benison and Bim were often at the cottage and Roddy stayed occasionally. Nancy Phelan and her husband, Peter, lived in the mountains, at nearby Lawson, and shared visits and lunches with the Hillside Farm occupants. Bim was showing signs of mental illness and his unhappiness cast a shadow over the lives of both parents.

Jane Grant wrote that Hillside became a 'sanctuary' for Kylie, who drove up at weekends with Elizabeth (who despite taking driving lessons seems not to have driven much). It was not the first time Tennant had attempted to live and work collaboratively with another woman. In the early days of her marriage, before she had children, Kylie had lived in a shack outside Melbourne with the communist painter Naomi Lewis. Grant noted that Blackheath seemed to work well for everyone 'and Rodd and Harrower appeared to have developed an amicable friendship based on their shared interest in Tennant's welfare'.[5]

That judgement is generous: there was ongoing friction between Roddy and Elizabeth.

The cottage opened a new phase in Elizabeth's life, one enabled by the wealth accrued by Richard Kempley through his accounting practice. Her mother had helped finance the cottage, using her own funds, but these had been generated by Kempley's business in which Margaret had been a partner.

Despite the tensions in her new relationship with Kylie, Elizabeth was content in these years. Lovat Dickson, general manager at Macmillan, wrote to her from London in May 1963: 'I must tell you how grateful I am personally for the wonderful way in which you have helped to set up and have competently run the Sydney office … I am sure that this job absorbs more of your time and attention than you meant to give it, because you are first of all a writer and not an office worker, but conscientious people always give more to a job than they are asked to give and that is what makes them so valuable.'

Kylie thought Elizabeth did a great job, 'presiding' at the publisher: 'Famous persons would come out from England, and Elizabeth and I would deal with them. Elizabeth was excellent at arranging parties for the firm's authors and the directors who wanted to meet them.'[6] Kylie was also important in the promotion of Elizabeth's short stories. She included 'The Cost of Things' in the anthology *Summer's Tales 1*, published by Macmillan in 1964. It was the first time Harrower had had a short story published. The following year Kylie included 'English Lessons' in the annual anthology.

Elizabeth's life in Sydney was very different from her years in London when she had had her head down writing books while trying to stay warm and solvent. She had revelled in the isolation and had been highly productive. Sydney's good weather and open skies were distracting, and she was much more sociable than in London. Her circle was expanding and included Sid Baker and editors like Ken Levis, who was responsible for the important *Coast to Coast* short-story anthologies promoting local writing. She knew Max Harris and the academic Ron Geering, and in June 1963 she met Melbourne-based writer Judah Waten when he came into Macmillan. A communist, Waten was already widely published and Elizabeth, some seventeen years his junior, grew to see him as a mentor as well as friend.

Born in Odessa in Ukraine in 1911, Waten grew up in Perth and Melbourne and was active in politics and Jewish affairs from his teenage years. In the early 1930s he spent time in Europe and at one stage did three months in prison in London following political actions. *Alien Son*, his first book of short stories, published in 1952, was based on his migrant experience as a Jew in Australia. He visited the Soviet Union many times and published several novels in the social-realist tradition, as well as non-fiction. In 1982, he released his final novel, *Scenes of Revolutionary Life*. Married and living in Melbourne, Judah was interested in Elizabeth's life and work. He was a straight man who did not fear friendship with a single woman. Elizabeth told Margaret Dick that Judah loved women 'in a most unusually straightforward and generous manner, with no – to use the ghastly term – hang-ups'.[7]

Waten drew Harrower into his milieu, telling her: 'We left-wing writers are a tiny group and we are obliged to carry a considerable load of work, journalistic and organisational.' He told her she was a better writer than her contemporaries George Turner, Randolph Stow and Thea Astley, because 'you write from life'. Elizabeth's world was changing in a way she could not have imagined. In London she had relied on Margaret Dick; other friendships, with landladies or part-time work colleagues, had been more peripheral. Back home she began to exercise her gift for friendship. She and Margaret joined a small pool of writers who were keen to build a distinctively Australian literature at a time when publishing was dominated by companies headquartered in the UK and local novelists saw their novels released in London then shipped back home. University curricula were dominated by British and American writers, and it was 1962 before the first chair of Australian literature was established at the University of Sydney. In the 1960s, Judah and Kylie were among those, like Max Harris and Geoffrey Dutton in Adelaide, who were not just writing the Australian story but pushing others to create a national culture.

Even before they bought Hillside Farm, Kylie and Elizabeth had spent time outside the city. In 1964, as they drove past Dogwoods, a small farm at Castle Hill, Kylie suddenly pulled up and dashed in to say hello to Patrick White and his partner, Manoly Lascaris. The couple were living there after several years in London. Elizabeth waited in the car. Patrick came out to say hello, and Elizabeth, who knew his work well, was delighted.[8] Tennant had been thrilled by White's 1955 novel, *The Tree of Man*, and had famously defended it, via a *Sydney Morning Herald* interview with White, after a highly critical review by the poet A.D. Hope.

Elizabeth was meeting exciting new people, but in January 1965 she was reminded of her past when she took a call from her half-brother. David Harrower, twenty years her junior, had left school and started work on the railways and was determined to meet the sibling whom he had never seen. Elizabeth was blindsided and told Margaret: 'I had a ring from a sixteen-year-old half-brother of mine tonight. David. He called me Elizabeth. He's passed the Intermediate and is getting a job tomorrow on the Railways! Quel famille! [sic] My first reaction when I heard he was to ring back at seven was to go out, bravely changed my mind. He was only a kid. He likes surfing. He has an older brother, Francis, who rides in go-karts. And is a pipe-maker at Kembla Grange whatever all that means.'

Undeterred, David travelled to Mosman to see Elizabeth but was disappointed. He recalled: 'She met me at the gate and told me she didn't want to see me; she blew me off.' Elizabeth had long ago begun editing her life and her past and she had moved far away, physically, emotionally and intellectually, from her father and his second family, with whom she felt she had little in common. David tried again on another occasion and again Elizabeth turned him away. Their father, Frank, was still alive, but it appears Elizabeth had no contact with him before his sudden death, at the age of sixty-two, in November 1968.

By the end of 1964, Harrower was fretting over the manuscript of *The Watch Tower*. Her mother, writing from Hawes, urged her to send it off to Macmillan, saying 'everything works out well in the end & worry doesn't help'. Harrower had worked on the novel for almost five years – far longer than she had spent on her three earlier books, each of which she wrote in a year. In Sydney, working full-time, she discovered 'it takes centuries' to write a book.[9] 'I would sit down after dinner, and it takes about an hour to shake the day's trivial events out of your head, and after about two hours, I found that I would be quite tired but still I could get into it, and I obviously did because I did finish the book, and then at weekends, I would just – almost every week-end I would write all day Saturday and all day Sunday, and in the end I thought I'd never get rid of this book!'[10]

She was also dealing with the expectations of her peers. In London, she worked in a bubble and had no connections with other writers or publishers. She was not part of the London literary scene. Now she was A Writer who was known to critics and academics and counted editors and reviewers among her friends. She had moved from the London fringes to the centre of literary Sydney. Her fourth novel would be scrutinised far more closely than her earlier work. Little wonder she hesitated about submitting it.

Harrower rewrote *The Watch Tower* several times, producing 'many more than three' drafts, and a year after its release said: 'The first [draft] I think, was practically a different book, I can't even remember it very well anymore.'[11] Finally it was finished, and

Elizabeth settled down to await publication in October 1966. 'It's rather a grim one,' she told Judah Waten. 'The next will have to be full of sweetness and light. It's no fun writing about hatred and evil.'

Kylie, too, had been busy in this period, writing *Tell Morning This*, which became a classic and was later serialised by ABC TV. She was also the subject of an important work by Margaret Dick, who had embraced Oz Lit with enthusiasm after she migrated from Scotland. In 1966, Dick published *The Novels of Kylie Tennant*, a work which challenged the view that Tennant was more journalist than novelist. The three women gave each other creative support: in 1964, Kylie included a short story, 'Summer Sunday', by Margaret Dick in the anthology *Summer's Tales 1*, which Kylie edited for Macmillan. But Harrower's work was very different from Tennant's. Indeed, Jane Grant argues that 'Tennant felt alienated by the interior psychological landscape of the younger writer's novels'.[12]

At times, Tennant tired of Harrower's focus on trauma. 'Elizabeth is typing industriously at her novel,' she wrote to her friend Mavis Cribb. 'If it is about a young woman suffering, I will hit her with a brick. I don't dare ask.'[13] Yet she recognised the younger woman's talent: 'Her writing is probably the exact opposite of mine, because I like to take notes – unless I write a thing down, I forget it, but Elizabeth goes in for much more subtle nuances of feeling and this is appreciated by erudite Swedes and Germans and others who come out here and want an article for their newspaper about Elizabeth Harrower. In Australia, I think Elizabeth is rather a rare bird.'[14]

Macmillan took a more proactive approach to *The Watch Tower* than Cassell had with Harrower's previous books. Patrick White provided a promotional comment: 'Elizabeth Harrower's characters don't fornicate under the reader's nose, but what they do and say is always true, sometimes subtly so.' It was, Harrower would write much later, a 'half-facetious comment that helped no-one'.[15] Indeed, the quote, which was used in an ad and on showcards for bookstores, was enough to agitate some. Not helping was the dust-jacket's statement that one of the novel's characters, Felix Shaw, 'outwardly a successful Sydney businessman is wicked'. It continued: 'One could say perhaps that he suffered a deprived childhood, is a homosexual, or offer any one of a number of excuses for him.' Three Brisbane booksellers refused to stock the novel. In *The Sydney Morning Herald*, Gavin Souter wrote that the word 'homosexual' was what did it, but said the 'baffled' Harrower had told him that 'there are no homosexuals in the book'.[16]

Souter, who became a personal friend to Harrower, interviewed her and found her 'a serious writer with a self-deprecating wit'. She told him the novel was about the mental torture of two women by an outwardly normal, but inwardly unbalanced, man. 'When I start writing a novel, I have no message in mind, but at its end, something seems to be resolved,' Harrower said. 'In *The Watch Tower* I hope I am saying to someone in a difficult situation: "There are ways out." And I am saying that it is too easy to judge others in unfamiliar circumstances.'[17]

The novel is set in Sydney at the tail end of World War II, when sisters Laura and Clare Vaizey, about to be abandoned by a self-centred mother after the death of their doctor father, must confront their suddenly impoverished futures. They have come down in the world and their mother's solution is to marry Laura off to her wealthy, if dubious, employer, Felix Shaw, who promises that the teenage Clare will be permitted to go to university. The sisters offer Felix respectability in return for financial security. As in *Down in the City,* Felix's decision to marry outside his class precipitates tragedy. Once again, Harrower drew on the trauma of her childhood and Uncle Dick for this story of coercion and entrapment.

In her 1985 interview with Giulia Giuffrè, Harrower did not name her stepfather but revealed some of her thinking behind her depiction of Felix. She had just seen the David Pownall play *Master Class,* about Stalin, and said she had known at least two people who reminded her of the Soviet leader: 'they're jolly, they're friendly, they almost win you over. You almost think, why, he's not so bad after all. He talks about his childhood, he does a little dance, he sings, in a gruff way he's quite a jolly fellow, and then instantaneously, it's the instantaneous switching from one thing to another that bogey men have I think.' Harrower's description of Felix as a man with scars on his forehead is also revealing: Richard Kempley appears to have had a long, distinctive scar on his forehead.

The reception of the novel was close to rapturous. The *Sydney Morning Herald*'s critic, H.G. Kippax, called it outstanding and positioned it with Patrick White's latest, *The Solid Mandala.* Kippax appreciated the scope of the author's ambition to write more than a story of a bad marriage, noting that the 'casual sadism and domestic tyranny are constantly counterpointed with references to the casual slaughter and betrayals of the wartime and post war world and with illustrations of the kinds of despotism at work in our Australian conformist, materialistic society. This is a dense, profoundly moral novel of our time, not just an exercise in suspense. Compassion indeed invades the whole novel, tempering Miss Harrower's uncompromising investigations of vanity, folly and spite.'[18] In *The Bulletin,* poet (and lawyer) Geoffrey Lehmann also compared her with White, noting Harrower's prose had a quality of intense compassion and suffering. 'White is savage, she is resigned. Her writing has an elusive femininity.' Harrower, Lehmann wrote, was 'not addicted to verbal pyrotechnics. Her writing had simplicity and purity, a quiet understatement.'[19]

Elizabeth had returned to Australia in 1959 and been 'taken up' by an older, more established circle of writers. She had the support of Australia's leading novelist in Patrick White and important 'influencers' in Max Harris, Geoffrey Dutton and Kylie Tennant, among others. *The Watch Tower* had been highly anticipated, and reviewers and friends were not disappointed. Some, like White, considered it a likely winner of the nation's top literary prize, the Miles Franklin.

Writing much later, the critic and publisher Geordie Williamson termed the novel a 'time-and-motion study of extreme violence and mental distress; a work where Australian masculinity is shown as a gibbering gimp. Its suburban living rooms contain intimations of Auschwitz and its endless skies glower with the threat of nuclear annihilation. All the gnarled baroque of Bluebeard's folktale is fitted to Sydney's harbour side streets.'[20] Felix Shaw, crudely mannered and narcissistic, is no murderer but he is an abuser, a man who must be humoured by those close to him, whose survival depends on submitting to his moods and inexplicable cruelties.

The parallels with Richard Kempley – who was able to provide Harrower with a comfortable life in Sydney's North Shore but who failed so many other tests – are obvious. Uncle Dick was, like Felix, a dodgy operator. He was much older than his wife, Elizabeth's mother, and family members wondered whether she had married him to provide security for Elizabeth. In the novel, the older sister, Laura, chooses marital serfdom to 'save' her younger sister, Clare.

Harrower did not link the novel to her family but did suggest it grew from her own experience. She told Hazel de Berg: 'I can't even remember how I chose the theme but I suppose I must have seen people trapped in rather hopeless situations and I knew that other people, more fortunate people, tended to judge people who were trapped in ordinary-looking situations, and I feel that there can be great tragedies going on in the suburbs and I feel that people should be more sympathetic towards sufferers.'

Harrower often talked about the repetition in her work: 'A blackbird always sings the same song. I just do have preoccupations, but you can come at them from so many different angles.'[21] An example was the short story 'The Beautiful Climate', published in *Modern Australian Writing*, a Collins anthology edited by Geoffrey Dutton in 1966, but written some years earlier, which prefigures an incident in *The Watch Tower*. In the novel, Felix Shaw announces the house that Laura and Clare have slaved over will be sold. In the short story, the father – Hector Shaw – drags his wife and daughter to a weekend cottage at Sydney's Scotland Island, where they spend most of the time slaving or relaxing – always on his terms. Suddenly he announces he will sell the property. It's a devastating example of psychological coercion, and Elizabeth's decision to write this story twice suggests her stepfather may well have done something similar. Certainly, the fictional cottage was based on fact: in 1978, Harrower told Judah Waten that the journalist and novelist Brian Penton had rented a cottage owned by the Kempleys at Church Point in Sydney, which 'was the background for that story, The Beautiful Climate'.[22]

Felix Shaw is a misogynist, but is he also a homosexual? Ron Geering noted his 'marked homosexual strain' and argued his attitudes towards young men grew from 'frustrated paternalism, possessiveness, a need for domination, a basic disgust with sex and contempt for women, a desire for recognition'. But Geering praised Harrower's skill in writing a character who was human, rather than a psychological type.[23]

Harrower resisted the notion that Felix was a repressed homosexual:

No ... there are those pieces in the book where he is nice, puts business opportunities in the way of young men, that was just an aspect. It was never really meant to suggest that you had to go down that track. No, it was never meant like that because that's, I think, a terribly obvious label and a very easy way out. So I really was suggesting that there was more even in Felix's character than was dreamt of in philosophy, that we [can't] just put a label on him and finish him off because as soon as you put that label on, or any label on, you can stop thinking about the person ... because you've put the label on them.[24]

The author cautioned against applying a template to the men in her novels, saying that they 'all seem quite different to me ... in every way ... people who have trouble with themselves and cause trouble' are all different.[25]

Harrower resisted the tag of feminist writer and said the oppression of women by men was 'incidental to what I'm really writing about'. But the timing of *The Watch Tower*, published as second-wave feminism hit Australia, meant some readers saw Laura and Clare as emblematic – Laura was the oppressed wife, while Clare, free of marriage, ultimately escaped male domination. In 1971, when Judah Waten told Elizabeth that Melbourne feminists were claiming her as one of their own, she said:

> I walked down the street reading your letter and had to laugh when I came to the bit about Women's Lib. Man, woman, child, cat and dog needed to be liberated from Felix … While it is obviously true that for historical and biological non-reasons women have often been oppressed and treated much like domestic animals, even in a state of most total equality between the sexes, individuals of both sexes will still from time to time overpower psychically other individuals of both sexes. I suppose we need to be liberated from the worst of human nature. Difficile.[26]

Harrower was writing after World War II, when some women were questioning their roles, but the middle-class nuclear family headed by a male breadwinner was still privileged. Older Australian women writers, those who had published from the 1920s to 1945 – people such as Marjorie Barnard, Eleanor Dark, Dymphna Cusack and Kylie Tennant – had written about women, exploring questions of sexual freedom, eroticism, abortion and oppression. But their feminism lacked a theoretical base and by the end of the decade it had been subsumed by wider political and economic issues, according to writer and editor Hilary McPhee.[27]

Harrower was ahead of her time in understanding why battered wives like Laura did not leave their husbands:

> People, I think, can be dragged along year after year in very bad situations because in an innocent way … you might say stupid, but still innocent way they keep being seduced by the jolly side

when it turns up and they rationalise it because they cannot bring themselves to face the truth of the other side, what they're really living with and facing … When *The Watch Tower* was not long out … occasionally I would come across someone who'd say, why didn't [Laura leave Felix]. Well, the people who said this … tended to be girls who had had a fortunate life, who were innocent in their own good fortune, who couldn't imagine a life so different from their own that the option of walking out into the world with no education, no money, no friends, that they couldn't quite believe that people ever have to make a choice like that.[28]

In *The Watch Tower*, Harrower displayed great understanding of the complex psychology of men and women and the choices facing women in their adult years, but she was struggling with her emotional involvement with Kylie. Fifty years later in media interviews, she talked of Tennant as a friend and offered no hint of the intensity of their relationship. Had she resolved her conflicting emotions? Were the memories of this time with Kylie still too raw or had they faded? Harrower could not point to marriage or children, and without an obvious sexual and romantic history she was hard to categorise.

She was prone to develop crushes on men as well as women but she 'didn't believe in happy marriages' and could never picture herself in that situation. At the same time, she said 'my life had not been free of men entirely … I have known an awful lot of very, very nice men who have been good to me and some of whom I have obviously cared about more than others.' She had never wanted children.[29]

The bleak marriages of Harrower's novels suggest scepticism about the institution, but she remarked to Giuffrè that some people were 'lucky'. She had seen people 'grow older together, grow older and wiser and happier together, certainly. I think it isn't easy. A good marriage is really hard to sustain these days which is a shame because I think it's the most desirable and enviable sort of state if it can work out … if you could say I could be guaranteed a terrifically happy marriage that worked from beginning to end, I'd say yes. I very much regret not having a marvellous marriage from beginning to end, but since that was never guaranteed …'

By the end of the 1960s, Elizabeth wanted more emotional commitment from Kylie than the older woman was able to give. Kylie struggled to define the relationship. She asked a mutual friend, Sydney art patron Ida Florence 'Bill' Cantwell: 'You're a woman of the world; is Elizabeth in love with me?' When Elizabeth heard of the incident, she related it to Margaret Dick and added an exclamation mark. It was an opportunity for Elizabeth to reveal more to her cousin, but instead she wrote: 'It just shows the utter confusion into which the situation had fallen.' Was Elizabeth's rejection of the idea she was in love with Kylie a reflection of her feelings, or more to do with the fear she would be labelled a lesbian at a time when there was still widespread social disapproval of same-sex relationships?

Unlike male homosexuality, which was illegal in the 1960s, there was no law against lesbianism in Australia – the assumption was that women could not be sexually involved with each other – but lesbians were sometimes harassed by police. Many hid their relationships for fear they would lose jobs or families or friends. It would not have been easy for Elizabeth and Kylie to have openly expressed any sexual desire at a time when the church designated it sinful and some doctors still saw it as a disease. Elizabeth mixed in fairly liberated circles of writers and artists and knew many homosexual men, including Patrick White and Manoly Lascaris, whose status afforded them a certain freedom in what was still a homophobic society. But lesbian relationships were rarely conducted openly, and gay women lacked the power of gay men.

## 8

# The Hazzards: Kit and Shirley

IN 1966, THE YEAR SHE COMPLETED *THE WATCH TOWER*, Elizabeth Harrower had one of the most consequential meetings of her life, one that would have an impact on her writing and her friendships. It was on 19 April when 69-year-old Kit Hazzard went, by arrangement, to the Macmillan showrooms in the city for a cup of tea with Elizabeth. The meeting had been set up by Norma Chapman, the proprietor of the legendary Clay's Bookshop (later Macleay Bookshop) – a Potts Point outlet which was a fixture in Sydney's literary scene. Chapman was concerned about some of the vague behaviour displayed by Kit, who lived in a Macleay Street block called The Chimes and was often seen wandering the streets in some disarray. Chapman knew Kit was the mother of the expatriate writer Shirley Hazzard, who was making a name for herself from her bases in New York and Italy. Knowing that Elizabeth was a successful novelist, Chapman thought that, despite an age gap of almost three decades, she and Kit might click.

Elizabeth was busy at her job and finalising *The Watch Tower* ahead of its publication in October. Her personal life was rich; every weekend she and Kylie drove to their retreat in the Blue Mountains and during the week she saw Margaret Dick and friends. She liked Kit, although she realised the older woman was 'not very happy'. But Kit, who was still strikingly beautiful, 'took the trouble to be entertaining, and to make me laugh, which I thought was very generous and gallant'. Elizabeth empathised with her, later telling Shirley Hazzard that she, Elizabeth, also had 'an excessive talent myself for happiness and unhappiness'.[1]

Elizabeth identified with the difficulties faced by Kit, who had been born Catherine Stein in Dunfermline, Scotland, just as the nineteenth century was ending. Kit was illegitimate – although her parents married when she was an adult. She followed them to Australia in 1925, after working as a tailor and a secretary in Scotland. In Sydney she found work in the office of Dorman Long, the construction company building the Harbour Bridge. There she met Reg Hazzard, who shared a similarly difficult past; he, too, was illegitimate and had been adopted as a child. They married in 1927, and Reg proved a good financial provider. As children, Shirley and her older sister, Valerie, enjoyed a comfortable life in a spacious house in Mosman, overlooking Balmoral Beach – not far from the Kempley house. But Reg was a drunk and the household was miserable even as his career prospered during World War II. In peace time he was appointed to trade positions in Hong Kong, New Zealand and New York, and by the time she was sixteen Shirley had left Australia. At the age of twenty she was in a job at the United Nations in New York. Later, Reg's long affair with another woman led to separation and divorce, and Kit, increasingly unhappy and unstable, began a pattern of moving backwards and forwards between London and Australia.[2]

Elizabeth's friendships with both Hazzard women were slow at the start. Kit was soon off to London and the United States, but she told her daughter about Elizabeth's kindness. Shirley wrote to Elizabeth, who responded on 16 November 1966 in a polite but slightly awestruck letter and sent Hazzard a copy of *The Watch*

*Tower.* She told Shirley that she and Kit had been 'well disposed towards each other of course, because of our common enthusiasm [a reference to Shirley] but it turned out that we would have been well disposed anyway'.

It was after 1970, when Kit was again living in Australia, that Elizabeth became more involved in her life and developed a regular correspondence with Shirley. Their letters in this decade, as Kit trekked between Australia, the UK and the US, were filled at first with details of Kit's emotional and mental distress and physical demands. As Kit's mental health worsened, Elizabeth organised psychiatric help and took her to medical appointments. At the Rozelle Hospital in March 1971, Kit was attended by 'Andrew Robertson, youngish Scotsman'. After a few weeks on antidepressants, Kit had a 'miraculous' improvement. Robertson remained closely involved with Kit's care and became one of Elizabeth's closest friends over her lifetime.

Kit was not easy to deal with, once again vacillating before finally boarding a ship to England in April. Elizabeth had written to Shirley a month earlier about Kit's plans and said: 'If your mother comes back to Sydney, and it's at all helpful, please do keep in touch with me. I don't know how I gradually became involved. (Partly my novel was finished, and my mother died, and I had some time between tasks when things began to fall to pieces for your mother. At other times, in the middle of a book, I know I've let other people sink or swim.) But although we are very different, I'm fond of your mother and understand the way she thinks, disastrous and one-sided though it frequently is.' It was an explanation of sorts, but even Elizabeth appeared unsure why she opted to take on so much responsibility for someone who was not family, and not really a friend. By August, Kit was indeed back in Sydney.

Soon Shirley and Elizabeth began referring to Kit as MM and YM respectively – my mum and your mum – as they coped with the frustrations of dealing with the fractious Kit. The writers shared an (unhappy) Australian childhood but also an estrangement from their families and a desire to create and curate their lives anew. But in other ways they were very different in temperament – a difference that allowed Shirley to leave the care of her mother to a virtual stranger in Elizabeth while Elizabeth, in turn, was almost too willing to take on the care of a virtual stranger in Kit. Shirley and her husband, Francis Steegmuller, were grateful for the load Elizabeth carried, and their letters of praise surely reinforced her commitment. In December 1971 Francis wrote: 'Of course you must by now realise that you have become part of our folklore – a kind of literary & household goddess: & as such I pay you all kinds of tribute, including thanks & affectionate greetings.'

Unsettled and resentful of Shirley's life in New York, Kit had become increasingly dependent on Elizabeth, who gradually assumed the role of surrogate daughter. Elizabeth had only brief respites: in 1972–73 and in early 1974, Kit spent time in New York with Shirley and Francis, who was a writer and translator of some note. Elizabeth was genuinely fond of Kit and a natural carer, but she also enjoyed the entrée Kit gave her to the glamorous intellectual life Shirley and Francis (known as the Steegs) had carved out for themselves.

After six years of letters, the trio met for the first time in London in April 1972, when the Steegs were on their way to Italy for their annual visit and Elizabeth was staying with Sid and Cynthia

Nolan in Deodar Road, Putney. They talked over afternoon tea in the potted-palm court at the Ritz, Elizabeth sporting a chic suede jacket; they went to dinner; and they visited Macmillan boss Alan Maclean – the publisher of both women's work – at his home. Elizabeth was not disappointed in the Steegs and wrote to Margaret Dick: 'Francis is an angel of a man. He's marvellous. And Shirley is just the girl you would imagine from all you know.'

After that meeting the women began a deeper conversation about their writing, their letters increasingly warm as Elizabeth continued her involvement with Kit back in Australia. Kit's mental health was deteriorating and she would eventually be diagnosed with manic depression. Shirley was now more specific in her requests for help in sorting out her mother's life, and more excessive in her praise of the person who allowed her to continue her life in New York. 'What I dread is that too-much-Mum should becloud our friendship; or that one should trespass on your own goodness and your presence there,' Hazzard wrote. She was generous with praise: 'You'll get bored with every letter beginning with our marvelling at your qualities, but this is your own fault for having them.' Hazzard's words were flattering but she was also determined to create a world where she could focus on writing. Elizabeth became her long-distance enabler.

Harrower had struggled with her writing after the publication of *The Watch Tower* in 1966, and now she was distracted by Kit. Shirley (who understood the single-mindedness needed to create art) noted the sacrifices Elizabeth was making. 'How can you be so many things to all of us, and how can one express what this means?' she wrote from Capri. 'And how can you be so good humanly and do work at the same time? – you can't obviously.'[3] In these years Elizabeth helped Kit with medications, took her to psychiatric appointments, included her in social events and helped find her accommodation. Elizabeth's good works did not end with Kit: in 1975 Shirley thanked her for 'sending the form for the library royalties' for her books.[4]

Patrick White blamed the Hazzard women for Harrower's writer's block. The Nobel laureate had picked Harrower as a major talent when they met in the 1960s and believed she had more books in her. He admired Hazzard but felt she exploited Harrower's generous nature, and he berated Elizabeth for being a 'social worker' who supported and enabled others rather than focusing on herself and her writing. The women's relationship looked one-sided from the outside, but Elizabeth gained much from the connection with this talented, cosmopolitan expatriate. Brigitta Olubas's biography of Hazzard reveals her as personable, even charismatic, if not necessarily likeable. She controlled conversations as if presiding over a salon and was aware of her aura and protective of her status. Smart, strategic, disciplined, she worked hard for her brilliant career and was very much the performer in her own drama. Shirley had had a much livelier love life and career than Elizabeth when they first connected, but Harrower was the bigger critical success, even if working in a smaller pond. Both writers had released novels in 1966 – *The Watch Tower* was Harrower's fourth book, while *The Evening of the Holiday* was Hazzard's first novel. But the power balance would change dramatically as Hazzard continued to write big novels and Elizabeth published nothing but a handful of short stories.

From the start, the Steegs were an exotic couple to the girl from Newcastle. 'Art and the art world were mainstays' of their life, Olubas writes. 'There was, as [art historian and friend] Alison

West put it, "a sense of knowing cities, knowing museums, having a certain way of life, approaching things in the same way, knowing the same people".[5] It was a life of ordered days and the silence in which to think, as Hazzard put it, asking Elizabeth: 'Do you find, as I do, that all this being anxious or furious about The World takes away from time and silence and thought for real work?'[6] The security of marriage plus money provided by Francis, who had inherited a hugely valuable art collection from his late wife, assured a productive life.

In 1972, with the election of Gough Whitlam, the friends' correspondence became more political as Harrower revelled in the exciting social and cultural changes in the country. She was now more explicit about her writing struggles. 'I *am* trying to work and there certainly seems to be a lot in my head. If only I can sort it out and use it properly,' she admitted in 1974. 'If not, *everyone* will cast me off. And that would be a pity. I did a piece, a sort of story, unpublishable but fun to do. And I remembered that marvellous feeling of being interested and absorbed and feeling it mattered.'[7] The May federal election and the need to find accommodation for Kit once more intruded and she sounded desperate when she wrote to Hazzard: 'all I really care about and all that worries me just now is work. And I wonder if I'll ever sort out and find ways of transmuting … I'd better.'[8]

The two women were Australians and about the same age, with similar left-wing views. They were writers of highly crafted prose. But despite her years in London and her love of European culture, Elizabeth was very Australian, with an instinctive dislike of class hierarchy. There was nothing pretentious in her writing and she exhibited no 'side' in her interactions with people. The same might not be said of Hazzard, who was conscious of her role as a public intellectual. Hazzard had few contacts in Australia; she had not cared to develop them and saw her future in Europe and the United States, not in her birthplace. Elizabeth quickly became her conduit to Australia, typing her pages and pages about politics and the literary scene and mailing wads of newspaper cuttings to New York.

Elizabeth had strong views on Australian books and writing and in the 1970s brought Hazzard up to date on a country she had left decades earlier. 'Some promising youngish men are writing plays,' Elizabeth wrote in 1974.

> I, myself, haven't read a new Australian novel for a long time (apart from *The Eye of the Storm*) … None of us (US, whoever WE are) much like Thea Astley's work or, indeed Thea Astley. There was, a few years ago, a huge fuss about Thomas Keneally, but that is over. The literary entrepreneurs look for someone to boost and often in their excitement do everyone a disservice. When I first came home from London in 1959, the quarterlies were putting Randolph Stow through the mill. It happened to Patrick, too, but he was older and better able to withstand the pressure of so much analysis and attention. For some years there was (and in some of those already mentioned) considerable Patrick-copying. They seemed to feel that the significance of his work lay in its syntax. Then there was a lull and now we have a very few youngish men writing in another peculiarly Australian and peculiarly awful style. Perhaps it's supposed to be hilarious and shocking. Hal Porter of course is – Hal Porter and stands where the real ones stand.

Through Kit, Harrower now had access to a glamorous intellectual world; this impressed her Australian friends, who saw Hazzard as a celebrity, a trophy. In some ways, the relationship between the two women was a trade, although one that lost its attraction for Elizabeth. Over time she did not hide her annoyance at the pressures Kit placed upon her; and she was disappointed by the relationship with Shirley – although she retained a deep affection for Francis Steegmuller. Stephanie Claire recalled:

Elizabeth had this very strong and combative relationship with Shirley. She was frightfully competitive and jealous of Shirley, and she felt Shirley was often putting her down. But she was linked to Shirley. It was as though Shirley had had the life Elizabeth could have had, because Shirley married this old famous guy, and then also became much more famous. Elizabeth constantly felt, I think, that she was the ugly duckling in the whole thing, and she went through times when she really hated Shirley. Yes, quite vivid. She was angry with her, just feeling Shirley was a person who used her. The subtext was that she was a much better writer than Shirley and Shirley had got all the fame and had got this life in New York.

Their neatly typed correspondence was extensive and intense and carefully composed – as if they knew their letters would become part of their public archives. Sometimes Elizabeth wrote two or three times a week; sometimes their letters crossed; always Elizabeth was diligent about answering Shirley's questions. Elizabeth's letters were often detailed descriptions of her involvement with YM, but she also revealed, on an almost daily basis, her own travails (shingles) mixed with political analysis (Malcolm Fraser).

In January 1976, as the Steegs prepared to visit Australia for the Adelaide Festival Writers' Week, Elizabeth updated them on the 'who's who' of Australian writing and advised that 'the only person that neither Patrick nor I would urge you to meet is Professor Leonie Kramer, Aust Lit., Sydney University. She has all the bone-deep dislike of art of the dedicated right winger, is positively damaging to (living) Australian writers … there is talk she may be appointed Chairman of the ABC. Horror! Patrick and Christina Stead call her Goneril.'

Hazzard had been commissioned by *The New Yorker* to write a 'Letter from Australia' based on her visit, and asked Elizabeth to collect press articles on the government. 'Do you think I would be able to see Whitlam for an hour?' she asked. On the way to Adelaide, Francis and Shirley spent time in Sydney, where Elizabeth threw them a party. Guests included Kylie Tennant, Nancy Phelan, David Malouf and Geoffrey Lehmann, who was struck by Elizabeth's generosity in introducing this 'star' writer to a broader group. Patrick White hosted the Steegs and Elizabeth for a dinner at his home in Martin Road, Centennial Park. Elizabeth also enjoyed a dinner with the visitors at La Causerie restaurant and later wrote to Shirley: 'It was a happy time. It seems to me all the times were – delighting, and often euphoric. All the more so perhaps because, as you said at Patrick's, "we've been through so much together."'

Elizabeth kept up a supply of press clippings and commentary to Shirley over the next few months as she wrote her *New Yorker* piece, which finally appeared in December 1976. Elizabeth noted: 'You must be so immensely relieved to have that out at last. It must have begun to feel like your life's work.' The essay was well received when copies eventually reached Australia and the expat writer, still not particularly well known in her home country, developed a higher profile here. Having enabled the essay and facilitated Hazzard's trip to the Writers' Week, via its chair, Geoffrey Dutton, Elizabeth surely had mixed emotions about Shirley's growing celebrity, but she remained generous in her letters and relished the conversations about books and writing.

'I've been falling in love with novels all over again,' she wrote to the Steegs. 'I love them. You hear sociologists and specialists of different sorts, struggling to discover or make clear ideas set out wonderfully years ago (in different words, to find different audiences) by great, and less than great novelists. They don't know what they are missing. All of these beautiful, severe, true things, lying about waiting to be understood. There should be Billy Grahams for The Novel, on soapboxes, on street corners.'

Often Elizabeth's letters mixed gossip of social events with deeper happenings. She was off to meet Christina Stead; was going to a rainforest with Margaret Dick; Patrick and Manoly had been over for dinner. But she was also 'trying to work' and was 'wrestling with Great Moral Problems, and finding everything very interesting'. She was reading a book by Elizabeth Bowen; apologised for a gap in the correspondence but said that 'dear friends nearby have had tragic things happening to two or three people in one house'; confirmed that YM had her new hearing aid; revealed Margaret Dick had a 'swain' in Sydney who was 'not ideal'; reported that she had been to her friend Yolanda Davies' home for dinner and that she liked Jean Rhys. She had taken Kylie Tennant and Christina Stead to lunch and realised that all three of them were 'exceedingly different'; and 'Yes, some writing is happening. Not very euphonious, quite cement-blackish, but going on anyway!'

The duty towards Kit was a constant through much of the decade as Elizabeth and Andrew Robertson rallied to support her. There were regular dramas to do with Kit's physical and mental health. Her resentments towards Shirley caused more tensions, and Elizabeth also expended time and energy trying to settle Kit into accommodation. Elizabeth and Shirley had by now developed a strong connection that did not depend on their mutual worry and frustrations about Kit, but Elizabeth was at times bothered by the unspoken transactional elements of the relationship. As Kit prepared to return from yet another overseas trip at the end of 1979, Elizabeth wrote to Judah Waten: 'Where can I hide?? … Patrick said, "She's a destroyer!"'

*Elizabeth Harrower (left) with Shirley Hazzard in* Look & Listen Magazine, *1984.*

Elizabeth's view of Shirley grew more jaundiced over time. In an unpublished note about their friendship, Elizabeth wrote:

'Remember asking Kit what S was like. Her mother said, "gentle and sensitive". That was when she was v. young, and I think that was the girl who wrote the early books and stories. When she was here at first, we met almost every day, or every day and talked and talked and had a huge amount in common. We were friends. She changed; I suppose. Other friends, famous, dealt with it differently.'[9]

'Other friends' appears to be a reference to Patrick White, who was critical of Hazzard's later writings and distanced himself from her over time. But the entry is most revealing of Elizabeth's difficulties as she watched Hazzard grow more successful and famous. The 'divorced child's' capacity to feel rejected was never far below the surface.

# 9

## The Miles Franklin Affair

ELIZABETH HARROWER HAD HIGH HOPES OF WINNING the Miles Franklin Literary Award in 1967.[1] *The Watch Tower* had been enthusiastically reviewed and friends, including Patrick White, were supportive. Could this be her year? She had missed out with *The Long Prospect* a decade earlier, but she had a higher profile now and was also living in her home country. Her main rival appeared to be White's own novel, *The Solid Mandala*. He had won the inaugural Miles Franklin in 1957 for *Voss* and was a dominating presence in the culture. But a decade later he decided he had enough accolades and would not enter any more book prizes.

That message did not get through to his publishers, Eyre & Spottiswoode, who entered *The Solid Mandala* on his behalf. It was promptly named the winner by the judges, headed by legendary Angus & Robertson book editor Beatrice Davis, who exercised considerable power over Australian literature during her long career. White was told the news in a congratulatory phone call from his publishers. He was livid, demanded the novel be withdrawn and telegraphed Davis: 'Must emphasise cannot accept award for book submitted without my knowledge.' He told her to divide the prize and the money between *The Watch Tower* and *Trap*, the first novel by Peter Mathers, an Englishman who had lived as an adult in Australia.[2] White said in a letter to his agent that both works were well above the average book which usually won the Miles Franklin. The arguments over what should happen went on for a couple of days by telephone.

In the end, the trustees of the prize decided on a single winner and awarded it to Mathers, who had relocated back to the UK. There, on 13 April 1967, he received a telegram saying he had won $1000 and could he please let the organisers know who would accept the prize on his behalf in Australia on the following Tuesday.[3] *Trap*, published by Cassell Australia, was Mathers' first novel. It tells the story of Jack Trap – 'an awe-inspiring mixture of Irish, English, Aborigine, and even Tierra del Fuegan. But he looks Aboriginal.' The book's dustjacket described it as a 'biting, very funny novel' and the eponymous hero as a symbol, surrounded by 'a variety of characters who represent the different aspects of an oppressive society'. When it was released, Cassell ran a promotional advertisement in *The Sydney Morning Herald* saying that *Trap* was 'the first big success Australia has had with the new and youth experimental style of the novel of today and tomorrow. Few writers have had the courage to look at contemporary Australia in this hard, satirical light.'[4] Mathers was thirty-five and struggling to write full-time while supporting his wife and two daughters, so the prize money was very welcome. White had backed Harrower strongly but wrote to his cousin Peggy Garland that he was glad *Trap* had won because it was one of the 'few creative novels' about Australia.[5]

Harrower was bitterly disappointed, and some friends were dismayed. Judah Waten stayed silent in public, but Margaret Dick wrote a scathing letter to *Australian Book Review*. She did not reveal she was a second cousin and close friend to Harrower, with whom she shared a flat. She did not mention *The Watch Tower* or its author but instead attacked the judges for their 'chauvinism'.

So, the Miles Franklin Award has come and gone once more, and the judges, forced by Patrick White's withdrawal to exercise the function for which they were appointed, have bestowed the accolade on the author of 'Trap'. I have no desire to criticise unkindly a young man's first book and would never have done so if 'Trap' had been properly received as an imitation in Australian terms of a style and attack already employed to better effect elsewhere, but still, an attempt with notable merit and certainty not excluding the possibility of better things to come.

Instead, it has been hailed as a brilliant satirical tour-de-force, as a 'breakthrough' in Australian writing, a turning-point after which – according to one critic – not only Australian writing but Australia itself 'will never be the same'. All this is pathetic, indicating as it does that chauvinism blinds many of our intelligentsia more effectively, if anything, than the man-in-the-street. Because 'Trap' by technical peculiarities deceives the unwary into supposing that its style is 'new' (foreheads to ground, please!) because it defends the aboriginal [sic], lays about the affluent, proves that in its handling of sex Australians can be sludge merchants like anybody else, it has apparently been overlooked that the satire is crude, applied with a wooden mallet, that the sex and humour are at the level of a lavatory joke, that the characters are galvanised cardboard, only alive insofar as they fit stereotypes that evoke happy recognition, and that reading the book is like running a three-legged race in a ploughed field.[6]

Margaret went on to compare *Trap* to Joseph Heller's *Catch-22*, published in 1961, noting it attempted the same thing – 'satire handled in a truly original and unconventional style' – but Heller's work was so much better, with its 'slashing satire, but with a diamond-cutting edge', its 'Rabelaisian sex', its 'energetic style' and 'ferocious wit'. The difference between the books, she wrote, was the difference between originality and gimmickry, but those who lacked critical standards or whose critical standards were parochial were unable to recognise that difference. 'It is sad', she concluded, 'that a prize which should be the major prestige award of the year is in growing danger of falling into disrepute.'

Margaret's letter showed her intellectual confidence. She had read widely, published several books and in a few short years in Australia had become something of an expert on Australian literature, including writing a book on Kylie Tennant. When *ABR* ran the letter, Waten wrote to Margaret, whom he knew personally:

This is to say that I liked your letter in *Aust Book Review*, very much. I would have liked to have said something about the award but dared not as I would have been an easy target, considering that I had a book out myself last year. I don't even know whether Cheshire [publisher of his book, *Season of Youth*] put it into the contest; often they don't as there is some friction between them and Beatrice [Davis] and they think Beatrice has made up her mind anyway. Personally, I have nothing against Peter Mathers. I met him in London, and I found him a nice lad albeit with a big chip on his shoulder and pretty humourless ... You made the point, which is really one of principle ... Joyce and Henry James sired a school of writers who seem to have a positive horror of a clear sentence and an obvious construction. Mathers is one of the school; the saintly Patrick is another, admittedly more formidable ...[7]

That sideswipe at White was not surprising. The communist Waten was a writer who valued ideas and advocacy above literary style.

The incident over the Miles Franklin came as Australian writing was changing – moving away from social realists and more political writers like Waten, Tennant, Ruth Park, D'Arcy Niland and Katharine Susannah Prichard, who had been so popular in the immediate post-war period. In some cases, their stories were told from a left-wing, sometimes communist, perspective. By 1957, when the Miles Franklin was launched, Australian writing was already moving into modernist territory. The judges signalled where the prize sat in the literary landscape when they chose White's *Voss*, followed by Stow's *To the Islands* in 1958. Since then, it had been won by White (again), Vance Palmer, Thea Astley (twice), Sumner Locke Elliott, George Johnston and George Turner. *The Watch Tower* would have sat happily with that cohort. *Trap* was a more adventurous choice.

But Harrower was hot, and in her October 1967 interview for the National Library of Australia's oral history program, she seemed to revel in her image of instinctive writer, telling Hazel de Berg:

I don't have a blueprint, very, very scrappy notes and I do much more sitting in silence over a typewriter than typing, I can spend, oh, seven hours more or less brooding over it. I'm always quite impressed when I hear other writers describing their theory and I feel there must be something lacking in me because I have very, very few theories. I feel what I'm doing is, I'm tracking something down, what I think is true about life. That sounds a terrible cliché, but it is a fact. I want to write terribly accurately as a scientist might do something, and yet I think I write with strong feeling, because I am a person of strong feeling … I don't start

with a specific plan or plot, but I usually have one or two characters, and above all I have a strong feeling about some situation
in life …

The source of her material? That was hard to identify because
'in a way anything, everything, every situation, everything you do
is useful to you if you're a writer, and the only things that are useful
to me, though, in a way, are the things that I take in unconsciously.'[8]
Harrower needed the money but found her Macmillan job tedious. She told Margaret: 'The extreme, extraordinary quietness of the
office has been hard to put up with. The boredom is quite something.'
She had word that one of her short stories had been picked up for a
London Penguin anthology and wrote to Margaret, who was lecturing for the Arts Council in Armidale, northern New South Wales:
'Why don't I, for heaven's sake write some more???? Why don't you?
We must be brighter than we act if you know what I mean.'
She was offhand about her short stories and did not rank them
with her novels. On 19 February 1968, she sent a story to Geoffrey
Dutton, who was editing an anthology: 'As I have no feelings about
short stories, and know nothing about writing or selling them, this
is rather like an uneven work of fiction. If this is too far from the
sort of thing they expect, please scrap it and say I was run over by
a taxi before I could finish the job.'
A year later she was equally jaundiced in an essay for the Ohio-
based literary magazine *The Kenyon Review*: 'So, to the question:
Is there a paying market for serious short fiction in Australia? The
only answer at this time is: Emphatically not … Australia is not a
metaphysical country. Ideas that might be right or wrong are anath-
ema. All this questioning, and moralizing, and hair-splitting that

writers indulge in: these allegedly superior perceptions and sub-tleties; the too-extensive vocabularies are no more than morbid and wearisome to straight-forward minds … In tennis or one or two other sports, we feel certain of our ground, having been told in print that we are champions. But how are we to know what to think of our artists and oracles?' One problem, Harrower wrote, was the cultural cringe; most Australians approached the work of 'any untried overseas writer with greater confidence than they do the work of any untried Australian'.

Harrower argued that young people who were 'good at English' at school were turning to journalism, criticism, non-fiction of every description: 'Up and coming pundits, pronouncing easily on real life and real people rather than on imaginary persons and situations, will have taken command of considerable celebrity and certain affluence while a gifted new writer is producing one publishable collection of fiction, and supporting himself meanwhile in some other occupation.'[9]

Even so, Elizabeth was not about to exit the country she had returned to almost a decade earlier. She had grown used to Australia and told Hazel de Berg that she had 'no desire to go away again. I think that writers don't have to rush all over the place, at least the sort of writer I am doesn't have to go away all that often, because it's not new sights exactly that stimulate me, and people come to Sydney more and more and there are other writers living here.'

*The Watch Tower* enjoyed great critical success but sold poorly and was remaindered. Sun Books, set up as a paperback publisher by Max Harris, Geoffrey Dutton and Brian Stonier in Melbourne in 1965, rereleased *The Long Prospect* in 1966 but it sold only 3400 copies over the next couple of years and was also remaindered.

Elizabeth was still working at Macmillan but was aware she would have to live dangerously again – that is, leave full-time work – if she were serious about writing. Friends urged her to apply for a fellowship from the Commonwealth Literary Fund, where Kylie Tennant was still an advisory board member, and in October 1967 she received a telegram to say she had been successful. She would be paid $6000 in twelve monthly payments. She wrote to the chief of the National Library, Sir Harold White, to say she had hesitated to apply for grants in the past and had felt 'puritanically, that it was better to do everything the hard way'. By 'working full time, saving then leaving work and living frugally, I have done most of my writing full time, but it was an arduous course. Now, having proved my perseverance to myself, I look forward with relief to the year's worry-free freedom to write.'

'I am supposed to write a book,' she told Shirley Hazzard and confessed the thought of the grant was alarming. She would resign from Macmillan but: 'The future seems dark and precarious, and the application quite restless and silly.' Even so, her new novel could steer her into new territory. Friends urged her to flick the switch from the darkness of *The Watch Tower*. Sid Baker suggested she stop writing about 'mindless good girls, who are left in the lurch and/or trampled into the dust by nasty, horrible, evil, selfish males' and reverse the roles.

In March 1968 as Elizabeth prepared to leave her job at Macmillan, she had 'seven or eight pages of notes' for the novel. She told Judah Waten she would not do any writing before she left her job: 'You can't start a novel in odd half-hours, really.' Her idea, she told him, was 'so amorphous at this stage I'm almost afraid to look at the notes in case they disappear, you know, whisp away'. Yet she felt she had a strong central idea, and this would 'magnetise all the other things that are floating around in my mind and in due course it will make a book, but this remains to be seen.'

Harrower had just turned forty and *The Watch Tower* had shown her at the peak of her powers. Now, the question was whether she could do it all over again.

# 10

# Crisis of Confidence

Elizabeth Harrower once told Patrick White that writing a novel was like 'digging a ditch with your brain'.[1] Nonetheless, it was a process that a born writer like her was driven to, and in 1968 she had cause to be grateful as the Commonwealth Literary Fund money began to flow. Yet she worried that her life was now so filled with other people that she would struggle to find space to write amid all her distractions. There was her mother, Margaret, and Kit Hazzard, who was both friend and burden. But it was her close relationship with Kylie Tennant that was most emotionally draining. The women supported each other in their writing but Elizabeth was constantly caught up in the problems of her 'second family'. Their Blue Mountains cottage was designed as a writers' retreat, but the women often spent weekends cleaning the house and doing outside chores.

Still, Harrower was hopeful she could carve out the time to write. In July she told the fund that she was 'still working away on the first draft of my novel. There is not very much I can tell you about it at this stage – until they are finished, novels are rather amorphous and undiscussable – but I am writing all the time, and glad to be writing.' At the end of 1968 Harrower was still positive, if a little guarded, as she again reported progress to the fund: 'This is to let you know that I am still working full time on my novel. I am writing slowly, as always, but seem to be progressing fairly well, although past experience tells me there is still great deal to be done.'

It had not been an easy year. Her father, Frank, had died in November 1968 and while she had not seen him for some time, his death prompted a renewed connection with her Newcastle past. Her half-sister, Yvonne Harrower, learnt of Elizabeth's existence only after Frank's death when family members decided it was time for the teenager to meet her older sibling. Yvonne took the train from her home in Wollongong to meet Elizabeth at Central Station. They ate pancakes with maple syrup in a city cafe and spent the afternoon across the harbour at Elizabeth's flat in Want Street, Mosman. Yvonne was impressed with her older sister but other than exchanging a few Christmas cards they did not keep in touch after this. Yvonne realised that her mother was a very jealous person who had never wanted Frank to have a relationship with Elizabeth. Ongoing contact between the half-sisters seemed an impossibility. Yvonne told me in 2023: 'It wasn't worth the drama that my mother would have created.' The meeting must have been disruptive for Elizabeth, even though she appeared to make no effort to continue contact with Yvonne. As with Yvonne's older brother David three years earlier, it seems she had little interest in forging links with her half-siblings.

Elizabeth's relationship with Kylie was intense in those years. In 1968 they spent time together at Diamond Head near Port Macquarie, where Kylie and Roddy owned a small shack used as a writing retreat. Kylie was working on *The Man on the Headland*, about Ernie Metcalfe, an eccentric resident of the area, and Elizabeth was working on her novel, at that stage possibly bearing the title *Slowly Spreading Circles* but which would become *In Certain*

*Circles*. Kylie was also doing battle with a mining company which had the right to mine for rutile on her 1.5 acres. Elizabeth joined the fight, writing a short essay on Diamond Head. 'There is always the silence, yet you often remember the slush of the wind in the grass, and the birds noisy before sunrise … The track through the grass smells strongly of honey, and yellow and white everlasting daisies grow everywhere. And of course, on the walk up from the clearing you rise right into a view of a Pacific empty of everything but invisible fish below and clouds above. Deserted beaches stretch for miles.'[2]

Harrower was under pressure from those who were financing her writing. By 5 August 1969, almost eighteen months after she began accessing her grant, the fund again asked for a progress report. Harrower wrote back on 11 August to say she had completed the manuscript and was in the process of working it over: 'I hope the re-writing won't take a great deal of time now.' She was still trying to visit Kylie at Diamond Head on weekends, and one day in October spent seven hours on the train to join her there. The trips north proved therapeutic. 'You wouldn't know Elizabeth for the same girl,' Kylie wrote to Mavis Cribb. 'One week has relaxed her no end.'

Around this time Harrower met another great Australian novelist to whom she would grow close. Ron Geering, who taught English at the University of NSW, and his wife, Dorothy, introduced her to Christina Stead when Stead visited Australia in 1969. Geering was championing Stead's work at a time when Australians had not truly appreciated the expatriate author's output – despite the fact she had already written nine novels, including *The Man Who Loved Children*. Later, Stead read *The Long Prospect* for the first time and wrote to Harrower: 'You have a remarkable sober acerbity, and almost historical view … you are unique.'

Stead had had a more upper-middle-class upbringing than Elizabeth, but both had lived with extremely difficult men as children. In Harrower's case it was her stepfather. Stead, who was born in 1902, suffered under a domineering father, David Stead, a marine biologist and conservationist. The family was financially comfortable, and Christina qualified as a teacher, but she had an unhappy time till she left for Europe in 1928. Then her world changed, and she revelled in a big relationship, culminating in marriage in 1952 to William 'Bill' Blake. She shared his Marxist views and they pursued politics and writing in several countries until his death in 1968. Back in Australia in the 1970s, she and Elizabeth would grow close.

In December 1969 Elizabeth was looking forward to Christmas but told Judah Waten that there was much to do and the first item on her list was 'finish the novel. So I had better obey.' On 6 January 1970, Kylie reported to Roddy from Diamond Head that 'Elizabeth is working. Yesterday she did four pages. When I said four pages were not enough, she said if she did twenty like me it wouldn't be worth reading … she got to her typewriter at six so she could get the best of the day while she was fresh.' Two days later she added: 'Yesterday Elizabeth and I went swimming and got so exhausted that we couldn't work.'

By March Elizabeth was in Sydney, suffering a stiff back and headaches and trying desperately to finish the book. Kit Hazzard drained her of energy, one day visiting 'in a state of pre-suicidal depression and self-pity'. Elizabeth told Margaret Dick: 'I started sympathetic, as often before, and ended repelled, as often before.'

She confessed to her cousin: 'I've done next to no work because I haven't been well and have had my first headache-free day today. I may go up to Blackheath with Kylie and Benno [Benison] on Friday night, either for the weekend or for a few days – yet to be worked out … Mum is coming over Thursday night … I suppose I am to be looked at like an idol or something. Another of my least favourite things. The very thought makes my head sore.' Struggling to complete her book, she had been cheered that week by separate visits to her Mosman flat from Roddy, who brought her some Soneryl sleeping tablets, and Kylie, who brought a chicken. She told Margaret she had been 'very pleased to see Kylie' and, in a comment that hinted at the complex strains in her relationship with Roddy, said, 'Anyway, he must have wanted to come over, and seemed to enjoy himself.'

In April Harrower began typing out a 'fair copy' of the novel and told Waten: 'I have no strong feelings about it, I am simply relieved ever to have brought it to this stage. These two years (!) have been full of personal distractions with relatives and things. Certainly not all that time has been spent writing.' Indeed, it had not. Elizabeth had dealt with many pressures from Kylie's family as well as her own. Her parents, who had spent time in the UK, now appeared to be living separately – Richard in Essex, where his son was based, and Margaret back at the family home in Mosman.

Elizabeth's relationship with Kylie and Roddy continued to be intense: on 5 May 1970, Roddy wrote to Kylie, who was at Blackheath, to say the financials in the future would be enough 'for five of us to live on (I am including Elizabeth)'. He suggested changes to Blackheath to expand the house. Harrower was still grinding out *In Certain Circles* (with early versions carrying the subtitle

*The Vantage Point)* and Kylie wrote to her husband: 'Elizabeth is still halfway through what must be her third last clean draft. She'll be buggering about for a few years yet at the rate she's going.' On 2 June 1970 Harrower told Waten that another ten days or two weeks were all she needed now to finalise the manuscript. She had enjoyed some 'celebratory lunches' because 'Whatever the book is worth, finishing a task is important'. She confessed that: 'It isn't the book I like most of what I've written. But it has its own validity.' At some level, she suggested, it was the only book she could write even though 'If I had any choice I'd have written something more cheerful.' Kylie wrote to Hunters Hill: 'Dear Family, Elizabeth has lit the two little candles on the mantelpiece to celebrate the finish of her clean typing of the novel.'

On 9 June 1970, Harrower sent the manuscript to the Commonwealth Literary Fund. She had missed her 'deadline' and blamed 'minor illnesses and one or two other things' for the time taken to complete the book. She was grateful for the fellowship, which 'made the difference between never writing another book, and deciding to write more, regardless of the odd difficulties: and to a person to whom words, and ideas, and books matter, this is a very big difference'. Her publishers were equally keen to see what she had produced and Harrower shipped a copy of *In Certain Circles* to Alan Maclean, at Macmillan in London.

The novel is set in Sydney. Unlike her earlier works which focus on central, almost claustrophobic relationships, it follows the intertwined lives of two sets of siblings from the end of World War II to the late 1960s. The atmosphere is more benign: Harrower was still wrestling with the familiar themes of coercion and submission, but the men in this novel are not always monstrous, her women not always victims. Immense social and political upheaval had begun in the second half of the 1960s and would continue into the next decade. In Australia conservative politicians were running out of steam as Gough Whitlam led a Labor Party whose time had almost come. In Europe a new generation was ready to detonate old structures in the name of equality. Traditional gender roles were being tested at the same time as modern marketing and advertising promoted consumption and materialism. Harrower had been back in Australia for a decade and was a very different person from the 23-year-old who had mined her past for her London novels. She had aimed for a more complex structure and plot for *In Certain Circles*; she wanted to break free from the stories and characters that shaped her childhood and produce a more global, outward-looking novel.

Although it had been a struggle to complete, Elizabeth was not unduly worried about the reception of the book. She had fulfilled her obligations to the fund and waited now for London's response. Feedback proved slow, but Elizabeth was philosophical and in August wrote to Robert Cross, who ran the Australian branch of Macmillan, saying: 'It may not be his [Maclean's] cup of tea – in which case we'll have to do better. News is bound to arrive soon.' Her equanimity was soon tested with her mother's death on 13 September 1970. Margaret Kempley was only sixty-one when she suffered a stroke. 'She died overnight,' Elizabeth said decades later. 'I still feel resentful. I vaguely knew she had migraines … It took me a long time to recover … It was horrific, I thought nothing would be so terrible again. I think you only get shocked like that once … You realise something then and you don't really recover, you just change.'[3] Elizabeth had not always found her mother easy, telling Shirley Hazzard 'I have a gentle, intractable mother who worries me too … it's rather hard all round.' But mother and daughter were very close, having formed an alliance in the early years of Margaret's marriage against the difficult Richard Kempley. In 2012, when she read my biography of Australian expat writer Madeleine St John, who suffered as a child after the suicide of her mother, Elizabeth emailed me: 'How lucky are those of us who have/had loving (and stable) mothers!'

Her mother's death unsettled her and a week or so later, with still no word from Macmillan, she wrote to her new London agent, Michael Horniman, at A.P Watt & Son: 'I have never written a novel I liked less.' She wondered whether she should withdraw the manuscript. 'This is rather a hard decision to arrive at, because there is no doubt that a lot of work went into the writing of the book as it stands, and here and there it seems to have been worth the effort. What do you think? Should I withdraw it? I am used to liking my own work better than this. If the general opinion is unenthusiastic perhaps it could be scrapped.'

On the same day, 28 September 1970, Harrower wrote to Robert Cross in Melbourne to say that she had suggested to Horniman that 'the novel should, perhaps, be scrapped'. She told Cross: 'I think Macmillan's have published worse (far worse) novels, but I am not attached to it greatly, which probably means something or other.' Cross was on his way back to London, having finished his Australian posting and Harrower asked: 'Do let me know what you think, if there's time before you leave.' Harrower was pre-empting a rejection of the manuscript but she surely did not expect the response three days later from Cross's replacement, Gordon Ross. Ross said while there had been some 'toing and froing' over the manuscript, with London wanting to publish, it was not possible to go ahead. He suggested Harrower would not be 'unduly sorry about this decision'.

Then a few days later a contradictory letter arrived from Alan Maclean in London. He 'certainly' wanted to publish, even though 'I don't believe the novel is going to make your fortune, but I hope we shall get some really good reviews for it.' Harrower wrote to him on 24 November, asking if she could do some 'judicious cutting'. She told her agent: 'I was never very happy with the writing of this novel and was briefly cheered to have brought it to any sort of conclusion.' She felt she could do better and now wanted a month to sort it out. Even so, her faith in the book was evaporating and she told Waten in December: 'People (non-writers) say you have no idea of the quality of your own work, but I don't think that's true. I know whether I'm doing what I intend or not. This last book never pleased me at any stage – for very good reasons. Such is life.' Years later she told Giulia Giuffrè that the novel had been written from willpower: in a good book, the characters should 'force it along … but that didn't happen in that other book and I knew it … It was quite readable, but the point is, it wasn't interesting to me.'

Life intervened again as Elizabeth heard she would have to move from her Want Street flat. Kylie told Mavis Cribb on 6 December 1970: 'Elizabeth is looking for a flat and says if she doesn't find one, she will live at Blackheath. As she and Roddy can't conceivably live in the same place I don't know where that leaves us but no doubt it will settle itself.' On 10 January 1971, as she began the rewrite, Elizabeth revealed to the Steegs that while Maclean had accepted the novel, 'we both know it is disappointing … There was an interesting book to be written, but I blocked it for all sorts of reasons and my concentration disappeared. People.' The suggestion that she had been distracted by 'people' was somewhat pointed, given the amount of time and energy she had expended on Shirley's mother.

It had been an annus horribilis on a professional and personal level for Elizabeth and there was more distress in the new year. On 19 January 1971, just four months after the death of her mother, Elizabeth's stepfather died in a London hospital. After Margaret's death, Richard had suggested he return to live with Elizabeth in Sydney, a proposition, she told Waten, that left her 'ready to book a passage to Siberia'. The death of this man who had been the model for Harrower's most aggressive male characters, Stan Peterson and Felix Shaw, must surely have been a relief.

Harrower was busy tinkering with the rewrite of *In Certain Circles* but was still running defence when in March she met with Alan Maclean, who was visiting Sydney. Maclean, whose brother was the Soviet spy Donald Maclean, was renowned for his English charm and diplomacy, but over lunch Harrower did her best to turn him against her novel. She followed up with a letter complaining about Macmillan's marketing of *The Watch Tower* in 1966. It had been remaindered, she reminded Maclean. There had been a 'lot of free attention in the press' but distribution had been hampered by the lack of a salesman in Sydney or Queensland for six months before or after its publication. 'The excellent reviews were out before the stock arrived … the office received more inquiries and orders for it than for any novel since I have been working at Macmillan – but all pre-stock.' She told Maclean: 'I have always felt a little sad about the timing of that book's appearance. Not a world tragedy, but novels can have happy or unhappy circumstances.'

Her misgivings about *In Certain Circles* were compounded by grief at her mother's death. 'So many things have happened to me since … that its [the novel's] importance has receded to just about nothingness,' she told Waten in March 1971. 'I wouldn't feel like that about a piece of work that satisfied me. Such is life!'

Harrower had given Maclean plenty of rope with which to hang her and on 25 March, having read the revised manuscript, he wrote her a 'Dear John' letter. 'I found that the book fell away sharply in the second half,' he said. 'Somehow what had started as a fascinating story of a group of characters whose lives interlocked at different and interesting levels seemed to change gear and speed, and to lose its form and concentration; it became almost part of a saga, and I felt its strength was dissipated and its tautness lost. I therefore feel disappointment in the book, both in terms of plot and character, but I remain a most fervent admirer of your writing and your very real gifts of observation and dialogue.'

Maclean went on: 'I cannot say that I think the novel is successful – and to say that it is fifteen times better written than many novels that are published every year is neither helpful nor comforting, although it is certainly true. Now, what are we to do? We have already made an offer to your agent Michael Horniman to publish the book, and I am certainly not going to go back on that. We have both a moral and an actual commitment to publish, and although we would do [so] with less than a desirable degree of confidence, it often happens that a publisher is proved quite wrong in his estimate of his own wares.'

Harrower must have been appalled by Maclean's next suggestion: if she were able to find another publisher, Macmillan would let the book go. If she couldn't, he would publish it. It was not exactly a vote of no confidence, but it was close. 'I am not pressing you to put the book to one side,' Maclean told her. 'But I know this is a course of action which you will consider … if you decide to stick with us and want us to go ahead then I say again that we will do our very best to prove ourselves wrong!' He included a reader's report from someone 'who is something of a Harrower fan'.

The reader, C.H. Derrick, had read Harrower's first version the previous July and now said the revised version was 'essentially the same novel'. He found the rewrite to be 'more distilled, sharpened, polished … it's the same book but it has found its identity more precisely: a sharp and intense abstract study of personal relationships within and without marriage, among well-to-do Australians with some emphasis upon the destructive effects of (a) egoism (b) pity, self-pity included … Very good marks to the author's intelligence, her observations of people, her wry, precise, and economical use of language.' But did it work as a novel? 'Throughout I get a feeling of unreality, of diagram, of theory,' the reader reported. 'But I may be wrong: it may be that the author's mode of perception is simply too feminine to connect with my hairy old mind. The subtlety and brilliance of the author's mind is obvious [but] I find the book at once empty and stifling. I can only fumble, as above, in search of a reason why.'

It was a decidedly negative, indeed patronising, report but Harrower adopted a measured tone when she wrote to Maclean to withdraw the manuscript. 'Your assessment is more than just and kind … As I said at lunch that day, I do know the difference between a good and a bad novel, and it is a model of what a novel should not be,' she said. 'All I regret are what I can only call "the true things" scattered through it here and there, that I am addicted to as a physicist might be addicted to quarks. But, quite possibly, in the long run, they won't be wasted.'

She was 'interested and not irritated' by the reader's report; she always knew *In Certain Circles* was flawed. 'When it was first completed, and even at the end of the cutting, I warned my two readers here, that it was like a blueprint, a theoretical thing, that – breaking all my own rules – everything was told and nothing demonstrated, that the people were not differentiated or visible, and that it was dead. You will see that after my own criticism, your reader seems positively kind … If you can believe me, I am relieved by this decision. I have felt all along that this novel shouldn't see the light of day. Other people around me will moan, and I'll have to reconcile them to it [but] I feel rather as if a disaster had been averted.'

Harrower was now in full damage control. Three days later she wrote to her agent, Michael Horniman, to say that her publishers 'think I can write but that this particular novel does not come off. I feel bound to accept their fair and impartial judgment and withdraw the novel from circulation, although Alan said he would not withdraw his original offer to publish. I am sorry to have involved you in such an unsatisfactory business and, of course, regret on my own account the time and effort wasted. Next time, I must make sure to do better.'

Maclean was relieved that Harrower had 'taken our criticism in this generous way' and decided to put the book to one side: 'It must be the hardest thing in the world for a writer to do. The important thing now is to get started on the next one and I hope that you feel ready for the fray.' He suggested an advance for the next novel: 'I don't know whether you actually like this sort of pressure, but you are far too good a writer for any publisher in his right mind to let slip … I really do admire the courage of your decision and the grace with which it has been made.' On the same day, Horniman wrote to Harrower urging her to 'put the book behind you and turn to another'.

On 3 May, she rejected the advance from Macmillan: 'I do hope to start another novel soon but naturally feel cautious about committing the same sort of crime twice. At the moment, I'm hovering.' She told Horniman: 'I do not think I am the sort of writer who responds well to knowing that money has been paid for work not yet produced. It seems best to work off the government's $6000 Fellowship before accepting an advance from Macmillan.' It is agonising to read this correspondence, so carefully filed by Harrower in her papers, and so revealing of her efforts to retain agency. Her public comments in later years would gloss over the failed novel, but the letters show how damaging the incident was to her confidence and ability to continue writing.

Pulling the book on the eve of publication had seemed the only option for a work she claimed as 'wrought, manipulated, not organic'.[4] In April she told Judah Waten that 'since I never liked the thing as whole, only stray reflections, this isn't the tragedy it ought to be. In the past I've had a feeling for what I've done that has simply never been there this time. Such is life. I'll put it aside … Had better go off now and do something like washing or shopping, or even considering the next book. Because there had better be one.' She had another book in mind, 'notes and all', but didn't want to make another false start. 'The worst of it is, in a way, having that ghastly CLF thing in the back of your mind. If the one written for it doesn't come off, I mean. Because, of course, there are always sixty people who feel they were more deserving. Ah, well!' She wrote to Hazzard: 'After a reader's report and a letter from Alan (in which he generously did not withdraw his offer to publish) I decided finally to shelve my novel. Alan wrote so kindly, such considerate, morale-building letters, that it almost seems nothing bad has happened. But it does make you hesitate to dash into the next thing.' In June she insisted to Waten that she was neither 'hurt' nor 'cast down' by events: 'If it [the novel] had been utterly rejected, then I would have been mortified, I suppose, but even then – only if I had regarded it as a good piece of work, which I don't. So, here we are. Being the sort of person I am, I certainly do get hurt, but not by books. There, only my own opinion really counts for much, and I can put up with any amount of criticism from myself about my work. It is my own feeling that doesn't want to see it in print.' She said she had not started work on another novel.

Was Elizabeth a reliable reporter of her own emotions? She wanted it on the record that she was the only reader of her work who mattered but she was struggling after the disappointment of the shelved novel. 'I'm writing notes, sifting notes for a novel,' she told Waten in August. 'But I'm not plunging in till I feel like plunging on, though I spend a lot of time thinking about it all. In between times, I see shows, read a lot, and give my pint of blood to the Blood Bank and have my hair cut.' A few months later she told Shirley Hazzard that she had 'written two poems and seen people and wasted my time badly, which is why I had better be exiled'.

It was an upbeat, almost flippant comment, but Harrower was hurting badly.

# 11

## Lovers and Friends

THE BEGINNING OF THE END OF ELIZABETH HARROWER'S career as a novelist coincided with the unravelling of one of the deepest relationships in her life. The author never connected the two, never suggested that as the tensions grew in her friendship with Kylie Tennant she began to lose her impulse to write. In comments Harrower made over many years explaining why she had dumped *In Certain Circles* there was no mention of Tennant and the crisis the couple experienced in the early 1970s. Yet her decision cannot be seen in isolation from her emotional turmoil in this period. The two women had shared much since meeting in 1962 but as she drew a line under *In Certain Circles*, in 1971, Harrower felt 'despair and desperation' about their 'peculiar', even 'destructive', relationship. Her mother and stepfather were dead, and after three years of work so was her fifth novel.

Elizabeth thus had many reasons to grieve. She had lost one of her biggest supporters with the death of her mother. Margaret could be irritating: 'God! Mothers are enough to make you commit suicide with sheer irritation,' Elizabeth once wrote to Margaret Dick. But the women had had a strong bond. More than thirty years later, Elizabeth told her cousin Thurza Snelson, in Newcastle: 'In my experience you just don't "get over" the death of your mother. I still miss my mother and wish that she could still be here … I have friends who never liked or got on with their mothers and I feel sorry for them.' With her parents dead, Elizabeth's last link with her past was her maternal grandmother. Elizabeth had a sense of duty towards Helen Burns Hughes Lamb Wilson, who was living in a nursing home in Queensland, but she was sometimes impatient at MumMum's 'tragic letters'.

Margaret Kempley had left money and property to her daughter, but by the end of 1971 Kylie reported to Mavis Cribb that 'Elizabeth is being rather difficult and weighed down by the cares of probating her mother's estate'. Elizabeth was fretting about Kylie. She was still paying rates for the cottage at Blackheath, but it had lost much of its appeal; she felt outnumbered by the Rodds and the friends of Bim and Benison, whose sleeping bags and bodies took up all available space at weekends. She had spent countless days at the cottage 'cutting back stupid blackberries that came back every year' and had 'waded' through emotional weeds for years, carrying Kylie's worries about her troubled son Bim as if they were her own. She tended to take on the cares of others. Jinx Nolan told me: 'She feels other people's pain, she knows their pain before they do. She is one of these people who is sensitive to others' feelings … Like the leaves of a tree. Any wind that is around, she responds.' Nancy Phelan had a similar view, telling Elizabeth: 'You have such wonderful understanding and ability to put yourself into the skins of others that I feel you must be in danger at times of being completely weighed down with their troubles … all very well for them but not so good for you.'

Elizabeth wanted more independence from the Rodd family and was reassessing her feelings for Kylie. She was tired of being 'the twenty-fifth spear carrier' in the Rodds' dramas, an observer whose 'only part in life is to express surprise, indignation, etc'.

When the women were out together, Kylie dominated and Elizabeth felt she could not open her mouth. She was determined 'not to trail about after [Kylie], fitting all my plans to her'.[1]

It's not clear whether Kylie was going through similar introspection. She appeared to shy away from self-reflection. Her biographer, Jane Grant, wrote that Tennant's 1986 memoir, *The Missing Heir*, was 'unsatisfying [because] although she records the surface events of her life, she deliberately frustrates insight into her interior life'. Grant suggested the extreme research Tennant had pursued for her books – the long rural treks and the time spent living in squalor in the city – were 'a form of psychological release and escape into other lives and, by implication, a mechanism through which she could avoid examining her own life too closely'. Tennant, she wrote, had constructed 'the self-protective myth of the humorous but tough-minded maverick'.[2]

In 1971, however, Kylie could not dodge reality. Bim was diagnosed with schizophrenia, adding pressure to a marriage that was now 'at breaking point'.[3] Kylie retreated to Blackheath and wrote to her husband, who had been a mentor, an editor and a facilitator of her writing career but had become a 'domestic tyrant' in her eyes, that she had felt like a 'complete serf' at Hunters Hill. 'You merely said what was to be done and I did it if I could,' she wrote. 'This has been the condition for so many years that you ignore the possibility of consulting me. You merely give orders … you do not know what scalding acid you pour over me.'[4]

With her difficult family issues, Kylie had little bandwidth to help Elizabeth through the disappointment of *In Certain Circles*, nor the grief at her mother's death. Instead, the Rodds appeared to take Elizabeth for granted. Margaret Dick had urged Elizabeth to go away for a break, but the Rodds did not believe she was strong enough to be apart from them. They must have been surprised when, in December 1971, she accepted an offer from Sidney and Cynthia Nolan to stay with them in London. Elizabeth booked her passage on the *Fairstar* for 3 January 1972 and arranged to give up her flat, planning to be away for four or five months. It would be her first visit to London since leaving in 1959. She wrote to Shirley Hazzard: 'I'll hope to do some work … Home about May. It's a fearful wrench to go … Heaven knows how a person passes a month (!) on a ship. I wish, I wish I could switch my mind to work again. Forgive all this egotism.' Elizabeth had gained much from the close relationship with Kylie, but a decade on she was exhausted, not so much unhappy but 'somehow crushed'. The trip to London was an attempt to 'do something constructive about it', she told Margaret.

Elizabeth was overwrought as the ship left Sydney. Within a few hours she wrote to the Rodds and began an avalanche of letters to Margaret revealing the depth of her anguish about Kylie and her family. 'If anyone had wanted my company in Sydney I wouldn't have gone,' she told her cousin.

> If anyone had believed I'd go away in January somewhere closer –
> I wouldn't have gone to the UK. If Cynthia hadn't been the only
> person to say she would like my company, I wouldn't have gone –
> I think, just the same, that I had to get myself out of that peculiar
> situation for a while, though not so far. And letters today from
> Kylie and Roddy confirm that, though so affectionate. But in
> despair and desperation I simply acted at last for the reasons
> given above … I intend to make a great effort to do something
> constructive while I'm away.

The letter was among dozens, sometimes pages long, sometimes written on every day of the week, that Elizabeth wrote to Margaret. She was desperate for love, telling her cousin: 'LIE if you have to and TELL me you miss me. I miss you.' These letters written over a six-month period in 1972 are among the most revealing documentation of Elizabeth's emotions and desires. They show a relaxed, intimate and trusting relationship between the cousins. They had almost always lived in the same city since meeting twenty years ago in Scotland, so the Putney correspondence is a rare record of their closeness. Elizabeth was open, vulnerable and unguarded as she poured out her distress in these months. Her correspondence with Shirley Hazzard is much larger and covers several decades but it offers far less insight into Harrower's state of mind. The writers were friends and intellectual equals, but Elizabeth did not reveal the raw emotions exhibited in her letters to Margaret. Those letters, held in a subset of Elizabeth's archive in the National Library, also show just how much her struggle to write was due to her anguish over Kylie. Forty years later, Harrower would say she suffered post-traumatic stress disorder after her mother's death, that she was 'knocked out for at least two years' with the shock, that she 'felt absolutely no affection for anyone'. [5] But in 1972 her focus was Kylie, not her mother. As the *Fairstar* sailed to the UK, Elizabeth wrote to Kylie: 'You're an angel writing to me all the way,' but she began to realise her friend did not share the same distress at their separation. Kylie's letters were cool: she did not acknowledge Elizabeth's 'doings' and seemed determined to put some emotional distance between them. Elizabeth was accustomed to dashing off letters two or three times a week to friends, but she now limited her correspondence with Kylie and her letters became less personal.

She was trying to establish a new relationship with the woman she loved, perhaps recognising that she would always have to share Kylie with Roddy. The Rodds were bound together despite their difficulties and any hope of a solo relationship with the older woman was a fantasy.

Elizabeth was, however, determined not to play the 'role of pawn'.[6] 'Of course, I'm still fond of Kylie,' she told Margaret, 'but I want to survive.' She was not prepared to have her life taken over again, and 'listen as though to tales of wondrous heroes, to the tales of Bim and Co'. The Rodds were overwhelming, and she could not 'cope with both of them, all of them'. Yet she was afraid of being abandoned and confessed to feeling unwanted by the family. It was a strange comment, given Roddy especially had made it clear he wanted to knit Elizabeth into their lives and envisaged them pooling financial resources as a single unit. He and Elizabeth clashed but he was positive about their future, perhaps recognising the depth of the women's relationship. Was he trying to shape an unconventional domestic arrangement or did he see Elizabeth as a convenient carer as he and Kylie aged? Kylie, always the pragmatist, reminded Roddy that he and Elizabeth did not get along well enough for them to live in the same house: 'I think if Elizabeth is coming back, we need some separate living quarters for either you or her. You would not live well together. But you might dwell in propinquity. Or we might be able to keep one ménage in Sydney and one up here.'

Elizabeth must have understood that as the single, childless woman she would always be on the margin of this household, with no real status. She resisted Roddy's effort to draw her in closer to the family. 'An irritating letter from Roddy this morning,' she told Margaret. 'I've been showered with love poems and chat I could do without – analysing Kylie – I only glance at them once.' Her comments suggest that while Kylie was more emotionally distant in this period, Roddy was seeking Elizabeth's support in this three-way relationship. She felt the Rodds were campaigning for her to stay with them at Hunters Hill when she returned from London. They were doing their best, Elizabeth believed, 'to see that I stay forever'. Among other things, Kylie was becoming too old and arthritic to rake up the leaves at Blackheath and 'they badly need someone to join the family and help'.

Elizabeth's grandmother Helen offered sympathy from afar and urged her to come back to Australia by plane: 'I am a poor thing at writing, but Betty, I could fill a newspaper … I hope to God you feel a bit better in every way. Cheer up dear, we can't bring back what has left us, cheer up you are young …' Was Helen sympathising with Elizabeth for the loss of her mother, or was this a reference to the break with Kylie?

In her letters (and some phone calls) to Margaret, Elizabeth wrestled with her feelings: 'I think it was necessary, essential to come away. No-one thought I could do it. But I had really been alone all my life in lots of ways, till I was 23, and so I am not unused to it basically, although I don't care for it.' She was clearer, too, about the reality of life with the Rodds. 'When I receive letters from Blackheath and Hunters Hill, full of rain, drains, disasters with cars and animals and boys, and battling on, I wonder how I can cope with all that again,' she told Margaret. 'I'm struck by all sorts of reactions – the monotony of it from Kylie's point of view and the awfulness of that and the great danger of returning if nothing had really changed – except that I have proved that I can go away, which no-one really believed.' An indication that the relationship was more intense than Elizabeth's other relationships is contained in a letter from Margaret in which she encouraged her cousin not to rush home: 'What I am saying is that *everybody* (Kylie, too!) wants what's best for you.'

The insecurity Elizabeth had felt as a child returned: 'It is difficult for me to believe from one day to the next that someone who likes me won't pull the rug out from under my feet … At the back of it I feel cautious. I am not sure that I could be disillusioned again, and I'm not sure that that's a good thing.' She was angry about the Rodds' demands. 'A lot has gone on that might have had someone cut her throat in despair.' London was calm, with 'whole hillsides of daffodils in the parks' and on the river at Putney 'swans floating by and magnolias blooming'. Just as important, people were 'being just so considerate and pleased to see me'. Elizabeth wondered if she could ever return to Sydney 'without falling into the same destructive situation'? There were hints Elizabeth was depressed. She had consulted a doctor in London about her skin, which had long been troublesome, and had been prescribed sleeping tablets. Margaret wrote to her: 'Your last two letters have sounded rather low-spirited and there have been indications that all is not well. I sincerely hope you are better, but if not, see doctors and get properly looked after.'

Life with the Nolans in Putney was very different from life in her Mosman flat and at Blackheath, where 'I was always in the wrong, and always making way for more important beings, and (on the telephone) not reacting to declarations (by R. for instance) intended to wring negative reactions from me'. Again, there is evidence of tensions between Elizabeth and Roddy and her sense of being treated as an addendum to events. She wanted a new arrangement, but she struggled to see the future: 'I can't cast off [Kylie] … We are too involved. But things have to be made possible. I must work, that's the answer. Must work. Must write. I am encouraged by the way everyone here likes me and thinks I'm good. There I felt the lowest of the low.' Since she left Sydney in January, Elizabeth had battled on two fronts – her relationship with Kylie; and resumption of her writing career after the disaster of *In Certain Circles*. She told Margaret she did not want to be a person who was 'perpetually not writing but always thinking of myself as A Writer, and everything else being second-, third- and fourth-best'. She understood the solitude needed to write. A few months later she wrote to her cousin about the struggle to get her work back on track: 'how many years of sitting alone thinking about human beings and motives go into the writing of even a few books.'

The question of how and where to work was tied to her future with the Rodds. Work meant writing: 'I can't break off in midstream like this in the prime of life??? Can I? I don't really know. And I don't know at all how my life can be arranged when I get back …' In June, almost six months after leaving Sydney, she was still mulling the issues: 'I must simply learn to have a life quite separate from Kylie's. I mean independent of her while (I hope) still seeing her (not at Hunters Hill, for preference) … Anyway, I must work, wherever I am, I can't just keep living this idle life.'

The letters revealed a clear link between her problems with Kylie and her writer's block. 'I wouldn't mind the stress if it let me write,' she told Margaret. 'Above all, what sort of situation am I going to be in when I get back? Kylie is one thing, the situation is another. I can't stay away forever because of it. I would like to have started a book before I return … I dare not sink into that destructive situation again.'

Some of her anguish lifted when she connected with Christina Stead, who was now living in Surbiton in Surrey. Elizabeth saw her several times, visiting her in 'an ancient flat with old stone stairs', and wrote to Margaret: 'She lives in a gaunt Victorian house in a gaunt Victorian crescent. Most of the other tenants have moved out; the street has been bought by developers and places are crashing down on all sides … She has a small pension from America and "earns a little". The writers also met in central London for meals. Harrower realised the older woman was not well, and ferried 'wine, bread, butter and flowers' to Surbiton. She sent Stead a copy of a talk by Margaret on Stead's work and Stead responded that Margaret 'has the gifts that go with imagination, generosity, insight, the power of recreation. She distils the spirit of the writer.' Stead had lived a much more radical and liberated life than Elizabeth, but the women hit it off and Elizabeth appreciated Stead's resilience and courage in the face of poor health and precarious finances.

Her stepfather was dead, but Elizabeth could not escape the Kempleys. Richard's brother Jack rang her from the country: his voice reminded her of her late stepfather's and 'my hair curled faintly'. In March, Jack travelled into London from Essex for lunch in Leicester Square. They walked to Hyde Park and sat in the sun. Jack was teary but clear-eyed about his brother, and Elizabeth told Margaret Dick: 'Apparently R's [Richard's] son at one time said if he'd been Mum, he'd have stuck a knife in his father [Richard]; Jack thought he [Richard] was born that way but added that strangely he and Richard had never had a quarrel, scarcely a harsh word. Just at the end Jack told him he wasn't a tin god here whatever he thought he was in Australia, but that's about the worst that ever passed between them.'

As the months passed, Elizabeth became calmer. In May she was anxious not to lose 'all this renewed whatever it is that I've got. What a relief to feel like this. You know, I think partly I've been in recent years so terrorised that I am not astonished if someone behaves in a very odd way.' She revelled in the respect shown to her in Putney: 'It is fun to be in a house where things are happening and to be part of a little routine. I had spent so much time alone waiting for people to want my company. And they bloody didn't! (Slight exaggeration!) … Yes, this is like a process of re-discovery. Initiative.'

Then, amid Elizabeth's anguish over Kylie, it seems she had a romance, albeit brief. When she had left Sydney on the *Fairstar* in January, a former work colleague from Macmillan, David Cleaver, was among those who waved her off. Elizabeth had 'unwisely kissed' him goodbye, and had been startled by the importance he attached to the gesture. He had then sent her a telegram 'mourning my departure'. But Elizabeth was not interested and decided she should be silent in order to 'disillusion him'. In an undated letter to Christina Stead, she indicated she was not interested in a romance: 'As for you only wanting a boyfriend – I had a letter from one yesterday who is travelling in New Zealand at the moment: he said he looks at everything twice, once for me and once for himself. What a pity I don't love him! He's nice too. But, but, but …' She wrote in similar vein to Margaret: 'Oh dear, David's letter today was from N.Z. … told me he looked at everything twice, once for himself and once for me. Help, help.' About this time, her grandmother, the formidable Helen Hughes, wrote to Elizabeth: 'Margaret gave me all the news About you having a nice companion.' It's not clear who this was, but it seems Elizabeth's friends were aware of a suitor. In July, her publisher, Alan Maclean, responded to an earlier letter saying he was pleased Elizabeth was still in London. 'I was feeling a little underprivileged because I thought you had departed for Australia, leaving not only your friends, but your fiancé in some unspecified doghouse.' Had Elizabeth invented a suitor simply to avoid questions about her singledom or was there a true romance underway? She had known David Cleaver for some time in Sydney; he went to her flat for dinner and they saw movies together. It seems unlikely they had an affair given the anguish Elizabeth was experiencing over Kylie. But Cleaver was close to her and wrote to her several times in London, telling her to travel home via Bulgaria and offering to send her money if she needed it. They would remain in touch back in Australia.

Elizabeth had gained perspective in London. 'Since everyone has been going on so much about unhappy childhoods so much,' she told Margaret, 'I feel bound to say I must have cast off mine (and it really leaves me unimproved and has for years) partly because of writing and partly because I told you and you listened and thought it hadn't been right or fair.' Later she talked of how the creation of her novels had allowed her to free herself of much of the sadness of her childhood. 'Perhaps it wasn't writing my books, but the deep consideration, the tremendous going-over I had to give those early years that sloughed off my youth and its grave trials,' she said to Margaret. 'Don't know. But it is true that it's years and years and too long ago to remember [when] I last felt sorry for myself on that score.'

Margaret could scarcely keep up with the flow of letters. She was pleased Elizabeth was experiencing a bigger world in Putney and urged her to work on her fiction. The Nolans are 'so good to you and for you. You really needed – I felt this strongly for ages before you went – to be seeing and talking to people who were creatively active and positively involved in life and work.'

Elizabeth had told her cousin that she was almost ready to start writing and had enough material for a dozen books. Once again, the author had realised there was never any shortage of things to say. The problem, as always, was how to say it.[7]

# 12

# Living with the Nolans

ON A SUMMER'S DAY IN JULY 1972 ELIZABETH HARRO-wer flew first class from Heathrow to Marseilles. Sitting alongside her was Sidney Nolan. At fifty-five, the artist was at the peak of his career, feted in his home country and part of an elite circle of painters, writers and public intellectuals in London. Elizabeth was forty-four with four books to her name but suffering a bad case of writer's block. She and Sid and Cynthia Nolan had enjoyed some wonderful events in recent weeks and had been scheduled to travel to France that day for an overnight stay in Aix, about 30 kilometres from Marseilles, but Cynthia was unwell and was advised by her doctor not to travel. She insisted Elizabeth fly with Sid, who hated travelling alone. It proved a glorious jaunt to the French countryside, reminding Elizabeth of motoring there with her mother and stepfather almost twenty years earlier. On the flight home, fashion designer Mary Quant was seated across the aisle.

That summer, Elizabeth was pretty much in love with the Nolans, the 'immensely likeable' couple she had met in 1967.[1] Elizabeth loved to tell the story of that meeting and, as with many of her anecdotes, the details scarcely varied in the retelling across the decades. Macmillan had just published Cynthia's memoir of her American years, *Open Negative*, and a book about Nolan's work. The couple were in Sydney for the opening of a retrospective exhibition of Sid's paintings at the Art Gallery of New South Wales. They were the talk of the town when Patrick White suggested they go into the Macmillan building and meet Elizabeth. 'Cynthia and Sidney came into Macmillan's where I was alone,' Elizabeth often recalled. 'I gave them a hand each and said "welcome". Patrick and the books had brought them in to see me. We talked for a while and Sidney went off, Cynthia staying for coffee, Cynthia staying for the first of those many unique and uniquely intense conversations. They had come into the big empty showroom stepping lightly, not quite prowling, alert for danger, finding none.'[2]

*Cynthia and Sidney Nolan in 1967.*

It was a typically acute Harrower observation about the couple; they were cool and detached yet keenly aware of their status. Elizabeth felt a strong connection to Cynthia and told White that: 'She is the person I know who most reminds me of myself.'[3] It was similar to her reaction to Margaret Dick, years earlier, when she had talked of the relief of meeting someone like herself.

On the Nolans' annual trips to Sydney, Cynthia and Elizabeth dined often at the Town House in Kings Cross. Cynthia urged Elizabeth to visit London, saying Putney would be perfect for writing. There was a separate flat and a typewriter and Elizabeth could plan on returning home after a few months with a draft manuscript. So, on 10 February 1972, the Nolans were at Waterloo to collect Elizabeth off the boat train. The plan was for Elizabeth to caretake their house while they spent several weeks in Africa and Australia. Before they left, there was much rushing about – a counter lunch at Peter Jones in Sloane Square; a visit to Kensington Antique Fair; Regent's Park for dinner; Burlington Arcade; Hatchards; a Chinese restaurant in Wardour Street; the British Museum for a Dürer exhibition; the Albee play *All Over*; a concert at Festival Hall. Cynthia even organised a skin specialist and a dentist. Elizabeth was delighted by the Nolans and their lifestyle in the house on the river: 'The Thames is maybe 25 or 35 yds away; the back garden wall is the embankment. When the tide is low, C. climbs over the wall down a ladder and walks on the Thames sand …'[4] But after the Nolans left, Elizabeth felt she was 'on the fringe of someone else's life'. Marooned in a house some distance from the centre of London, with poor heating plus regular power cuts, thanks to the miners' strike, and no television set in her separate quarters, she mulled over Cynthia: 'I think if C can't feel she is the most important person in your life, she switches off.'[5]

In the next few weeks, Elizabeth caught up with old friends. Her second cousin Stephanie (Margaret Dick's younger sister) and husband Alec came to stay. Cynthia did not want Elizabeth to reveal ownership of the house, and when Stephanie and Alec saw Nolan's paintings on the wall, they remarked they must have been produced by a child. Elizabeth went in search of the almost forgotten books and household goods she and Margaret had left with friends in 1959, when they had expected to return to London in a year or so. Thirteen years later, the books had disappeared but the 'mugs we used to use, the chair I sat in to type *The Catherine Wheel*, the green glass lamp with the dimples pushed in' were still there. 'It was so, so strange. Time!' Elizabeth told Margaret.

As she struggled to begin writing again, Elizabeth was often despondent and keen to return to Australia, even if unsure about the Rodds and where and how to live. She had previously worked at John Brink's Anchor Books in Sydney, and soon Brink wrote to her: 'I need you very urgently indeed to work for me for 5 or 6 weeks … there is nobody at all except you who'd be able to do it … mostly typing invoices, letters and orders. PLEASE.' Elizabeth did not take up the offer, nor an offer to work at Macmillan in London. Margaret Dick suggested they should live together when Elizabeth returned to Sydney, but Elizabeth, still clearly unsettled, did not pursue the idea.

When she left Sydney in January, Elizabeth had packed a copy of *In Certain Circles* and now reread it with fresh eyes. 'What a pity to entomb so much – whatever it is – in such a wooden and unconvincing and slight framework,' she told Margaret. 'Must see what I can do with another one. I wonder if I've lost the knack. You never know. I'll try again before I come to that conclusion (hope I don't have to!).' But she had not given up on it entirely. She sent the manuscript to Richard Simon, a London literary agent, but her accompanying letter was full of misgivings. He wrote back: 'I don't think this one is really at all successful. I think the basic trouble is that the family is just not interesting enough, so you have started off with a great disadvantage … it seems to me to lack life and conviction. So, I think you are right to absolutely put this one out of your mind and get on with the new one.' It was an honest response, but it must have been depressing for Harrower to accept this assessment, especially after producing four successful novels.

After more than two months alone, Elizabeth looked forward to the Nolans' return on 4 May, but when they arrived Cynthia was offhand. Elizabeth, heading to Scotland to see relatives, was convinced she was not wanted. 'Dismayed' and 'disconcerted', she contemplated staying at a hotel when she returned from Edinburgh.[6] But then, peace. Cynthia telephoned her in Scotland and all was forgiven – the Nolans did want her after all. The incident, easily blamed on Cynthia's weariness after her travels, offered a hint of her complex, more controlling side. It also revealed Elizabeth's 'touchiness' and readiness to take offence.

The next three months in Putney were 'total heaven'. The painter drove the women into town on most days where they lunched at Fortnum & Mason's and shopped at high-end fashion outlets. Elizabeth had her hair 'done' regularly in Sloane Square, picked up a pair of expensive Charles Jourdan flats – a find for her large feet. At Harrods she bought 'two cloth coats … pale brown fitted coat with gold buttons and a white, navy and black silky sort of tweed fitted coat', she told Margaret. In July she bought a green chiffon summer dress at Jaeger, and Cynthia later gave her a green necklace to wear with it. Elizabeth had to watch her spending in this period but had inherited money from her mother.

Often in the evenings, Cynthia climbed the stairs to Elizabeth's flat for a drink while Sid worked, read or listened to music. Cynthia warned Elizabeth about returning to Sydney: 'You're finished if you go back.' These were warm encounters, but Elizabeth did not talk about her childhood and would later say she did not have an 'emotional friendship' with Cynthia.[7] How did Cynthia see the younger woman in these months? Was Elizabeth a companion, someone to distract her while Sid worked? Did they see her as their project, their protégé? Cynthia wanted Elizabeth to write her biography, but Elizabeth turned her down. The Nolans were generous but had Elizabeth once again opted for a supporting role, just as she had with Shirley Hazzard and the Rodds? Was she again a bit player in other people's dramas?

She tried to explain her relationship with the Nolans to Margaret Dick:

> C loves having a friend in the house, loves having someone to go shopping with and do things with and talk to. It's nice for me, too. Because as you know, I had been spending far too much time alone … I don't feel really that they are fond of me, as you say, only that they think I am conscientious and trustworthy and tidy and Australian and friends with Patrick and Bill [Cantwell] and like them and have written and may write and so on … S knows that C loves to have a friend in the house for company in the evenings or for odd shopping and so on … And now that we've talked a bit more – S and I – I think he mildly likes me too.

Sid, who was renowned for his singular focus on his career, advised Elizabeth, still unable to begin writing, that when it came to work you must 'make something up and start from there and keep on, and not stop working'.

Elizabeth had witnessed some bad marriages but was impressed by the Nolans' relationship: 'C and S are so likeable together and have such a relaxed and sweet (no other word for it) association … C couldn't be nicer. She is very gentle and insecure, and quick-witted. I do like her. And I like S. too. He is so equable and is never tired. He reads & reads.' Elizabeth noted how Sid and Cynthia were 'so easy and live their lives so lightly somehow. They are so unsecretive, so uncautious, so trusting, so open … they are so casual [and] go about their busy life so calmly, in a very disciplined way, accomplishing a lot, but never making much of it. Never blowing anything up into a world-shaking extravaganza. It is nice.'

She liked Sid's personality: 'S is never tired, but he is never violently or aggressively energetic, either; he is just always wide awake, eager, good-humoured, and funny. He makes us laugh all the time … [he]has a way of not being got down whatever happens and that is likeable and something to learn … What there's never time to say is how light-hearted and funny and loving C and S are always to each other. Heavens, it is nice.'

The only thing that really mattered at Putney was art, and while Sid was 'playful and humorous' he was not given to idle chatter or gossip. The household was organised to allow him to pursue his work yet engage with the powerful people who assisted his career. This ordered life allowed for 'the production of work', with Cynthia as the enabler. Few questioned Sid Nolan's right to the security and support of marriage with an intellectual and artistic equal. A supportive wife was taken for granted. It was a relationship that Elizabeth, as a woman, was unlikely to achieve.

Critics have argued that Cynthia controlled her husband, fending off people he might want to see, but Elizabeth had a more nuanced view. '[She] certainly protected him … he probably liked company but for a painter the work has to come first … I cannot tell you how calm and controlled and enjoyable it was and how they floated along somehow but in the course of that produced great work,' she told documentary-maker Catherine Hunter in 2009. '[Cynthia] looked at the world in a unique way and appreciated art, flowers, literature, but more than that, I can tell you, because she was so intense. She was tremendously intense, and you wouldn't say mercurial because she was very calm. There was a lot of steadiness and calmness, but you always felt underlying that there was a great deal of electricity. Between Cynthia and Sid I was very conscious of the closeness and the great bond.'[8] In her time at Putney, Elizabeth saw what intelligence, talent, discipline and a certain ruthless commitment could deliver – especially if one had a 'wife'.

Elizabeth wrote to the Rodds to say she would not move in with them when she returned to Sydney, but she was worried how Kylie would react and told Margaret: 'We've had so many good times as well as bad, she and I. It just gets too complex at H. Hill some of the time, though of course I've often had fine, lovely weekends there, too.' She planned to look for a flat in Sydney – a decision that signalled a significant break with the Rodds. 'It's so good of you to be all ready to receive me into Hunters Hill when I get back,' she wrote to Kylie. 'But I couldn't take Bim's or Benno's room. It's their home. And I'd get on your nerves, or Roddy's, in next to no time, just by being myself. You've forgotten how much I irritate you … must rapidly find a shack, hut, dwelling, flat of my own … You're an angel and you know how much I appreciate being welcome.'

Elizabeth was trying to move on, but in May she told Kylie 'I miss you', and again: 'It will be lovely to see you again; though you never say so to me.' Margaret Dick was wary. 'Don't know what you should do about Hunters Hill on your return,' she told Elizabeth. 'Even if you go for a few days (at the most) it doesn't solve the thing, because it will probably take a few weeks to find a place and settle down.' Elizabeth was struggling to show her independence and was clearly annoyed in July when she wrote to Margaret asking if she should stop over or fly direct to Sydney when she returned. Kylie had suggested that Elizabeth could not manage a stopover and Elizabeth wanted to prove her wrong.

Just before she left for Australia on 18 August, the Nolans took her to the international music festival at Aldeburgh in Suffolk, the town Benjamin Britten called home. It was a pleasant weekend, even if the town was 'desolate, flat, grey' and the nearby church at Blythburgh was 'isolated'.[9] After eight months away, Elizabeth was ready to return to Sydney and told Margaret on 6 August: 'I want, want, want to come home. It has been marvellous, but the time has come to settle down again.'

Harrower was at a crisis point in her life, personally and professionally. Months earlier, she had written to Shirley Hazzard: 'I'll go home and hope to find a way of living there and writing. Otherwise, I'll have to think again.'[10] She was about to test that resolve.

# 13

# Hunters Hill: Moving On

ELIZABETH HARROWER HAD TOLD THE RODDS SHE would not live with them when she returned from London in 1972 but in fact she stayed in the Hunters Hill house for two weeks before finding a flat nearby. She had always claimed to hate the suburbs, equating them with the entrapment described in her novels. According to Jinx Nolan, Elizabeth was 'not interested in suburban life, not interested in talking about doilies'. Yet she had lived on the lower North Shore of Sydney, in Neutral Bay, Cremorne and Mosman – all designated as suburbs, even if they boasted some of the most sought-after real estate in the city.

Hunters Hill was also on the harbour but it was not expensive, and Elizabeth paid $36 a week for a two-bedder in a red-brick block in Joubert Street, just five minutes' drive from the Rodds' bungalow in Garrick Avenue. Her time there would generate rich friendships and spark political involvement, but she had mixed feelings about where she had landed. Not long back from London and the cosmopolitan life of the Nolans, she told Shirley Hazzard she had looked out from her flat to see 'a terrifying, super-real, empty painting of suburbia, no sign of life'. Walking in the evening she 'loathed knowing there was a savage dog at the end of the street protecting someone's place and a terrible smell of roast cooking'. In her eighties, looking back at her life, Harrower equated suburbia with marriage: 'I just loathed that imprisoning domesticity.

Living with someone. Not good. There have been famous characters who lived separately, and I think that says a lot for their common sense.'[1]

But in 1972, at the age of forty-four, she still wanted Kylie Tennant in her life. In London she had recovered her confidence and found a modicum of independence from the Rodds, but home again she resumed her Blackheath routine. 'Spent Wednesday night at Kylie's then we drove up here on Thursday morning – the first time we have both been up together for 10 months,' she told her friend Bill Cantwell. 'The house was dirty but cleaned up by both of us in half a day. The garden needed and has been receiving much weeding and raking.' She wrote to Judah Waten: 'The blossom is out, and violets and so on. I mow the lawn, burn up masses of paper and stuff in the incinerator and TIDY as far as I am able, because too much chaos is alien and troublesome to me.' She told Cantwell:

We've had some radiant days in Blackheath and much housework. It looks much better for it, but if you aren't going to be here all the time you know it will be constantly sinking back. Such is life. There are still violets out, and the pear and plum trees are either coming or going, I can't remember which. Wedding veil (or some such name) is coming out, and daffodils are here, and japonica has just almost passed. Everything else is waiting to spring forth. We may drive down to Everglades one day next week – that National Trust garden at Leura. There's a deplorable art nouveau pseudo-Spanish style house, but sometimes the gardens can look lovely.

Kylie and Elizabeth were a couple again. They lunched with a visiting Japanese professor at Nancy Phelan's house in the mountains and invited him back to Hillside Farm. Elizabeth was 'magnificent, discussing Japanese novels with the Prof … Don't know how I would have managed without her,' Kylie wrote to Roddy, holed up in Garrick Avenue. When the women took Benison to Diamond Head for a holiday that year, Kylie wrote to Roddy that Elizabeth was 'neat and gentle and good company'. It was an odd statement, given how well the three knew each other but perhaps Kylie was reassuring Roddy that things were back on track after the pressures of the recent months.

Both women were strong Labor supporters, and Elizabeth was ecstatic when Gough Whitlam won the federal election on 2 December 1972. She wrote to Hazzard: 'My mob and half the population are THRILLED about the change of government. From not being able to read an Australian newspaper I am reading four a day.' The mood in Sydney was infectious: she boarded a bus and noted that passengers were 'all bosom friends by the end' of the trip. She and Kylie celebrated the Labor victory with champagne and balloons. It seemed 'miraculous', the most exciting thing 'that's happened in this country since I've been born'. Five days after the election, and there were 'things happening that should have happened years ago … even the wild geese on some island off the coast of Victoria have been saved! … [it's] as if everyone is in love, like after the war, in London.' Elizabeth was not alone in her delight at the Whitlam government: Australia had been ruled since World War II by the conservative parties and many Labor supporters had despaired of any change. Now Labor lost no time in implementing its program of renewal of the society, economy and culture, which Whitlam had championed and shaped over several years.

It was in these post-election days that Elizabeth met Helene Nolte, a local potter, at one of Helene's exhibitions in Hunters Hill. Helene had emigrated from South Africa via London with her husband, Ferdi, an architect, and their young daughters, Karin and Linda. They were left-wing and strongly anti-apartheid, and when Elizabeth met Ferdi later they hit it off immediately. Linda Nolte was thirteen when she met Elizabeth, who was quickly adopted by the Nolte family and their circle of white South African émigrés. Linda recalled: 'She was like another family member … and she took on the role of my other mother.' After school, the teenager often stopped by the Joubert Street flat. Elizabeth was almost always at her typewriter, but Linda sensed over time that her inspiration had 'dried up, that she was trying but maybe she didn't think it was any good'.

Elizabeth was talkative and drew people to her, but Linda understood she was a practised observer who was always making mental notes as she spoke to people. 'Whether she liked them or not, if they shed any little glimmer of interest, she would pull them in and then put them in one of her many circles,' Linda told me in 2023. 'She was like Planet Elizabeth, she had little groups who didn't know each other, she would pick people's brains, get information and then she would have something to talk about with somebody else … She never talked about herself: she was an amateur psychologist, and she would discuss things about various people, how and what made them tick.'

This is a comment made by many of her friends. 'She would ask you a million questions,' recalled Jane Novak, her former publicist, who knew her in the decade before her death. 'But if you ever turned around and asked her a question, she would find a way to flip so she would always ask you questions about your childhood or about your relationship. She was constantly mining. We talked about everything, but she would never talk about herself, and she would always find a way to deflect attention. You realised you were with somebody who was incredibly observant and very, very perceptive about who you were: there was nowhere for you to hide, for anyone to hide, because she saw everything.'

Linda noticed how the older woman constructed her life: 'She was very considered; she wasn't very spontaneous. She lived in her head and spontaneity wasn't really part of it.' Stephanie Claire found conversations with Elizabeth 'therapeutic, rather cathartic'. Elizabeth was fascinated by Stephanie's middle-class upbringing in a family of five children with a father who was a doctor. The women were friends over several decades from the 1970s, but their exchanges were often one-sided, with Elizabeth asking questions, trying to find the clues to life. 'I felt that she was almost exploring, like [anthropologist] Margaret Mead,' Stephanie said. 'She just did not have any idea of how a big family functioned. It was as though she was trying to [gain knowledge] about this other strange culture. She seemed such an intuitive person but yet she was asking questions that made it seem like she came from another planet.' Stephanie would drive home after a conversation with Elizabeth pondering 'the fact that there was nothing coming out of Elizabeth at all', so adept was the author at interrogating others. Elizabeth was particularly interested in Stephanie's relationship with the painter Salvatore Zofrea. She wasn't curious about the sex, rather the love. It was as if Elizabeth wanted to understand situations she had not experienced. Stephanie recalled: 'She seemed to have a few romances, but I gathered that they had been problematic or not satisfying.'

The Hunters Hill years were a fresh chapter in Elizabeth's life. She had gone through a personal hell in the aftermath of *In Certain Circles* and her months in London had been lonely and confronting at times. She was now an orphan rather than a 'divorced child' but she was also reimagining her relationship with her other family of Kylie and Roddy and their children. New friends in Helene and Ferdi Nolte and their circle of émigrés and activists helped her confidence. Her involvement with Patrick White and Judah Waten and many other writers would remain an essential part of her life, but the Noltes and their friendship circle consolidated around regular shared meals and other celebrations. She and Ferdi developed a special bond, based in part on their political activity during the Whitlam government. 'Elizabeth found Ferdi very interesting,' Linda Nolte recalled. 'He had a lot of depth, he had a lot of humanity, he had an enormous heart and soul, he was a lovely man, and she just took to him. I think that in many ways, he was her perfect man.'

On 23 December 1972, with Sydney sweltering in 104°F (40°C) heat, Elizabeth remembered the hot Newcastle summers of her childhood. She generally spent Christmas with the Rodds and Margaret Dick and this year she was to host everyone at Joubert Street, serving cold turkey and hot plum pudding. Whitlam (whom she praised for knowing Greek) was still top of mind after the stunning election day. She told Hazzard: 'None of us has experienced anything like it.' A month later her gang was still 'like a lot of Cheshire cats'.

It is hard to overstate the euphoria among Labor voters in this period. Elizabeth's letters to Hazzard captured the excitement, a unifying moment when people recognised their tribe. In 1980, she told Jim Davidson that the election allowed a lot of like-minded people to discover each other: 'Many people who were very isolated in that uncongenial sort of Australia found themselves at home in their own country for the first time.' New friends and old, a growing passion for politics and a joy in building a new Australia, and her involvement with Kit Hazzard left her little time for writing. She tried to get back in the swing after New Year, typing from old diaries and notebooks in an effort to re-establish work habits. There was plenty of advice from Patrick White, who told her sternly she should be writing more books. She ploughed on, telling Hazzard that 'the typing of ancient stuff continues, and it didn't feel purposeless though not immediately useful either'.

The old anxieties about the Rodds returned, although Elizabeth was guarded when she told Hazzard of a personal crisis which 'started the day I returned from London – tragic, heart-rending. It's been like being in a war, receiving startling dispatches at all hours, and often contradictory ones.' It's likely the 'dispatches' were about Bim, whose behaviour was increasingly erratic and who was taking recreational drugs despite his diagnosis of schizophrenia. Elizabeth told Hazzard: 'You do what practical things seem possible and that's all right. But if people you care about suffer, you suffer with them and for them – probably excessively, sometimes possibly more than they suffer for themselves – and this is what's wearing and tattering.' The Blackheath cottage was impossible at weekends. 'What was once meant to be a place to work [had become] a sort of halfway house for hippies. Long-haired boys who take drugs and think (and worse, keep telling you) that they're the Universe drift tiredly from bed to table.'

It was then that Kylie decided to take a six-week cruise with her father and Benison to Japan, departing Sydney on 21 March 1973.

Her father would foot the bill. She invited Elizabeth, who didn't really want to go but found it hard to say no and threw tantrums when she realised what she had agreed to.[2] Worse still, she would be away when Sid and Cynthia Nolan were on their regular visit to Sydney. When she heard about the cruise, Cynthia urged Elizabeth not to go: she was doubtless worried that a six-week voyage would damage Elizabeth's emotions. Elizabeth was stunned and told Hazzard that Cynthia seemed fragile and ill and was 'so incensed about [the cruise] that she has refused to see me. It's quite staggering to me'. There was a standoff, then one day before the cruise departed Elizabeth ran into the Nolans in the city. She talked to Sid briefly, but Cynthia remained seated in their car. The women looked at each other 'ruefully' and Elizabeth noted that 'nothing C does really surprises me, though I couldn't believe at first that she intended to keep up this embargo as a kind of punishment'.[3]

There was more stress when Elizabeth and Kylie dealt with Bim's declining mental health, only just preventing him from being admitted days before the cruise departed. It was not the only time Elizabeth was involved with Bim, who spent periods in the large psychiatric hospital in Gladesville. She visited him often and was horrified by the conditions: 'Abandon hope all ye who enter here! More or less', she told Bill Cantwell.

Bim's condition burdened the Rodds for years and framed much of Elizabeth's relationship with Kylie. In an undated letter, Elizabeth wrote:

Dearest Kylie, I should have the kindness to leave you alone since that's what you want, and I do understand that you should feel like that. This is just to say that I'm here, anyway, if there's anything I can do. How could I be seeking light entertainment or gay outings if there's anything wrong with you or Bim or Roddy? You can't just switch off feeling for those closest to you because you're told to. Don't harden your heart towards me because I tried to help and at one time got worn down. If there was anxiety about Bim it was because I truly cared what happened to him, not because of indifference. And I do care, as you really know when you see me. Don't secretly reproach me for anxiety and failings that only come from profound affection. I try to take some comfort from the thought that if Roddy is still planning to go to Blackheath on Monday, perhaps nothing can be very much worse than before. Or he wouldn't be going. But you sounded – not good. When you can say something – do. Till then I'll just wait and wonder and send my best thoughts. I had thought we might be able to be hopeful.

And in an apparent reference to Bim, she wrote: 'He's going to be all right. I'm thinking of Roddy too and tell him so. Dearest Kylie, we've all had terrible turmoils, but never doubt me.' It is likely this letter was written after Elizabeth's return from the Nolans and before the Japan cruise, at a time when Bim was in crisis. It reveals not just the deep care Elizabeth showed to Kylie but the extent of her emotional involvement with Bim.

Somehow the travellers made it to the dock, and the trip started smoothly enough. The ship was very comfortable, small but not crowded, and the service was 'amiable and the food excellent'. The three women – Kylie, Elizabeth and Benison – were together in a four-berth cabin, while Kylie's father was next door. They were used to camping in small places, such as Blackheath, and they settled in for the trip. But as Elizabeth later told Judah Waten, she was torn:

> My one real objection has been that I don't like the sea and six and a half weeks of it struck me as rather bad news. On the other hand, I knew Kylie badly needed a rest and a break from the ghastly times here, and if it could make any difference in a good way, I would go. Well, I did go after driving my friends mad with my indecision and doubts, and we all enjoyed it, and liked the ship, and got on well, as we expected to, because we all know each other very well. Then the ship lingered in Brisbane from Friday morning till Sunday at noon. And it was that ghastly lingering in Brisbane that got me down … Anyway, also it seemed to me – and this was really the deciding factor – that my presence wasn't going to make much difference to anyone at all … Of course after I had said (suddenly at about 11 and it sailed at 12) that I had to get off, everyone was startled and felt I must go if I felt I must, but after I'd been to the office and made announcements it was then very sad, for it then appeared that my presence did make a difference, and my absence would make a difference and so on. And if it had been possible to go on and on, getting off and on the ship, I suppose I'd still be doing just that! What a friend I am! I was (of course!) overcome with remorse and regret at having let everyone down.

It was a dramatic departure. Elizabeth waited for five hours at the Interstate Station in Brisbane, brooding about her character defects – 'bad, and sad, too'. The train 'rattled and clanked its way back to Sydney'.

The aborted trip weighed on Elizabeth. She told Hazzard on 10 April. 'Although I felt horrible, rushing away, I'd have permanently despised myself if I'd stayed. (And there were some other reasons, apart from boredom and sea: I couldn't take any more stress.) But you see the confusion! Of course, when you are usually reliable and not excitable, it's all the more staggering to other people when you do something so apparently out of character.' Elizabeth had worried she would not have time in Sydney to see the Nolans, but she did not rush to contact them. For her to turn to Cynthia now would be a betrayal of Kylie. It was not a love triangle, but the attractions of these two powerful women was confronting for Elizabeth.

A few days later she came down from the mountain and saw Roddy, who wrote to Kylie, still on board the ship, that Elizabeth was 'ghastly thin', her trousers hanging off her. The cruise, however disastrous, seemed to reignite Elizabeth's passion for Kylie. She wrote to her on board the ship: 'Well, I've sent five thousand loving letters to you, and I've meant them, life being short and so on. I could as soon cast off half of myself as cast you off, but I'm not so cruel that I could want you to feel you couldn't cast me off, if I really irritate you too much. My greatest wish has always been to please you and make things better and to have happy or any other times together when possible. If you want to be free of me, you must feel free to be free of me. I can't imagine it somehow – our ever being changed or far apart. But things have to be mutual and spontaneous, really felt, or it's no use, I suppose.' On 23 April, she wrote: 'How's my darling?' and a day or two later: 'I miss you. Dreamed of you the other night. I was on the ship. This has happened often since I got back.' In London Elizabeth had questioned the relationship and almost walked away from Kylie. Now she seemed to have fallen for her all over again. Elizabeth did, however, want to separate her finances, and Roddy told Kylie on Anzac Day 1973 that they might have to buy Elizabeth out of her share of Blackheath. He advised his wife, who was still on the cruise, that she must try to be kind: 'I think it best to forget everything about Elizabeth's return from Brisbane [and the cruise] … She was obviously in a very rundown condition.'

Elizabeth never truly recovered from that trip. Writing in the third person, she noted that 'Elizabeth who did not obey, has been "cast out".'[4] In July she told Hazzard she felt she had been 'run over' by Cynthia: 'I'll eternally wish she had spared me that extra stress earlier this year. All that tumult really wrecked my health.' Years later she wrote of Cynthia: 'On a good day there was absolutely nothing that she didn't understand. We had marvellous conversations, and the atmosphere around her while intense, was never heavy, the very opposite.'

Elizabeth had some financial freedom thanks to her inheritance, but she was struggling to write. Margaret Dick told her to either start a book or get a job. Patrick White told friends Elizabeth was living a novel instead of writing one. Harrower was still in the swim, however: Geoffrey Dutton, a key backer of the Adelaide Festival Writers' Week, suggested she attend the 1974 event and mingle with John Updike, Nadine Gordimer, Peter Porter and Sumner Locke Elliott. Elizabeth began holding dinner parties at Joubert Street with regular guests including White and Manoly Lascaris, along with young poets like Geoffrey Lehmann. He and Manoly bonded over a love of gardening, and Lehmann and his then wife, Sally McInerney, included Elizabeth in their dinners at

Lindfield on the upper North Shore. Writers Bruce Beaver, David Malouf and Roland Robinson were often present.[5]

Amid this social life – and her efforts to write – Elizabeth was also dealing with the demands of Kit Hazzard. In August 1973, she spent time and energy sorting out Kit's pension. It was the sort of thankless task she performed often in these years as Kit declined in her physical and mental health. A month earlier, Elizabeth had found Kit in a bad way in her flat at The Chimes: 'I thought Kit must have taken ten tranquillisers all at once, she was so sunk and inert,' she told Shirley. 'If you can give your mother something to look forward to, some idea that she'll see you again, this will be what will settle her and calm her … So I suppose we all see the sadness of Kit's situation, and care about her, and feel she's a demon, all at the same time.'

Elizabeth's friends were keen to help her write and in September Judah Waten told her the new Literature Board of the Australia Council, on which he sat, would give her a two-year fellowship if she applied. The board had taken over the work of the Commonwealth Literary Fund and was now well resourced by the Whitlam government. Its board read like a who's who of Australian letters – Geoffrey Blainey as chair, Manning Clark, Geoffrey Dutton, Richard Hall, A.D. Hope, Nancy Keesing, David Malouf, Elizabeth Riddell and Richard Walsh, as well as Waten, who had been brought back into the fold by Labor. Elizabeth was not keen to accept another grant, given her failure to publish *In Certain Circles* after being supported by the Commonwealth Literary Fund. But eventually she put in an application and was granted $6000 a year for two years.

It was a psychological boost as well as a financial one, and Harrower hoped it would end the insecurities about writing that had engulfed her since *In Certain Circles*. She told Hazzard she would change her routine and only socialise at night. Thanks to the inheritance she could afford to stay at home and not go to an office, but the grant was nonetheless welcome: 'I have to be very careful with money, so this will mean a certain loosening up, which will be nice; but much more than that, it will provide a spur and an obligation of the kind that most people can recognise. It could be – quite non-financially – a lifesaver.' She wrote to the director of the board, Michael Costigan, to say she was 'astonished and startled and did a great deal of brooding' before she accepted: 'While I would not have applied for one, I must say that – after great thinking – I feel this could be a lifesaver for me. The last novel … was actually accepted but I cut it and was still dissatisfied with it and withdrew it. Too many things in general had gone wrong. Now I suddenly feel hopeful again and as if I have a good many books yet to write.' She told Waten: 'I really do think it could literally save my life. Not that I was starving to death although I was counting my cents, but things had reached a pass that was not good at all.'

She wrote from Blackheath to thank Judah: 'Things have not been marvellous – in spite of quite a happy social life between dramas. It is my conviction … that I'll have to take myself off for at least a few months. Not overseas, just out of an area where I feel myself and my work "taken over" because too much questioned, jollied, and otherwise put off. This happened last time [with the grant from the fund]. It may be that I could keep the H. Hill place on – try to sub-let or something, so that I still have a base where I can come back for weekends. It's not clear in my mind yet – the details – but the necessity is very clear. I haven't discussed this yet with anyone except M. [Margaret] a little, on the phone. We'll see.'

Kylie Tennant suggested that the Blackheath cottage might be the place for writing, but Elizabeth considered this impossible. She told Judah it would be 'rent free, since I nominally own half, but in truth it hasn't much to do with me anymore. And the noise and rushing in and out! … Benno lives here all the time with many ducklings, hens, cats … They need a lot of attention and cause considerable excitement. As I can't send any friends here for weekends or holidays because there is usually a full house, I don't any more feel greatly called on to contribute much except my half of the rates and plenty of food and stuff when I am actually here.' Waten counselled her against using the cottage to write: 'I wouldn't go there if I were you. Almost anywhere but Blackheath.'

Once again, her relationship with Kylie threatened to derail her writing. 'Somehow, somehow, I have before [the grant starts] to wrench my mind and heart away from those who do not really want me but won't let me go,' she told Waten. 'Heavens, this is becoming something of an ancient story, and I should spare you. It's just so weird and sad, and destructive … of peace of mind, concentration …' Elizabeth was experiencing the confusion at the end of an affair. In her fiction, she wrote with honesty of the gap between reality and desire. Humans, she knew, could be 'very faulty' and people had disappointed her profoundly. She told me in 2012: 'I have come up against reality and people think if they push hard enough against it they will win, but they don't. I think most of the important, fundamental lessons that you learn in life, they are not enjoyable, but they are things perhaps you have to know.'

Now, in her early forties, struggling professionally and personally, she was learning some of those fundamental lessons.

# 14

# Gough and Elizabeth

IN 1966 IN AN INTERVIEW AHEAD OF THE PUBLICATION of *The Watch Tower*, Elizabeth Harrower told Gavin Souter, the literary editor of *The Sydney Morning Herald*, that she was a pacifist. However, she was content to let her books speak for her. 'I suppose you could make a full-time career of protesting, but if you are a writer one way or another, protests get into your book,' she told him.[1] She had been interested in politics since her time in London with Margaret Dick in the 1950s and she found like-minded people in Kylie and Roddy Tennant and others. She and Kylie attended anti–Vietnam War protests in the 1970s, and Elizabeth became more politically active when she met Ferdi and Helene Nolte.

Harrower's fiction is personal and psychological rather than political, but, in the 1970s, politics crowded out her writing. With the election of Gough Whitlam in 1972, politics became almost an obsession: 'I think I just spent a lot of time just … being enthusiastic and doing my best (for Labor).'[2] The election not only changed the nation; it rescued Elizabeth from the despair she sometimes felt in the aftermath of *In Certain Circles*, providing an acceptable distraction from the typewriter. Harrower, a lifelong fan of Whitlam, knew him well enough to invite him to a couple of parties. But her novels touch only lightly on contemporary events, and there is a timelessness about them. She never wanted to write about politics or to directly reveal her view. 'I think [you must] show society as it seems to you and it either is or isn't obvious what's wrong with it,' she said. 'I think you mustn't tell people what they are to make of your work. There it is, they make what they like of it, don't they?'[3]

Her most intense period of engagement with Labor was from the December 1972 election to the Dismissal in November 1975 and Whitlam's defeat at the subsequent poll. She attended rallies, donated money, handed out material and immersed herself in the excitement of the period. She had joined the party in 1973 'out of happiness' after Whitlam was elected (and remained a member for forty years, leaving in protest in 2010 when then leader Kevin Rudd was 'axed').[4] Whitlam's intelligence and 'crash through' approach appealed to Elizabeth, who, like many others in her circle, saw in the Labor leader a sophisticated politician who could appreciate the past – its books and its culture – but who had a vision for the future. Like others who had spent time in the great European cities, refugees from an Australia that seemed unformed, Elizabeth saw in Gough a deliverance from the stasis of the post-war Menzies era. Many of her friends welcomed Labor for its commitment to social and economic justice; others saw a government ready to fund the arts and launch a big conversation about what it meant to be Australian.

Elizabeth and Margaret and the Rodds knew many people, including Judah Waten and Christina Stead, who were communists or Marxists. Through the Noltes she met other South Africans, including anti-apartheid activists such as Margaret and John Brink, who ran the Anchor Books store in the city, where Elizabeth worked at one time. The leading communists Audrey and Jack Blake were friends. Elizabeth had been raised in working-class Newcastle, but she did not refer to that background when she talked about her politics. She had not displayed much interest in politics in her teenage years and in many ways, she was the product of a small business mentality and self-made migrants rather than the industrial working class. As we have seen, her grandmother Helen, with whom she lived as a child, ran boarding houses and small hospitals and her stepfather, with whom she lived from the age of twelve, was a businessman. Elizabeth linked her political awakening to her time in the UK in the 1950s, when the country was undergoing huge social change. Across the West at the time, various versions of communism and socialism were seen by many as answers to the fascism that had devastated Europe.

A year into Labor's reign, Elizabeth told Hazzard that 1973 had been 'extraordinary … Even on days when nothing was personally wonderful, I was still feet off the ground (though that's quite wrong, for never in a way did feet stand so cheerfully on the ground) and many, many felt the same way. That we were experiencing something too good to be true.' She was mad about the 'prodigious' Whitlam and full of praise for his 'excellent Ministers … It is uncanny to feel there are men like these in power with an idea of what they're doing and some plan – rather, plans, that are flexible, subtle, human. And he is witty in addition to all that.'

The Whitlam government moved quickly to transform the nation, but by 1974 it was under pressure. Elizabeth and Ferdi were in the front row of the Sydney Opera House on Monday, 13 May, to hear Gough rally the true believers for fresh elections – a double dissolution poll to resolve issues around supply. He told the crowd that, 'we are trying to build an Australia where all can feel involved … an Australia that belongs to all Australians.' Elizabeth had already attended the launch of Labor's campaign at Blacktown and a Lane Cove meeting featuring Whitlam. But this one was 'MARVEL-LOUS' she told Hazzard – with 3000 people inside the Concert Hall and 15,000 on the concourse outside.

Patrick White was among the luminaries at the 'Come and meet the Prime Minister' lunchtime gathering. The Nobel Prize winner strode to the stage to endorse Gough, and Elizabeth was thrilled at the sight of her two heroes joined in the fight. White, as the scion of a wealthy grazier family, had been seen as a conservative, but he backed Labor in the 1972 election and was now a pin-up boy for the left. At the Opera House, he and historian Manning Clark were part of 'a stunning display of democracy in action'. Elizabeth wrote 'indignant' letters to the papers during the election campaign and organised to spend six hours at the polling booth with Ferdi on polling day. She threatened 'to change my nationality' if Gough lost. Election day was cold, dark and wet: 'People queued in heavy rain at 7.45 am to get into the local church hall to vote … We were sodden, and the officials hadn't even enough ballot boxes to hold the papers.' She told Hazzard: 'There was an extraordinary feeling of – oneness. The radicals and conservatives of Labor drew together, and the meek spoke up, and the most wary admit to a great (if wary) affection and admiration for Whitlam.'

When counting halted on Saturday evening and television coverage ended, 'Australia retired with a head-cold and a sore throat and stayed in bed most of Sunday. We've been in limbo all week, with huge headlines contradicting each other every day about which party would be in power … it has been so strange.' Labor was returned but Elizabeth walked on eggshells until the Dismissal – and she discovered politics did not mix with writing:

'Being anxious or furious about The World takes away from time and silence and thought for real work. Yes, it's very noisy and creates conditions in which Great Thoughts come and, especially, go, all too quickly. It's quite something to resist …'

Harrower's grant from the Literature Board would finish at the end of 1975 but she was still struggling to produce anything. She told Margaret Dick in September that year: 'I have typed the first bit of a new short story and I'm enjoying it. A [quota] of work had been set and will be adhered to.' She wrote three pages that day and four the next, smoked Sobranie cigarettes to help her concentrate, reported she was 'working steadily' and declined dinner invitations from the Lehmanns and Kylie: 'I want to press on till I feel something is properly written … I have finished the second draft of that story and don't care for it so well now.'

Many of her friends were worried about Harrower's writer's block. One day in June 1975, Christina Stead, who was now living with her brother in the Sydney suburb of Hurstville, wrote to her: 'How are you, Elizabeth? Does genius burn?' It was a reference to Louisa May Alcott's *Little Women*, in which aspiring writer Jo squirrels herself away for intense 'scribbling' while family members occasionally venture to ask: 'Does genius burn, Jo?' It was a nice touch from Stead, who considered Harrower had a unique voice and now asked: 'When will your genius and your conscience allow us to see another of your delightful absorbing books?' Stead had returned to Australia in 1974 and over the next few years would live with family and friends in Canberra, Sydney and Victoria. 'She darted about a good deal. All of that moving about was sad, it was difficult to write in those circumstances,' Elizabeth told Stead's biographer, Christine Williams. Once again,

Elizabeth's caring instincts surfaced, but Christina, unlike Kit Hazzard, was not demanding. Help came from Patrick White, who awarded Stead the 1975 inaugural Patrick White Literary Award for writers whose work had not been sufficiently recognised. There were tears all around when Harrower took the train to Hurstville to make sure Stead was happy to accept the prize worth $25,000 ($200,000 in today's value).

In 1975, Christina and Elizabeth spent time with Canberra friends. The capital boasted fewer than 200,000 residents and was still a country town with scarcely a restaurant to be seen in the commercial centre of Civic. But there was a rich intellectual life centred on the Australian National University and the writers and artists clustered around it. There was a stimulating mix of working poets, painters, writers, historians and philosophers, many of whom lived in the same garden suburbs.

On 11 November, Elizabeth and Christina drove with friends into the bush for a mid-morning picnic and returned in time for a phone call telling them, 'Malcolm Fraser is Prime Minister. Kerr has got rid of Whitlam.' There was 'horror and stupefaction. People very nearly fell in the street with amazement and dismay,' Elizabeth told Hazzard. 'Manning Clark (our most splendid historian) said he was literally sick. Switched on radio which was dooming away in stunned voice. Chris [Stead] offered gin, brandy, sherry … took taxi to Parliament House. People surged there from everywhere. It was so AWFUL. Everyone was outraged. Our votes meant nothing. Moderate reform is not allowed to take place here … Whitlam came out and it was a relief to see him alive and valiant. To say that Kerr and Fraser have welded the Labor Party together is an understatement.' The next day Elizabeth was back at Parliament House for a rally. The police were out in force and Whitlam and most of the Cabinet spoke from the back of a truck. 'The sun blazed down. People handed up ten-dollar notes to Whitlam, who put them in his shirt pocket. I met Manning Clark. We all got sunburned.'

The Dismissal was unprecedented in Australian politics, the country was in uproar awaiting fresh elections on 13 December. Elizabeth wrote to Hazzard: 'We're in a fever. What days, what days!' She went to a rally in Sydney's Domain, to a fundraiser at the home of architects Harry and Penelope Seidler, and told Hazzard: 'We have been sunburned, blistered, very nearly made bankrupt, for Labor, have caught chills and lost voices from standing in the rain.' To no avail, the Coalition achieved a record win. 'Death and destruction have often, if not ever, been the fate of visionaries and idealists but few of us had expected to witness anything so sad and amazing here and now,' Elizabeth told Hazzard. Normal life was on hold. For weeks, Elizabeth read nothing but newspapers: 'we had all stopped writing here and now must try to remember where we were and what we were doing. I looked back at some writing yesterday with interest as if it had been written in the last century by someone else.'

The Labor years deepened her friendship with Patrick White, and she was drawn further into academic and literary circles. Margaret Dick was almost always included in lunches and dinners. Elizabeth had found her tribe and relished this lively, if at times, slightly claustrophobic, environment. She had many friends who were, like her, novelists, although they never talked about books or writing, she told Giulia Giuffrè. That would have been far too incestuous.

Her relationship with Cynthia and Sid Nolan was never truly repaired but she joined them for dinners at White's home when they were in town. Sid represented White in Stockholm when his 1973 Nobel Prize was announced. The following March, Elizabeth and Margaret joined the Nolans at White's for a dinner when the Swedish ambassador and his wife travelled from Canberra with the Nobel medal and diploma to bestow on the novelist. There were only eight people around the table for this significant event in White's life, and Elizabeth was among them – an indication of their great friendship.[5]

Later Cynthia and Elizabeth had a 'longish talk' on the phone, but their former intimacy was gone, and Elizabeth could not forgive Cynthia's earlier behaviour. 'At a time when I was bludgeoned half to death and so needed some personal appearances, presences, and kindness, there was an inclination to bully me by telephone,' she told Hazzard. 'I couldn't make out C's actions and reactions because, although at some level we knew each other very well, we didn't have at all an emotional friendship. C was witnessing at a distance something disastrous and might have acted differently but didn't. It was complicated.' But Cynthia 'isn't well. She only weighs 6 stone 7 lbs … Like you, I feel there's mortality, and I know Cynthia well.'

Two years later, in November 1976, in a London hotel, Cynthia Nolan took a fatal overdose of sleeping pills. When Sid married again just fourteen months later, there was a very public split between White and the painter. In his 1981 autobiography, *Flaws in the Glass*, White was brutal: 'If I have not been able to accept him since Cynthia's death, it is from knowing the Cynthia in myself, and that I might have acted in the same way. What I cannot forgive is his flinging himself on another woman's breast when the ashes were scarcely cold.'[6]

The split between Nolan and White meant Elizabeth did not see Sid for several years. Then on a Saturday morning in September 1984, she was waiting for a bus in the city when she saw a familiar figure enter the duty-free shop in Hunter Street. 'Before the bus came, he emerged – Sidney Nolan. We hadn't met for years. Because of Cynthia above all, and time, and his and P's awful public quarrel, it was sad. We spoke of Cynthia, and it seemed possible he doesn't all that often hear her name. He said he drives down Deodar Road and looks at the house.'[7] In May 2009, with Sid, Cynthia and Patrick dead, Elizabeth took a phone call from filmmaker Catherine Hunter who had interviewed her for a documentary on Nolan. Hunter told her that *Mask and Memory* would go to air in a few nights, but Elizabeth could not bring herself to watch this story about a man she had known so well. It would be too stressful, she told her diary.

# 15

# Other People's Lives

I N THE MID-1970S, ELIZABETH BEGAN CLAIMING INDEPEN-
dence from Kylie. She wanted to end the Blue Mountains
living arrangement and liberate some cash. Roddy wrote to
Kylie: 'Elizabeth is facing a bleak financial future … Blackheath is
one of the major problems. Nobody would buy that old ruin if they
had the money to buy a home and yet it is to Elizabeth a kind of
last resource when her finances are dwindling. You can't buy her
out at any sort of price she would place on her share.'

Kylie did eventually buy her out and later noted that Elizabeth
'was not a rural type. She is elegant and slender and intelligent.
Her books are appreciated by Europeans as well as Australians.'[1]
In contrast, Kylie threw herself more deeply into rural Australia.
She believed the only hope of rescuing Bim was to provide a rural
living space for him. In the mid-1970s, she bought a bigger property about 70 miles (113 kilometres) from Sydney. The idea was
that Cliff View Orchard at Shipley would be a permanent home for
the Rodds, which they would run as a profitable farm. The house
was in poor shape and friends were horrified, but the woman who
walked hundreds of kilometres in her younger days was unmoved.
In notes for an unfinished novel, quoted in Jane Grant's biography,
Kylie wrote: 'Elizabeth who was in the process of moving herself
said, surely I wasn't going to call it Cold Comfort Farm. "You can
do better than that." She wouldn't even go and look at it because

she thought there was some treachery in our moving so far away, a full seventy miles of the old reckoning. Other friends who did go and see Cliff View Orchard were inclined to stagger back.'[2]

However amicable the separation of their Blackheath finances, this was a period of readjustment as Elizabeth began to spend less time with Kylie. She tried to reclaim letters she had sent to her friend and was successful – up to a point. In an undated 1976 letter to Kylie, she said: 'Roddy asked me today if I was going down to collect the rest of my letters. I said, no, that you no longer agreed to this. It doesn't matter. It wasn't worth a single hard word.'

This was also the year when Harrower had to deal with her delay in producing work under her two-year Literature Board fellowship. In February 1976 she wrote to Michael Costigan at the board, saying: 'I have written a number of short pieces, enough – I believe – to make a collection. The novel I have been working on is nearing completion. Macmillan (London) have an option on it. I have notes prepared for another novel.' She sounded optimistic about her progress and a few days later, Costigan wrote to invite her to a meeting of present and past fellowship holders at the Adelaide Festival. The idea was to have 'a drink and discussion on the pleasures and problems of being a long-term Fellowship-holder'.

A few months later and Sandra Forbes, the executive officer of the Australia Council, which administered the Literature Board grants, wrote to check progress. Elizabeth had nothing to show her and told Judah Waten, who had been a board member, that she was considering returning the $12,000 grant. Waten was horrified: 'That letter was a pure formality. All you need to do is tell them briefly, that the novel tentatively titled ? is in the process of revision and you hope to have a completed version ready for the publishers before the end of the year or next year.' He explained the board did not want to apply any pressure to fellowship holders. 'So, if you write to say I have sinned, and I haven't finished my novel and I am returning my grant, it would not only throw consternation into the ranks of the Board but you might open up the possibility of a change … So, in the interests of the writers' body don't – take my advice and write as suggested.'

It is not clear what action Elizabeth took, but she seemed to airbrush the grant from her CV. She commented often that *In Certain Circles* had been doomed because she had accepted a 1968 Commonwealth Literary Fund grant and felt she was being paid to write. Given that, it is a mystery why she applied for another grant a few years later. She was embarrassed by her failure and rarely mentioned the second grant. Indeed, she often remarked about the lack of assistance for writers, neatly avoiding the fact she had received generous assistance on two occasions.

Harrower had been distracted by politics and the high emotions of her relationship with Kylie Tennant, but in 1976 she was a little distracted by Herbert Cole 'Nugget' Coombs, the legendary public servant and head of the Reserve Bank. Nugget, who was based in Canberra, had met Christina Stead through Jack and Clare Golson, who also became friends with Elizabeth. Jack was a professor of anthropology at the Australian National University where Clare was also an academic. Christina was smitten with Nugget. She had never made a secret of wanting a boyfriend and had a reputation for not being very interested in women (particularly those without careers) and of being somewhat unfriendly to feminists. She was not unkind but tended to dispense with them if she didn't find them interesting, according to her biographer Christine Williams.

Harrower had a more nuanced view and told Williams that Stead 'didn't like being claimed by feminists, it hurt her feelings, it hurt that aspect of her that was so devoted to men that she should be remotely thought to be against men with some gang of women'.

Christina certainly liked men. She knew she talked too much about her male friends but could not help herself, because: 'I am so staggered and delighted that they even look at me!' For years, she had a crush on Don Dunstan, the South Australian Labor premier, whom she worshipped from afar. She 'adored' Coombs, all 5′3″ of him, and he took her to lunch several times. She called him 'a darling, an echte Mensch', who was 'warm, cheerful, natural and very bright'. She was upset about her bad hair day when they met at Balmoral Beach for lunch.

Elizabeth was hungry for details of Nugget, but some years later she would also lunch with him. Revered by many for his policy initiatives in the arts and Indigenous affairs, as well as economics, Coombs was seventy-seven years and Elizabeth fifty-five in 1983 when they lunched at Balmoral, just down the road from her house. She wrote to Christina: 'He's exceptionally nice, as who knows better than you do!' Nugget was married and in a 25-year-long secret affair with the poet Judith Wright, but at some stage in the 1980s Elizabeth had a meltdown over him. In one of her Sunday morning calls to Andrew Robertson, Elizabeth was distressed. 'I never quite understood what it was,' he recalled. 'She didn't say "we've been having an affair" but she said, "I won't be seeing him again."' An affair seems unlikely, although Linda Nolte remembered Elizabeth saying Coombs had once asked her to marry him. True or false? Elizabeth was capable of flights of fancy and given his marital status a proposal sounds unlikely. When Nugget died in 1997, Elizabeth wrote to Shirley Hazzard: 'Many regarded him as the most outstanding Australian of the century. It's sad when people disappear.'

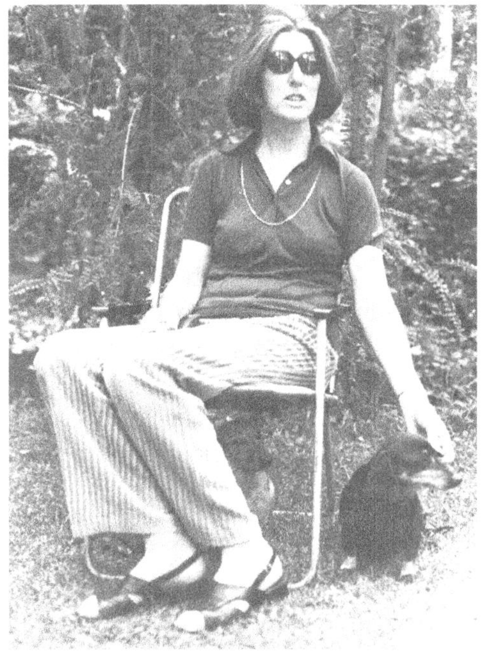

*Elizabeth at Ferdi and Helene Nolte's home in Hunters Hill, 1974.*

The years in Hunters Hill had been enriching in terms of friendships but a desert when it came to her writing. In mid-1976 she decided to move back to her family home in Mosman, which had been rented out since her mother's death in 1970. Elizabeth considered it far too big, even if Margaret Dick planned to join her there for a time. But back on the North Shore she began to revise her time in Hunters Hill, blaming her writer's block on the suburb, and questioning why she had not decamped earlier to an environment more conducive to writing.

Elizabeth had a personal income at this stage. She had inherited a block of four flats in Middle Head Road, Mosman, from her mother as part of an estate of $44,283.36, or about $640,000 in today's terms. The flats yielded a weekly income of $92 (about $1340 in today's value). Richard Kempley left his estate worth $7545.13 (about $110,000 in today's value) to his son from his first marriage, Richard John William Kempley.

At first Elizabeth and Margaret rattled around the 'biggish house', which looked 'neglected'.[3] Even so, it had a 'marvellous' position: 'all that blue, the birds, clouds, moon-on-water, sunrises, tiny curved, deserted beach with little sailing boats at anchor all week. It's a constant surprise. Seeing it when I'm alone, I envy myself and want everyone else to see it too.'[4] Elizabeth did not have a great interest in decorating homes and friends remarked the furniture at Stanley Avenue was inoffensive and spare. She had realised when young that 'mine was not a life in which buying things would make me happy, this wasn't where my happiness lay, in acquiring things. I'm not really all that interested in objects … I'm not very good visually.'[5] Elizabeth was also not very interested in food but she loved conversation. The poet and Sydney University literature professor Vivian Smith remembered a salon-like atmosphere at her gatherings. Artist Salvatore Zofrea recalled that Elizabeth would focus on one guest at a time and was happy to be a listener: 'You felt very comfortable.' Elizabeth told Giulia Giuffrè in 1985: 'I'm much better at interviewing people than being interviewed by them … Having questions asked of me is one of my weaknesses because I know from other interviews – not always – that my whole intention seemed to be to give nothing away, to disguise myself.'

By now, friends were aware of her struggle to write and began finding her roles such as writer-in-residence or judge of book prizes. Years ago, she had moved out of Mosman because she feared being seduced by the middle-class trappings. Was she back-sliding? Was she too comfortable back in this spacious house with water views? Kylie, living among the mud and animals in the Blue Mountains, told her: 'You need more squalor, then you would write.' Ken Levis, an English lecturer at the Alexander Mackie College of Advanced Education in Paddington, and his wife, Eve, had known Elizabeth since the early 1960s. In 1978 Levis helped organise a writer-in-residence role for Elizabeth at the college. The position was funded by the Literature Board and paid $4000 for nine weeks, spread over about four months. But it did not suit Harrower: 'I can't write one word surrounded by hundreds, thousands, of people ... even thinking of writing fiction, seemed a strange thing inside a university, college,' she told Judah Waten. A colleague had warned her not to let the residency interfere with her writing, but she found it difficult and only wrote 'pieces of [a] novel and pieces of short story'.[6]

Harrower had many academic friends but was somewhat dismissive of the academy and often claimed she had had no powerful friends from university days to promote her career. Writing in the 1960s, she suggested, had been an unsupported calling. This was a tad disingenuous, given she had accepted two literary grants and one writer-in residence appointment and was part of a powerful circle of people whose books were reviewed in *The Sydney Morning Herald*. 'I didn't want to be part of that rather bitchy literary world,' she told me in 2012. 'It was not for me. I was the outsider. I stayed the outsider except that I was an outsider with some very good other outsiders. I did find some very good friends and we understood each other and you were in tune, and this was a huge pleasure, and I was inside this important, interesting and loveable and loved group of friends.'

Harrower published only a few short stories in the 1970s but retained her currency with the republication by Angus & Robertson of her novels in 1977 and 1979. Even so, her 1980 interview with Jim Davidson for *Meanjin* was notable for its focus on the past, even though she was still only fifty-two. She was, in so many ways, living off former achievements. She talked to Davidson about her obsession with writing *The Catherine Wheel* at the time of the Aldermaston anti-bomb marches:

'I thought even if the world's coming to an end I must finish this book, which is really strange and yet it seemed terribly important that I had to get all of these things down.' And she told Giuffrè, 'No matter if the world was blowing up next week, I had to finish that book … whether the book was good, bad or indifferent. It's an enviable feeling for a writer to have, the book matters so much, that … they've got to finish it even if the world blows up … I look back in a nostalgic way on these days, I look back with envy on my former self because this is a marvellous way to feel, that you are so absorbed in your work.'

She told Davidson that 'friends, the written word and the natural world' were what most sustained and enlivened her. 'Otherwise, theatre, films and singing have meant most to me,' she said. 'From an early age I was taken to the theatre a lot, and loved it, and I was an ardent movie-goer. I also listened to singing on every possible occasion.' She was determined to curate her image. When she checked the *Meanjin* transcript she told Davidson she was 'faintly alarmed to have described myself as "often happy". "Often happy!"

In case the gods are listening and honing their well-known dislike of hubris, it might have been safer to say, "Sometimes happy". Do the gods read *Meanjin*?'

In the 1980s, several quarterlies published surveys of Harrower's work, and while she told Hazzard that 'it makes me feel I must be going to die', she was surely gratified. Her novels were studied in English departments, with papers delivered at conferences of the Association for the Study of Australian Literature in 1980 and 1982. Every now and then a letter turned up from a university researcher. In 1981, Frances McInherney was preparing an article in *Hecate* about the feminist elements in Harrower's work and asked for biographical details. Harrower had basically stopped writing but, perhaps to save face, told McInherney: 'I hope to do more work. There's a good deal more I still want to say.' [7] Nola Adams sent a copy of her master's thesis to Harrower. It noted that the writer resisted any attempt to place herself in an 'Australian tradition'. Rather she saw herself as a 'free spirit grazing on many pastures'.[8] Harrower enjoyed her self-appointed role of the outsider: in 1984, she told the Steegs that she was off to a lunch to 'talk about a six-thousand-word autobiographical piece I'm not going to write for inclusion in a book. All the other women are academic women. I'd be like an orange in a crate of apples, or vice versa. My writing, life and approach would be too peculiarly different.'[9]

Elizabeth was still close to the Rodds in these years. In 1976 when she was hospitalised with a severe case of shingles, Kylie and Roddy invited her to stay at the farm at Shipley as she recovered. Her writing struggles were soon overshadowed by Bim's drug addiction and erratic behaviour. In October Elizabeth told Judah Waten that Shipley must be 'grim' because Bim was agitated and creating a 'strange and stressful atmosphere'. By June the next year, Bim was in the Parramatta Psychiatric Hospital and Elizabeth wrote to Waten: 'All remains unread, untrue, uneverything.' Bim was twenty-six and on a permanent invalid pension. Then early in 1978 there was terrible news. Bim was in hospital in Sydney, badly injured after having jumped or been thrown from a second-floor window in Potts Point. Kylie had driven him to a bank in the mountains to withdraw about $1000 before he took the train to Central, with a plan to travel to Nepal. Instead, he had been attacked in the city, his money and possessions stolen. For four days he lay unconscious, till his death on 6 March. Elizabeth identified the body of the young man she had met when he was just ten years old.

Nine months later, a 24-year-old man was jailed for life for Bim's murder, a crime the judge described as 'callous and indifferent'. He said the convicted man had assaulted and robbed Bim and 'terrorised' him to a point where he jumped from the window, and had then gone downstairs and dragged him 'like a sack of potatoes' to a laundry.[10] The two-week trial ended on 21 December, and Elizabeth wrote to Hazzard: 'At the end of the first week, at the weekend, which was the last before Christmas, we went out to the shops for food and things, and people were buying presents, and the tinsel everywhere was looking pretty sick in the hot sunshine, and we were really like visitors from another planet. All the week we'd been in the world of life and death, and truth and lies, and the real world made this seem so flimsy and nightmarish.'

But the real world was not far from Elizabeth's thoughts in these years when she was deeply engaged in national politics. It was three years since the Dismissal, but she was still seething.

On 22 November 1978 she had a letter published in *The Sydney Morning Herald*: 'Something tragic for Australia, and irremediable happened on November 11, 1975,' she wrote.

Harrower remained connected to many of the leading creatives in the country. At least once a week she hosted or attended a dinner or lunch or drinks with people at the top of their game. The view from her Mosman garden was superb, and she threw memorable parties for Shirley Hazzard, Francis Steegmuller and Christina Stead. In early 1984, when Hazzard was in Australia to deliver the ABC's Boyer Lectures, Elizabeth invited Gough and Margaret Whitlam, among many others, to meet them. Elizabeth treasured a thank-you note from the former prime minister: 'Elizabeth, a splendid soiree! With abiding affection, Gough.' Among the guests that day were the director of the Art Gallery of NSW, Edmund Capon, and his wife, Joanna, and the writers Murray Bail, David Malouf and Richard Hall. She included close friends Andrew Robertson and Clem Yap and Yolanda Davies but omitted Ferdi and Helene Nolte, admitting later to their daughter Linda that she did not want Helene to attend. 'I think that she would [have been] a bit concerned about the worlds colliding,' Linda told me. 'Maybe it was part of the creation of her life … She could treat people who are supposed to be good friends and part of the inner circle quite shabbily without really thinking about it. Like it didn't really occur to her, or maybe it did. I don't know, but it could be quite cruel.'

The Noltes were excluded, but Kylie was there for the big party at Stanley Avenue. She and Elizabeth had remained close after Bim's murder, although the relationship was now more on Elizabeth's terms. The years since her son's death had been difficult and Kylie was soon also grieving for Roddy, who died in July 1979. She mourned, too, the loss of her only grandchild, fathered by Bim not long before his murder. There was no talk of marriage and the baby was put up for adoption, although Kylie tried, unsuccessfully, to adopt him.[11] A couple of years before her death in 1988, she told journalist Patricia Rolfe that she hoped that when the boy was eighteen he might seek her out 'as she has tried to seek him out'. Kylie was still on her 26-hectare Shipley farm, but she was tired of rural life and keen to 'find a handy slum to live in'.[12]

What a wrench it must have been for Elizabeth to distance herself from this larger-than-life woman. They were very different people. Elizabeth, outwardly conventional as she grew older, remarked in 1983 when Kylie had just turned seventy-one that her friend would 'always be a Wild One of about twenty-three'.[13] In a 1985 documentary, Tennant was pictured sitting outside her house in the mountains. She was seventy-three, a little overweight, her white curly hair unstyled, yet she was magnetic.

Andrew Robertson considered Elizabeth had been consumed for too long by Kylie and the Rodds: 'She spent a huge amount of time looking after this absolute mess … If she wasn't with them – when she rang you, she talked about them. She was very hooked into lost causes.' But Elizabeth's love for Kylie endured. In 1977, when Kylie was diagnosed with cancer and had a radical mastectomy, she recuperated with Elizabeth in Mosman. After she left for the mountains, Elizabeth wrote to her: 'I've been living on snacks since you left … You are very much missed. The house seems strange without you … stacks of love and hugs to you.' Their relationship was built on writing and talking. As they grew older, their exchanges were sometimes banal – 'How are you feeling? How is your weight? I'm ten stone again and it won't alter. Must be the scales. Must be stuck,' Elizabeth wrote. Sometimes they revelled in ideas: 'Dearest Kylie … Lovely to have a talk yesterday over gin and tonic about Heisenberg's Uncertainty Principle and other amazing topics.'

When Kylie fell ill again in the 1980s with severe emphysema Elizabeth travelled to hospitals all over Sydney to visit her. After almost six months in and out of care, she died on 28 February 1988. Elizabeth told Hazzard: 'Although I sometimes had to force myself to trek over to Chatswood to visit, I was almost always glad I'd gone because it did make a difference to her. She knew great quantities of poetry by heart, and I heard her say for the last time familiar lines she'd quoted hundreds of times over the years.'

Dorothy Green, a friend as well as a critic, said Tennant had 'one of the most penetrating, imaginative, original and independent minds in the country'.[14] It was a comment that could just as well have been applied to her greatest friend, Elizabeth Harrower.

## 16

# Patrick White: The Good, the Bad and the Ugly

WHEN ELIZABETH HARROWER WAS LOOKING FOR somewhere to live in the 1970s, Patrick White sent her pages torn from the real estate pages of *The Sydney Morning Herald* with flats near his house in Martin Road, Centennial Park, circled in green pencil.[1] It was the sort of detailed care and attention he gave to the novelist over their thirty-year-long friendship, a friendship of which she was both proud and protective. White was worried that friends at Hunters Hill were a distraction and was keen for Elizabeth to move to the other side of the city.[2] Over the years he found 'all sorts of people' for her – doctors, dentists, acupuncturists, painters, podiatrists, investment advisers. About a month before he died, he rang to put her onto a masseur.

Harrower knew about White well before she met him in 1964. She recalled that when she lived in London in 1955: 'There were suddenly some wonderful reviews of a book, *The Tree of Man*, about Australia, by an Australian. A miracle. In all the years in London, it seemed to me, the homeland was mentioned once and then (to me) adversely in that Mr Menzies [the then prime minister] supported the Conservative assault on the Suez. So, all at once there were numerous good things to be said about Australia, this book, and this writer.' Her mother queued in Sydney and got White to sign a copy of his novel for Elizabeth: 'She sent it to me in London and I thought it was marvellous.'[3]

After Kylie Tennant introduced them at Castle Hill, and after Patrick and Manoly moved to their home at Centennial Park, Patrick invited Elizabeth to dinner with Kylie and the theatre director John Sumner. Elizabeth recorded the date, 2 January 1965, in her diaries several times over the years. It was a significant event in her life and the first of many meals with White. 'He and Manoly were good guests and arrived sometimes, it seemed to me, spruce and brushed and curious and eager to know more about everyone who was there,' Elizabeth wrote in a short, unpublished recollection of White, written over six months from late 1991 to April 1992. The recollection was, in some ways, her personal response to journalist David Marr's biography of White, which had been published in mid-1991.

In her 'memoir' she wrote that eventually Patrick and Manoly met all her friends 'because they wanted to know what everyone was like that I knew'. Kylie Tennant was initially at all the dinners until Patrick suggested she no longer be included.

Elizabeth was not a natural cook, but White was seriously good in the kitchen, and over the years they regularly talked food during their Sunday morning phone calls. Those calls were part of White's ritual. He used Sunday mornings to keep in touch with several friends, all of whom had a 'slot' when they expected him to telephone. Elizabeth recalled the effort he put into dinner parties, when he would disappear into the kitchen while everyone else was having drinks, then emerge 'bearing a tureen, a platter or deep dish'. He would be 'concentrated, pale, perspiration in the hollows under his eyes'. Elizabeth wrote: 'During the sixties we had regular dinners, to and fro, meeting friends, acquaintances, overseas visitors.'

Patrick also liked the informality and lack of grandeur in her small flat in Mosman. 'In those days Patrick didn't see many writers, and he often asked me to dinner if he had some publishing people visiting from Europe or the United States.'

*Patrick White and Manoly Lascaris at Martin Road, 1978.*

White took her to restaurants and included her in big events. In October 1973, she went with him to the weekend party celebrating the opening of the Sydney Opera House. Elizabeth wrote to Shirley Hazzard: 'At last we have a building. To whom should we give thanks that our first building is not dedicated to sport?' White wrote to her when he was overseas in 1971, and when she was in London the following year, he typed long letters to her. In July 1976, when he was in Oslo, he sent her a five-page letter.

White often harangued Harrower about not focusing on her writing, but he was solicitous. One day when she was unwell, he arrived by taxi with food and the gift of a small antique gold brooch which had been given to him and which he and Manoly called 'the solid mandala' – a reference to his 1966 novel. 'On a good day, he was very fond of me,' she remarked.

Every Christmas Day for years she and Margaret Dick drove to White's Centennial Park home to exchange presents: 'He gave me a chunk of boulder [sic] opal, a heavy blue linen sunshade from Italy, a pottery Chinese teapot, many books, my kitchen table and six stools, a David Rose print of Bateau Bay, and one by Sally McInerney.' Elizabeth gave Patrick and Manoly ties, a cashmere scarf, bath towels and a marble rolling pin among other gifts. She treasured a book he gave her in 1986, inscribed 'To Elizabeth, luncher & diner extraordinaire. Shame you don't WRITE'; and a small drawing he had gifted her.[4]

There was undoubtedly a power imbalance, but the same could be said of most of White's friendships. Elizabeth had been awestruck when she met him in the early 1960s but over time she would come to know his complex, contrary nature, his reputation for verbal cruelty and argument as well as his kindness. White believed she was a major talent and was relentless in his efforts to get her to write more. His support was affirming, even if Elizabeth worried about proving worthy of his faith in her. He was protective and in 1980 wrote to Shirley Hazzard: 'Too many vampires, Elizabeth keeps her principles. Whether she is also writing, I have given up asking in case I get the wrong answer. Too many vampires make too many demands on her.' It was surely a dig at Hazzard, whose mother Kit had made heavy demands on Elizabeth's time while Shirley's career had raced ahead in New York.

Patrick and Elizabeth saw films and plays together and talked politics and books. She gave him *Out of Africa*; he told her to read

Flannery O'Connor's short stories. When Harrower was awarded the Literature Board grant in 1974, she told him: 'If I'd just written a wonderful book, I'd feel it was justified.' He told her: 'you might write a wonderful book.' One year, they were invited to the Soviet Union by the Writers' Union. White was 'theoretically charmed and fascinated' but was frail, and the idea faded. She didn't go but was slightly regretful. 'There was nothing to stop me making my own way to that fabled land,' Elizabeth wrote. 'And that was in the days before it was at all usual for writers to turn up in droves. Judah Waten had gone, as a Communist, and Manning Clark had gone with him, on one occasion. But it would have been a privileged glimpse of a system still self-protective, remote from the West, fearful and feared. Because of literature, films, what I'd read during the war of the courage of the population, most of all because of the temperament evinced in the writing of the great Russians, I felt predisposed to love them.'

Realising how much her friends hindered Harrower's creative life, White tried to shame her into writing, but he dented her confidence. 'These attacks and counter attacks went on for years,' she wrote. 'He seemed to want to incarcerate or quarantine me, perhaps misguidedly imagining that a life totally devoid of diversions, company, new experiences would prompt me to write. He should have known better. I was no more responsive to bullying than he was. So, this was a dark strand in our friendship.' On the other hand, Patrick was 'like a playmate' and they had wonderful conversations: 'Patrick liked to hear things, stories, idle thoughts that almost no one else would have heard with the right attention. Presumably, I listened to him in the same way … he could be sympathetic and sorry for people over specific events but again he showed a complete switching off of all warm currents when the person failed to evince some recovery, some toughness.'

Given the strength of the relationship, it was not surprising that when David Marr wrote in the White biography that Elizabeth was 'devoted' to the author she was 'mildly fed up'. She felt Marr downgraded her relationship with the Nobel Prize winner, as if 'the friendship was all on my side'.[5] In her recollection she wrote that White was 'a very important figure in my life. Indeed. A lovable man. An infuriating, unreasonable man. An endearing man. A terrible man. A many-faceted man. I am miserable sometimes that he's not here. It was certainly not a bland friendship, not calm and polite and dead. We sometimes shouted – he would start it of course … There were days when we bored and irritated each other, and he was perfectly capable of saying something slighting about me to David Marr, as he was capable of saying slighty things about David Malouf, Jim Sharman, Desmond Digby, almost anyone, to me.'[6]

White wasn't the only one of his circle with a waspish tongue. One day in May 1981, Harrower sat at her typewriter smarting from reports of a dinner party at the home of poet Elizabeth Riddell – who lived across Centennial Park from White. Harrower wrote to the Steegs that she had heard that the dinner, attended by Patrick and Manoly and other writers, had 'done me over' and that 'women novelists seem to have a thin time there'. Harrower was upset: 'ER [Riddell] told the company she'd met me in the street and I'd announced I wasn't going to be a victim any more. The others all joined in laughing and went on from there destructively.' Harrower was 'extremely cast down for days. Massacres, where no one stands up for you, are a bit grim. I think Patrick was taken aback that I minded so much.'[7]

When White died, he left Elizabeth a small legacy. At the Adelaide Festival Writers' Week in 2017, Elizabeth told the audience that their friendship 'irritated some people. Why does she know him? We just liked each other … I loved him, he loved me, we were really, really true friends.' 'He would be the counsel for the prosecution, I was the counsel for the defence. Those were our roles.' Elizabeth recalled: 'Patrick detested "warm" people, the word "warm" as applied to people … he was somehow thin, washed, clean, concentrated, even pure.'

In October 1973, when White won the Nobel Prize for Literature, Elizabeth heard it on the radio at 10 pm and dashed to the phone: 'He was in bed. I raved on with huge happiness. He was calmer … I stayed awake ALL NIGHT, heart beating.'

Christina Stead believed Patrick and Manoly were like brothers to Elizabeth and she agreed that 'I do count on them as if they were'.[8] Jinx Nolan thought Patrick was like a 'girlfriend' to Elizabeth, who in turn thought he was like a good friend much of the time and 'harmful like a bad friend for the rest'. Patrick 'became to me over time, like a relative, a good, close friend, someone who knew most things about me, recent and distant, and someone who was interested in the detail of my life, and who wished me well for my own sake. I confided in him, and he told me how he was thinking and feeling – as we both undoubtedly confided in other close friends. The thing was we both believed in friendship. He had many relatives and was detached and separated from them, and I had very few: friends were almost everything.'

Elizabeth was under no illusions about White: 'As is well-recorded, however, he was sometimes simply atrocious – irritating, unreasonable, irrational, damaging, patronising, hurtful, infuriating …

I came to understand that he was relieved after raging on about something, raging, raging, when you seized the initiative and changed the subject totally, and abruptly.'[9]

Elizabeth never forgot White's generosity in drawing her into his circles in the 1960s when she felt there was little support for Australian writers: 'Patrick White looked out for that rare bird, another writer … He invited me to lunch and after that we were friends. So then in addition to being patronised, I was cultivated, sometimes by the same people. Interesting and funny.'[10] She told the Steegs: 'He tried to rescue me from myself when no-one else did.' White could make anyone laugh when he set out to amuse, but he could also wound – and Elizabeth was no exception. 'He hated me to receive attention. He hated me to praise other people, unless perhaps they were dead artists, or living artists not personally known to either of us.' There is a touch of Harrower's fictional men – Felix Shaw and Stan Peterson – in this image of White, a gay man keen to limit the applause for his female friend. Elizabeth understood contrarians: 'Simultaneously this sometimes perverse and multi-faceted man, urged me to write, berated me for not writing, hated me for not writing, was mean to me because I wasn't writing, abused me because I wasn't writing, told me I was an artist, not a social worker (when I indeed unwisely spent time helping distressed friends and acquaintances like an unpaid welfare worker), told me I was depressed when he thought I wasn't writing, told me he'd thought of four books for me to write …'

When Marr was finalising a volume of White's letters, he sent Elizabeth a quote from Manoly Lascaris saying she had been one of White's 'Lady Disciples'. She was not pleased and wrote back to Marr: 'The quoted "disciple" credits me with a humility I've never possessed, indeed with an alien – unAustralian! – character that would startle people who know me. It's given rise to some deep thoughts about – well, the problems of the person who said it. Someone I'm fond of. Such is life.' The quote was eventually dropped for space reasons and Elizabeth was pleased. In his summary of Harrower for the book of White's letters, Marr wrote: 'Harrower knew not to be possessive. Her cool intimacy with PW was unclouded to the end.'[11] Marr noted that Harrower had kept twenty-six letters from White but that much of their long conversation had been conducted in those hour-long, Sunday-morning phone calls.

It's likely White's belief in Elizabeth intimidated her. She withdrew *In Certain Circles* in part because she felt he would be disappointed. But was she so much in his thrall that he can be blamed for her writer's block? David Malouf thinks not. He knew Patrick and Elizabeth well over many decades and believed that while White's opinion mattered a great deal to her, she saw her work clearly and was comfortable in drawing a line under her novels. 'In the time that I knew her, she was really quite certain that the books she had already published constituted a body of work that was cohesive and original, and very much that the books belonged to one another,' Malouf told me in 2024. 'At that time, she couldn't see that anything she wrote would amplify them in any way. Of course, she could write … and if you're a writer who's had a lot of practice, as she had, you can always go on writing another book or stories or whatever. But I think it's up to you to decide whether they would be done at the same level as the books you've already published, and if what you wrote would add to what is written, and in some way, amplify it. She thought not, and I had huge respect for that.'

After Patrick's death, Elizabeth told Shirley Hazzard: 'Of course, he was infuriating and hurtful and said many non-wonderful things about everyone, but equally he was extremely loveable, kind and funny… Another time, he said, "I get depressed when I think you're not writing". Not many deeply mind whether other people write.'

Elizabeth missed Patrick greatly and ten days after his death visited Manoly at Centennial Park: 'We went through the house, looking at books and pictures, and it seemed so empty and quiet. We seemed to be looking for Patrick.'[12]

# 17

# Life at the Edges

ALMOST A DECADE AFTER THE FAILURE OF *IN CERTAIN Circles*, Elizabeth Harrower was still processing the events and gently massaging their sequence. She still saw herself as A Writer. In her 1985 interview with Giulia Giuffrè, Harrower said she was still putting things down on paper: 'I haven't wanted everything to get away from me because, things do get away from you and they lose their freshness if you don't put them down. So, let's just say that on the one hand, I sometimes think, I don't have to say everything I know … Then there's the other aspect which says, that unless you write it down in a novel, unless you work hard to refine it and sit at it day after day, you don't know yourself what you know … You find out by the writing.' She told Giuffrè that she had written a novel but had no idea of the theme. Was Harrower referring to the writing she had done in the 1970s under her Literature Board grant, work that had never surfaced? Or was this another, later piece? What is clear is that Harrower was intent on maintaining a persona as an active writer, even though she had not published so much as a short story for a decade. This was also the time when she appeared to become almost jealous of a new cohort of writers who were able to access more government support for their work. In 1988, she told the Steegs that success in writing is 'such a lottery':

Younger writers don't realise some of this. The fact that huge amounts of money have been spent on writers' grants, publishers' grants, advertising, promotion, travel and so on because politicians and others of an older generation, interested in the arts, worked hard to bring this about doesn't occur to them. They think they are just naturally better than anything before and receiving what they deserve. The many prizes go to the head. There are, of course, genuinely gifted writers about, but the idea of becoming a famous writer is now as widespread as the desire to become a famous actress, model, TV personality … still justice surfaces from time to time and someone like Sumner [Locke Elliott] is recognised.

Harrower's 1950s novels, published in the UK, had preceded the development of a stronger Australian publishing industry in the 1960s and 1970s. In those decades, new entrants and older houses like Angus & Robertson expanded into paperbacks and brought Australian writers to a wider readership. After her return from London in 1959, Harrower had worked hard to have her work published in Australia. In 1966, the year in which *The Watch Tower* was released by Macmillan, her 1958 novel, *The Long Prospect*, was published as a paperback by Sun Books, the imprint founded by Geoffrey Dutton, Max Harris and Brian Stonier, but it sold poorly. Harrower waited more than a decade to see her work offered to a mass audience. After she signed with A & R, it released *The Watch Tower* in 1977 under its A & R Classics imprint. Two years later, the publisher's Sirius Quality Paperbacks imprint released *The Long Prospect* and *The Catherine Wheel*.

Harrower's books had not sat easily within the Cassell stable in the 1950s and once again, marketing was an issue. In her 1982 master's thesis, Nola Adams suggested the Sirius cover illustrations for *The Long Prospect* and *The Catherine Wheel*, designed to attract women readers, gave an impression Elizabeth was a Mills & Boon–style writer rather than one of Australia's most important novelists. The back cover blurb for *The Catherine Wheel* was melodramatic: 'Christian draws the two women onto the catherine wheel of his precarious existence, a whirling circle of immense beauty and danger that both entices and threatens the onlookers.' A & R rereleased all three titles in the late 1980s, with elegant covers more suited to Harrower's sensibility. Their publication prompted media attention and Harrower cut out and kept a 1988 column in *The Sydney Morning Herald* by reviewer and academic Don Anderson. He lamented she was not better known and that scholarly and critical articles on her work were few and far between.[1]

The 1980s also proved difficult for Elizabeth at a personal level. She had survived on her mother's inheritance since 1970 but was now facing financial problems. Andrew Robertson recalled her managing on a 'widow's mite', largely the rent from the flats she had inherited. In 1988 she was living on the annual 10 per cent interest from her Commonwealth Bank account and confided to Nancy Phelan she was worried about money. In March 1989, she told Phelan she had spent $6500 more than her income in the previous year and that this was 'not good news. It makes the move [from her Stanley Avenue, Mosman home] which was inevitable, appear closer … I am looking around the place to see if there's anything I can turn into cash.' Harrower had worked in small jobs, such as John Brink's Anchor Books, over the years, but had survived for decades without regular paid employment.

In the 1980s Harrower was in her fifties but many of her closest friends – Patrick White, Christina Stead, Bill Cantwell, Judah Waten, as well as Kylie Tennant – were twenty or more years older, and in declining health. By 1982 Stead, for example, was living between her half-brother at Lindfield and her half-sister at Cremorne. She had suffered several minor heart attacks and had to cart an oxygen cylinder around with her. Harrower told Shirley Hazzard that Christina was 'very frail but in brilliant spirits, saying she feels about twenty-five inside. She was making notes for a book yesterday.' Stead was an inspiration to Harrower: after Stead's death in 1983, she wrote: 'In recent months or years her life had ceased to be enjoyable, she was too ill. But her life was wondrously fulfilled.'

Harrower's connection with the increasingly famous Hazzard added to her glamour at this time. In 1984, when Hazzard delivered the Boyer Lectures, she dedicated them to Elizabeth, who had helped her with the research. The lectures proved controversial, as Hazzard criticised the growing nationalism in her home country along with its treatment of Aboriginal people, its prejudice and its capacity for derision and 'unexamined violence'.

When they returned to New York, the Steegs pressed Elizabeth to visit them there and on Capri. She reluctantly agreed but was worried about her finances. 'Earlier on, before I moved into this house, before I sold the flats, before I went to the aid of a friend, if I had been more interested in my own affairs and applied more intelligence, I could have arranged for more prosperity,' she told them. 'I might have gone away and stayed away for a while, but people had nervous breakdowns and died, and it didn't happen.' She knew she could afford a longer European holiday if she sold Stanley

Avenue but 'the bad experience of selling the flats at the wrong time makes me nervous of that'. Linda Nolte told me that Elizabeth had been 'ripped off' in that real estate deal.

In the end, the holiday in Italy, which was heavily subsidised by the Steegs, was a small disaster and Elizabeth cancelled her plan to stay with the couple in New York. 'I guess I don't like even beautiful islands as well as cities,' she wrote to Bill Cantwell. 'Don't fence me in! Still Donald Keene was there [on Capri] and Shirley and Francis seem to know every inch of Italy, so well that I learned more and saw more than you would expect to see and learn in months. No time was wasted. I met their friends (all rich, all charming) and we ate out every single day for lunch and dinner – out of doors often on Capri in surroundings of spectacular beauty.' That reference to Keene, the American who became a renowned scholar of Japanese literature, gave a sense of the elite circles around the Steegs. Just as she did with Elizabeth, Shirley Hazzard maintained a correspondence with Keene over more than thirty years. One memory remained with Elizabeth – the interest shown to her by the adored Francis: 'In Capri F. came and talked to me alone one evening or afternoon when S was doing something. He tried to urge me to write more, keep writing. Was very nice.'[2]

Elizabeth preferred Paris to Capri, because the Whitlams, who were there for Gough's stint as the Australian ambassador to UNESCO, were hospitable and fun, and 'even lovelier than we imagined'.[3] Rome, where she and the Steegs stayed at the Hassler, was equally satisfying, but she was unhappy to be the recipient of so much attention. Margaret Dick wrote: 'Dear E, please relax, be calm, try to have some pleasure and fun from your journeyings. Shirley seems to have been a trial, wanting to do you good whether you like it or not … It does seem they have tried hard to give you a happy time, even if misguidedly.' On her way home, via the UK, Elizabeth was struggling with the difficulties of resuming writing and wrote to Hazzard, 'I'm not going to wake up having written a good book unless I work.' The tensions continued and back home in Sydney in December, Elizabeth wrote a postcard to the Steegs filled with contained anger and hurt: 'I've cared about you both a great deal for years and refuse to be not cared for back because all of a sudden I got worn down and ran out of energy … So I came back from London, but I'm a constant friend.'

Years later, Elizabeth said she should not have agreed to go on the 1984 trip because it had been too rushed: 'Invitation, arrival, departure, all too pressing and sudden … S and F not pleased when I did not go to NY.'[4]

Elizabeth's friendship with Hazzard was also challenged when Patrick White became less impressed with her work and blamed Kit for distracting Elizabeth from her writing. Caught in the middle, just as she had been with Sid Nolan, Elizabeth recalled that White 'came to like Francis much more than he liked Shirley and spoke of her "terrible American sweetness"'. Elizabeth began to question Hazzard's authenticity:

In her letters, which were wonderful, there was also a level of flattery – was very hard to reciprocate. From time to time I tried, feeling that graciousness – in other words gross flattery – should be responded to in kind. But I couldn't do it very well, feeling awkward and insincere, though at the time I did feel respect and admiration and great affection for them both, but it was a style not natural to me. And as for Patrick, he really detested anything 'warm' or lush in the way of compliments and came to feel antagonistic towards Shirley. He also felt, knowing of my involvement with Shirley's extremely depressive mother, that I was being made use of. I defended Shirley to him for years, but now I think he was right. Sadly.[5]

Elizabeth was still a Labor devotee but her views were not easily categorised. The 1980s brought big political and economic changes. Sydney's Darling Harbour was reclaimed ahead of the 1988 Bicentennial. The debate on Indigenous Australians escalated as the Bicentennial Authority decided on a 'warts and all' reflection on national identity. It declined to support a re-enactment of the First Fleet, arguing it would give offence to Aboriginal people and supported historians in their efforts to uncover the past. According to Harrower, the authority wanted 'special and extended treatment' given to Aboriginal people. A week from Australia Day in 1988, she wrote to the Steegs about the celebrations, including *La Traviata* performed in the Domain and the 200 tall ships due to arrive on 26 January.

She had always supported the left but now questioned attitudes to Indigenous Australians. 'Far and away the worst aspect of 1988 and the celebrations is the irrational and sentimental attitude taken towards aborigines [sic] and the founding of the colony by self-righteous (but irrational) white Australians who always like to be "agin the government", she told the Steegs. 'Not one really plans to give his own house to an aborigine, or to sail back to Europe, but they rage and rage about something that happened in 1788. They want to do good and be good, but this is surely not the way to go about it. Some like Manning Clark speak so much of "blood staining the wattle" that it's difficult not to feel they'd find it interesting.' But on 26 January, Elizabeth was swept up in the celebrations, and reported that the Bicentenary was a day when 'human beings overcame the motor car and surged into the streets and walked in good natured crowds, lovely … I think it was psychically, psychologically good for us to see that 21 ½ million people can behave well, understand instructions, enjoy life without being drunk, appreciate the hard work and organisation that went into it all … and have some feeling for the past and the future.' She was still finding it hard to adjust to the new mood towards Aboriginal people and told the Steegmullers:

> There is much confusion, anger and activity. Some Aborigines are going to Libya to seek help – money, arms training and the cancellation of substantial exports from Australia to Libya. There is equality before the law, and positive discrimination in favour of aborigines, and that one per cent of the population own sixteen percent of the land outright. There is an almost touching amount of goodwill amongst whites, in and out of power, for aborigines, and this has been the case for many years. But for the moment, the leaders of the aborigines, black and white, are too excited to articulate exactly what it is they want. Yesterday one leader wanted to be able to hunt kangaroos in Melbourne. Fortunately, some individuals are flourishing, and they'll gradually help.

In the 1980s, there was also a divisive debate on immigration. Elizabeth did not share the views of many on the left about the controversy sparked by historian Geoffrey Blainey. His comments at a

Rotary meeting at the Warrnambool Capitol Theatre in March 1984 were made at a time of increased Asian migration. Blainey criticised the Hawke Labor government for the pace of entry and the 'preference' given to Asians. Elizabeth wrote to Hazzard:

> Geoffrey Blainey stirred everyone up by saying what many people think – that there is something unbalanced about the immigration programme. People from the UK and Europe have trouble getting into Australia. The feeling in the country is changing rapidly. They say (Bill Hayden for one) that it's inevitable that Australia will be 'Asianised'. Powerful people on 'multicultural' boards attack Sydney University when it tries to set reasonably high standards in English language courses. And so on. Ambitious people do attach themselves to 'liberal' causes and hammer certain topics almost to death. Whereas I admire Geoff Blainey for uttering a few words of good sense about aborigines, neurotic and trendy characters looking for causes have done so much harm.

A couple of weeks later, she reported: 'Immigration and race have taken over the newspapers and parliament and interviews and conversation. Blainey's more complex thoughts have been grabbed, simplified and turned into weapons by the stray maniac', but 'Hawke has spoken very well on the subject.'

The late 1980s were a time of upheaval in the communist bloc, and Elizabeth followed the moves towards glasnost and perestroika in the Soviet Union. Her friends Audrey and John Blake had been influential in the party in the 1930s, '40s and '50s. Jack was a former coalminer and former senior member of the Communist Party of

Australia; Audrey was an activist who led the Eureka Youth League in the 1940s and '50s. They remained politically active, and Elizabeth took a close interest in the gradual demise of Soviet power. She was somewhat horrified at the West's tactics: 'The lack even of enlightened self-interest much less generosity of spirit, shown in the West's dealings with the Soviet Union frequently stuns me.' She watched Clive James interview a Soviet and then an American commentator on television and noted 'such cheap jokes'.[6]

She revealed more of her political sympathies when she wrote to Audrey Blake:

> Thanks so much for sending *Moscow News* and the Aus–USSR Friendship Society Bulletin … It's a really fascinating issue of *Moscow News*. Like you, I was very taken by the article by Martin Walker, the *Guardian* man … Did you see *Four Corners* last night? What an unimaginable thaw that we should be seeing such programmes! Tonight, I'll miss Richard Carleton's interview with Sakharov, but watching that man is a health risk for me, anyway. This morning on ABC radio when he spoke from Paris, he sounded quite bemused. His preconceptions have taken a shaking up, whether he admits it or not. He could only have held some of those views by keeping himself wonderfully ill-informed.

In 1987, when Elizabeth was almost sixty, she decided it was time to declutter. Her roof was leaking and there were papers everywhere. She would not part with all her letters, dozens of them covering decades of her life, but some would have to go. She felt she needed to read them all before handing them over to the National Library. That was especially the case for a precious cache Bill Cantwell had given her for safekeeping. These were letters from Cynthia Nolan and dated from 1951 until just before her suicide in 1976. It was important history and Cantwell, who was eighty-eight, was worried about managing correspondence that could reveal Cynthia's state of mind and the state of her marriage to Sid Nolan. They had to be read, but Elizabeth confessed to Nancy Phelan: 'Owing to Cynthia's extraordinary handwriting, I've put off reading them.'

Many of Elizabeth's peers were wrestling with similar issues – and it was not just a case of unreadable handwriting. These writers and artists were confident of their place in Australia's cultural life and believed their legacies should be preserved. They desperately wanted to matter in the national story. Most retained their letters for posterity, some of them had typed them with carbon copies to create a record. Kylie Tennant threw nothing out, leading to her depositing one of the biggest archives in the National Library. Some writers and artists were chased by institutions for their papers, others negotiated payments or tax breaks, and some found libraries were not very interested in every Christmas or birthday card.

But in the pre-internet age, letters were the record of their lives. Many wrote several letters, notes or cards every day, conducting running conversations about the books they read; the gardens they planted; the concerts they attended; the casseroles they cooked; their sore legs and bad colds; their trips to the bush; their writing projects. The minutiae of daily life filled the correspondence, the letters operating as the connective tissue that held friends and colleagues together at a time when mail was delivered quickly and telephone calls were still seen as an opportunity to pass on specific information, to set appointments, or for emergencies, not for extended chats between friends.

Detailing her life and knowing the detail of others' was almost an addiction for Harrower and it is impossible to know which came first. Did she use the time spent on friendships as an excuse for not writing books, or did letters fill the gap after her fiction dried up? She told Phelan that her letters, some typed and some dashed off in an almost unreadable scrawl over three decades, were 'lovely'. The Nancy Phelan pile would go straight to the archive along with 'Christina's. Judah's'. There was no mention of Shirley Hazzard's letters, but these too would end up in the National Library. The correspondence with Christina and Judah and Nancy was more informal and relaxed than Elizabeth's correspondence with Hazzard. Nancy and Judah were mates, not icons; and while Christina was a star, Elizabeth was not overawed by the author. Elizabeth knew these three well. She regularly saw them face-to-face or talked to them on the phone. Elizabeth did not mention any correspondence with Kylie Tennant when she wrote to Nancy in 1987. Elizabeth had retrieved some of her letters from Kylie in the 1980s, but these are not in her archive. A handful from Elizabeth to Kylie are in Tennant's NLA archive.

Judah Waten, like Patrick White, was keen for Harrower to write more. 'Thank you for the literary "push"', she told him in 1975. 'I think athletic coaches "psyche" their runners, swimmers, like that, with talk.' At the end of the 1970s, Waten helped her win a writer-in-residence position at Monash University, but Elizabeth, scarred from her Alexander Mackie experience, declined. When Waten reread *Down in the City* in 1984, three decades after its release, he told Harrower: 'I still think it's splendid.' Unlike White, whose comments verged on bullying, Waten was constructive, gently instructing her in the art of making a living from words. Harrower took his advice that 'it's good to be able to turn your hand to anything', but novels rather than short stories were her metier and she told him: 'I am like a piece of earth-moving equipment that only knows how to dig large holes.'

Waten rarely missed a chance to acknowledge her work. In 1980, at a seminar on Marxism and literature, he cited her alongside Stead, Miles Franklin, Mary Gilmore and Katharine Susannah Prichard as women writers with progressive or radical ideas. Harrower respected his writing but there is little evidence that she worried much about his judgement; the critics who mattered to her were White and Hazzard. Waten was her 'Communist-Jewish-novelist-friend' who offered advice on everything from dealing with her enlarged heart and shingles to navigating a Literature Board grant. For years, there was little or no mention in their letters of his wife, Hyrell, a schoolteacher and activist, but over time she moved into focus and their daughter, Alice, a talented musician who had studied in the Soviet Union, enjoyed a strong friendship with Elizabeth.

Elizabeth's friendship with Judah went well beyond writing: she shared her concerns about Margaret Dick as her cousin aged; they gossiped about Kylie and Roddy, although Elizabeth, true to form, revealed little of the drama of her life with the Rodds. And, as she did with all her friends, she detailed her social engagements. In December 1979, Waten was overseas but she reported on a dinner at her place with 'MD, the Costigans, the Smiths, the Geerings. They didn't know each other but hit it off.' She had seen Kylie and would see the Beavers [Bruce and Brenda] next week; Patrick had given her two mezzanine season tickets for the next Sydney Film Festival; she was still looking for flats to buy so she could sell her Mosman house and kicking herself for not acting earlier. It was an enduring relationship, but in April 1985 a letter from Hyrell told Elizabeth her old friend had suffered a cardiac asthmatic attack and was in emergency. A couple of months later, Judah Waten died at the age of seventy-four.

Nancy Phelan was still engaged in life, churning out books and travel stories and pages of handwritten letters to Elizabeth from her home in the Blue Mountains. Unlike Elizabeth, who said that learning to touch type after she left school was one of the best things that ever happened to her, Nancy did not type her manuscripts (or her letters). She was prolific but handwrote first, before typing her books and articles because, she claimed, she could not really read her own writing. Older than Elizabeth by fifteen years, she had had a more privileged upbringing, studying at the Conservatorium of Music before travelling overseas, marrying in London and returning to Sydney after the war with husband Peter and their child. She threw herself into the arts community at Kings Cross, and at the famous arts colony at the Merioola boarding house in the eastern suburbs, she met people like the painter Justin O'Brien. She was much more middle class than Elizabeth, yet so much more bohemian. Nancy and Pete maintained a flat in Macleay Street in Kings Cross, but Elizabeth stuck to the other side of the bridge, preferring views of the harbour to the inner city.

When Nancy died aged ninety-four in 2008, having produced more than twenty-five books – novels, biography, memoir, travel books and even a cookbook – obituarist Angela Bennie noted in *The Sydney Morning Herald* that Phelan was consumed by her writing: 'Writing was her life, part of who she was; and transforming the world into language was her life's task.'[7] The same could be said of Elizabeth, yet for years she watched as Nancy published more and more books, partly to pay the bills. It must have been disconcerting for Elizabeth to see her friend streak ahead and garner more acclaim. Nancy also had what Elizabeth lacked – a supportive relationship, a calm home in the country for writing, and an occasional city life of dinner and book launches and events. They were close for decades, sharing domestic detail along with talk of books and writing. Elizabeth revealed she often just ate 'fruit and bread or fruit and Cruskits' for dinner. She told Nancy it was ridiculous to talk of a literary establishment in Australia because writing was so essentially *not* a group activity.

In the late 1990s, when Nancy spent time in London, Elizabeth's letters were like gossip sessions over coffee. She had been shopping and bought 'one pair cotton slacks, one striped top, heavy cotton jacket'; she had been to lunch at Mosman Junction at a new French cafe where the owners were so French they 'have trouble, with English'. After Phelan sold her flat in the Cross, the women saw less of each other and in about 2000, their letters petered out. Like every Australian, they now used the phone to stay in touch. But something was amiss. In 2003 when Phelan published her book *Writing Round the Edges*, it was subtitled *A Selective Memoir*, suggesting it did not pretend to be an autobiography. Elizabeth told Andrew Robertson that she would not read the book. 'I didn't ask why, I just knew that if she didn't offer a reason, not to ask,' he recalled.

If Elizabeth stuck to her oath and never read the memoir, she missed out on a lovely passage from Nancy: 'Elizabeth was the one who was always there to help and support Kylie through the dramas and tragedies of her life. Generous, loyal, affectionate and understanding she and Margaret [Dick] have also been my friends for over 40 years.'[8]

Harrower made an artform of keeping her friends apart. There were distinct circles and while Elizabeth linked them through her conversations, she structured her gatherings. One person who seemed to cross these invisible lines was Margaret Dick, who was at almost all social events. Margaret was special – a blood relative as well as a kindred spirit, and a calm foil to the intense Harrower. Initially, Margaret was the wise head in the relationship, but this changed over time and Elizabeth took on the role of financial as well as emotional support. She paid Margaret's strata fees when the retiree was hit with a big bill.

The duo took road trips to western New South Wales, dazzled by the light and the land, and were constantly together at films and plays and operas in the city. They enjoyed a similar eclectic approach to the arts and in one week in 1987 saw a Munch exhibition and the movie *Crocodile Dundee*. They swapped books and magazines and saw each other at least once a week. Margaret helped with the catering when Elizabeth entertained at Stanley Avenue and mixed easily with editors and critics and academics and writers. She was a full-time worker, teaching and lecturing and holding down administrative jobs, and had little time for writing. Laurel Laurent recalled: 'Margaret was bright. She had a lot to say. Elizabeth had strong opinions, but they had known each other so long and I felt that Margaret had her measure.' Laurent met both women in 1973 when Margaret worked with her mother at the Institute of Chartered Secretaries. Mother and daughter became regular guests for Sunday lunches organised by the cousins.

Margaret, unlike Elizabeth, had no family financial support and worked well past retirement age. Elizabeth felt it was a 'curse' that Margaret was often too tired at night to write and too busy with chores at the weekend. Linda Nolte said Elizabeth regretted not helping her cousin more: '[Margaret] didn't have a lot of money. She didn't have a lot of success. She was quite a humble woman. She wasn't egotistical. Elizabeth always said she was much cleverer than she was.' The two women were close for many years with the Greek-Romanian-Australian poet Antigone Kefala who served on the Literature Board of the Australia Council in the 1990s. Another long-term literary friend was Richard Hall, the journalist, author and Literature Board member who was an adviser to Labor politicians and shared Elizabeth's strong political views.

For years, Elizabeth had little interest in her extended family in Newcastle, but in 1981 the cousins travelled north to see Frank Harrower's younger sister, Dell, and her daughters Thurza and Verity and Dell's granddaughters. 'The two divorced sides of my family will meet after about a hundred years,' Elizabeth noted.[9]

Helene and Ferdi Nolte were loyal friends and regularly trekked across to the North Shore for dinner and a movie at the Cremorne Orpheum. Sometimes it was just Ferdi. Helene was not such a film buff, and Ferdi became Elizabeth's rock. 'Yesterday Ferdi came over twice from Hunters Hill to get up on my roof and try to fix the broken tiles and keep further rain out,' she told Nancy Phelan. 'Today he'll contact a tiler to finish the job off and he can tell him exactly what has to be done, which is a help.' Ferdi and Elizabeth delighted in each other's company and Elizabeth half-joked that Helene suspected an affair. In fact, Elizabeth, who adored this man with his 'lovely, good nature', had to stand by as he fell in love with a younger, Swedish woman in the mid-1980s. Elizabeth was drawn into the Nolte family's grief as they split and Ferdi planned a wedding in Sweden. That fell through and Ferdi and Helene reconciled.

In her sixties, Elizabeth, the child who had been so isolated, had become an adult with a strong circle of friends. At Christmas 1985 she told Hazzard her 'family' of friends had 'scattered all over the country'. She listed them: 'the Madigans, the Costigans, Andrew, Margaret, Salvatore and Stephanie, the Smiths, Yolanda, the Levises, Jane and James' and added, 'That's not to say there aren't rather a lot still around and still feeling sociable.' Even so, she confessed: 'I love it when the workaday world starts again after all the Public Holidays. As has been noted before, hedonism has its limits.'

She had left her Newcastle origins behind but still maintained a connection with her cousin Thurza. They would meet for lunch or afternoon tea when Thurza travelled to Sydney to attend the theatre. Thurza, twenty years younger than Elizabeth, found her warm and welcoming, but guarded. Elizabeth always led the conversation. She told Thurza: 'I've had lovers,' but revealed little. They talked about politics, Paul Keating and Patrick White. They exchanged cards and letters, and Elizabeth told Thurza: 'After childhood and youth [which] last for eternities, we all expect the middle part when we're allegedly in our prime, to last forever. It doesn't, so the thing is to make the most of it while it's around, I suppose.'

Harrower had been friends with many of the country's midcentury writers and now found herself in demand from biographers: 'More people have come to talk about Christina, Judah, Kylie and Patrick,' she told Hazzard. 'I haven't minded yet but could get bored if this keeps up.' Her letters in these years read like shopping lists, detailing the books and films consumed each week: 'I've read more of Julian Barnes, Ian McEwan, Rachel Ingalls, Martin Amis, the John Cheever biography ... I've read good pieces about/by Bellow, Genet, Duras, Milan Kundera ...'

Elizabeth was aging now and in May 1984 wrote to Hazzard: 'My face seems to have decided to follow the path of Auden's. I don't think this can be attributed to some inherent literary inclination of the flesh; it has more to do with the wondrous skin specialists of the late forties and early fifties who irradiated me with so much X-ray treatment for adolescent spots that it's a marvel I haven't been carried off yet.' She looked remarkably fit in her eighties when I interviewed her, but had health challenges over the years, beginning with heart problems and a serious case of shingles in the 1970s and high blood pressure in the 1980s, when she was in her mid-fifties. Her biggest challenge came in 1989 when she was diagnosed with colon cancer. She wrote to the Steegs on 4 November:

It's 10.00 at night and I'm alone in a 4-bed ward of the Royal North Shore Hospital. Big black windows off to my right with some scattered lights of St Leonards or North Sydney, Crows Nest. In the last few weeks, I've been rushed in twice – the first time following blood tests & x-rays – for blood infusions, then for tests as an outpatient & second immediate admission. Came in last Friday at 2.00 and didn't see the surgeon till 2.00 today. Tuesday. A tumour. Operation Friday. People have said some cheerless things, but friends have been wonderful ... I certainly haven't been lonely, so much loving support ...

18

# Coping in Cremorne

E LIZABETH HARROWER HAD DONE LITTLE WRITING when in the early 1990s Angus & Robertson asked her to write the introduction to a planned volume of work by Cynthia Nolan. The publishers had decided to bring together in abridged form the books that Cynthia had written about her travels with her husband in Africa, China and Australia in the 1960s and 1970s. After Cynthia's suicide, Elizabeth had forged a friendship with her daughter, Jinx. In 1991, for example, the two women organised a gathering for fifteen people, including the surrealist painter James Gleeson, in honour of the late Bill Cantwell, who had been one of Cynthia's oldest friends.

Harrower had had virtually no contact with Sid Nolan, who died in late 1992, after the painter fell out with Patrick White decades earlier. She must have had mixed feelings about tackling Cynthia's legacy. In the 1970s, she had declined to write Cynthia's biography. Harrower was well placed to capture Cynthia's essence, but she would have to grapple with just how much to reveal about her. Could she be objective about the woman whom she felt had 'cast her out'?

Born in Tasmania, Cynthia had been taught by a governess before boarding at an elite private school. She worked in a Melbourne art shop and spent time in London and Germany between the wars. In the 1930s, back home and still in her twenties, she ran an art gallery and interior design shop in Melbourne and showed her ability to pick a star when, in 1934, she hosted painter Ian Fairweather's first exhibition. She studied dance and art in Sydney then trained as a nurse in Chicago and London and at a New York psychiatric hospital. Back in Melbourne in 1941 she gave birth to Jinx, spent time at the artists' colony Heide outside Melbourne, moved back to Sydney and published two books. In 1948, Sid Nolan, whom she had met at Heide, sought her out and they quickly married. He was thirty, she was thirty-nine. Sid was marrying up from his own working-class background and the partnership proved one of the most productive in Australia's arts scene. But Cynthia's work as a writer, artist and gallery owner was overshadowed by Sid's fame. *Outback and Beyond*, containing abridged versions of four of her travel books, was designed to bring her work back into the light.

Harrower had once been in awe of the stylish Cynthia but now wrote about her with confidence. She had told Patrick White in the 1960s that Cynthia was the person most like her and she could well have been describing herself when she wrote of Cynthia's 'rare capacity to "listen like a scientist, to listen like a lover".[1] Cynthia was neither shallow nor self-seeking but had compassion, a sense of social justice and a lack of vanity. Intuition was perhaps her greatest gift, Harrower wrote. Cynthia, 'with a complex lifetime of experience behind her', had found in the marriage to Sid 'a task sufficiently demanding to fill her life for many years – a task at which she was supremely able and supremely successful: promoting, guarding and directing the establishment of her husband's international career. This was the public life in which she was unsparing of herself, and in which her great charm and accomplishments, her astringent intelligence, played an essential role.' Jinx Nolan was delighted with

Harrower's 'extraordinary' introduction and told me in 2012: 'She nailed it.'

Angus & Robertson asked Harrower to write a memoir, but she did not sign a contract. She wrote fragments for the 'non-memoir' but could not shake the dread she felt when writing to others' expectations or when she was funded by literary grants. 'Even when they're benign and friendly shadows, shadows hang over you when you're doing something to order,' she noted.[2] She maintained connections with several younger people she had met in the 1970s. Among them was Sydney painter Tom Carment, who painted her portrait and often took his young children to visit her at Stanley Avenue where she plied them with pastries. Tom and Elizabeth shared reading suggestions: 'Haven't read Tobias Wolff, but I'll watch out for those books you mentioned,' she wrote. 'Today there's a list of books I'll order up at the library – to read before buying: one is *The First Man* by Camus. Abbeys didn't have *Mystery and Manners: Occasional Prose* (Penguin) [by the twentieth-century American short-story writer Flannery O'Connor]. Patrick and I went through a Flannery O'Connor period, reading her letters and short stories. I miss his enthusiasm for things suddenly discovered or rediscovered.'

Elizabeth had recovered well from colon cancer in 1989 but felt physically vulnerable. She had suffered high blood pressure for decades and now her body was letting her down. In May 1995 she slipped in her back courtyard and broke a knee, spent ten days in hospital and wore a leg brace for six weeks. A few years later she broke her right wrist falling off a high kitchen stool (undaunted she wrote in her diary each day, using her left hand, the scrawl barely decipherable). On another occasion she fractured a femur.

Always, she worried about her heart. Life was more restricted: 'Somehow I never go to the theatre anymore and I used to love it.' She saw films and watched a lot of television. Her tastes were eclectic, and she enjoyed the American gay comedy/drama *Tales of the City*: 'There was something magical about it – the house, the off-beat lives.'[3]

She continued to wrestle with politics and society, telling the Blakes in the 1990s: 'There has to be another idea, other positive ideas, of how to live, to coexist with capitalism and consumerism … my optimism must be generic.' Her politics were not hard and fast; she was still keen on Labor but by the end of the 1990s was questioning progressive ideas like multiculturalism. She wrote to John Blake:

> When I see Greeks and Macedonians and Yugoslavs and Croats brawling away and looking ferocious in the streets of Sydney and Melbourne, I feel quite fed-up. And when in Canberra last week at some multicultural gathering an Asian man stood and asked Howard scornfully what this Australian character was they were supposed to identify with, I also felt irritated. Who built all these cities, factories, roads, railways, telegraph lines, mines and grew the food if not the Anglo-Celts of generations past. I think forelock tugging to 'ethnic' people is as tedious and as out of bounds as to the overlords of long ago in the UK.

As the Soviet Union faltered, she wrote to Clare Golson: 'Several marvellous friends with a particular passion for the USSR are dead – dear Judah Waten, dear Bill Cantwell, not to mention Christina. My whole disposition is drawn to Gorbachev – his genius and humanity and intelligent goodwill are all evident in his deed, in his eyes, in his endurance all these years.' She was distressed when the Gulf War started in 1991. 'It's incredible that another major war is in progress,' she told Nancy Phelan. About eighteen months after Paul Keating won the 1993 election against the odds, she told Shirley Hazzard that it had been a great time in Australia: 'Assassinations, unemployment, droughts and bushfires notwithstanding, I've never known a time when so many different people have recognised that we've been living through a period in this country that will be remembered very favourably. Something good under the surface of things has been going on.'

In 1996, Harrower won the Patrick White Award for writers who had not been sufficiently recognised. The media spotlight was on her. Asked if she would write again, given the twenty-year gap from her last short-story publication, she replied, 'I think I would feel very fed up with myself if I didn't.'[4] She told the Blakes that if she were to capitalise on the prize, she would have to find an agent. A couple of years earlier she had moved her novels from Angus & Robertson to publisher Tom Thompson's new imprint, Editions Tom Thompson (ETT), but had been unhappy with the exercise. Thompson and Harrower had met through Elizabeth Riddell in 1982 and later, when he became a publisher at Angus & Robertson, he had overseen her novels, reprinting *The Watch Tower* in 1991, and offering to republish *Down in the City*. She had refused and displayed some 'dreadful loathing' about the writing in her first novel, Thompson told me in 2025. When he left Angus & Robertson to set up ETT, he bought rights to a number of A & R Classics, including Harrower's works. In January 1995, ETT published *The Watch Tower* and *The Long Prospect*.

Elizabeth remained keenly interested in politics and was upset after Labor's loss of the 1996 federal election. 'From being an exceptionally surprising and enjoyable country to live in for thirteen years, Australia has now turned into something quite other, following the March election,' she told Hazzard. 'All the tattered Thatcher ideas, all the worst of the American religious right, have taken over … Now with the Liberals in power and the Olympic Games on the way, it's hard not to see this as a very Dark Age.' The following year, life was no better: 'Everyone I know groans about the state of the country, the incompetence and mean-spiritedness of the government, the ineptitude of John Howard … at home and abroad. That the feeling could change so much in twenty months is hard to believe.'[5] She told Clare Golson: 'Isn't it dreary and horrible with Liberals in power? And boring, too.'

Elizabeth was now almost 70 and had not published for 20 years and she relied increasingly on friends she had formed outside Sydney's literary circles. In August 1995, she told Shirley Hazzard that Andrew Robertson and Clem Yap had visited with French champagne and noted that Andrew, whom she had met thirty years earlier through Kit Hazzard, 'has the great gift of empathy'. As well, Ferdi Nolte 'has been phenomenally thoughtful and kind'.[6]

For many years, her Christmas mornings were shared with Andrew, Clem and Margaret, often followed by a telephone call from Shirley Hazzard in New York and celebrations with other friends. Sometimes the holiday hospitality was too much. As 1999 began, she wrote a list in her diary: '1. See less of the moody and neurotic (moody neurotic?); 2 Never persuade a spoilt moody person (remember neurotic gave bad and cheap and passed on presents); 3. Never invite 9 people or 11 to lunch/dinner at table.

Too noisy and table and chairs not sufficient.'

Her friendship with Hazzard had survived the unhappy 1984 trip to Capri and Elizabeth was pleased when Shirley made another trip to Australia in 1997 to speak at the annual Sydney Institute Dinner. This time she travelled alone: Francis had died after a long illness in 1994.

Elizabeth warned her friend that she would 'be coming to a very grumbly, discontented place in August – mean-spirited, grey. It has so changed since the arrival of the Liberals. Before that, no one wanted to be anywhere else, and now it's exactly the opposite.' But the 'grumbly, discontented place' embraced the expat and in 2004 Hazzard won the Miles Franklin for her novel *The Great Fire*. She asked Elizabeth to accept it on her behalf, surely a somewhat bitter task for Elizabeth given that she had missed out on the award in 1958 and in 1966. Elizabeth declined the role but attended the dinner.

For years, friends had urged her to sell her Stanley Avenue house, and late in 1999 she did, moving to a 1970s medium-rise apartment block in Cremorne with a harbour view. She was on the fifth floor, with three small bedrooms, combined sitting and dining room; a kitchen 're-made about three years ago, no common walls, cross-ventilation … two little bathrooms, two balconies (small) and a view. Camphor laurels grow up to eye level, so I see the birds nearby.'[7] It was 'geographically wonderfully convenient – to the city, transport, friends, cafés and so on'. Her apartment was close to a bus stop and she zipped into the city 'on Tuesday for Italian, Wednesday to Newtown to a Buddhist centre, other days for coffee with friends'.[8] But it had been a 'torrid' year, she told Hazzard, not only because of the house move but because Margaret Dick had been in hospital four times, including for surgery: 'There is no one else to manage things for Margaret – no relatives and contemporaries frail or departed.' It was all too much.

She was just a few metres away from Andrew and Clem. Around the corner was her hairdresser, Ulrik Funch. Ferdi Nolte was a constant visitor, bringing magazines, sorting household blips and ferrying Elizabeth to movies and medical appointments. Elizabeth regularly rang people on Sunday mornings, a routine copied from Patrick White. 'Everybody had slots,' Andrew Robertson recalled. Elizabeth was still interested in Italian, which she had begun studying in 1990, and Buddhism. She made new friends in Barry Willoughby, who worked at Abbey's bookshop in the city, and Brian Galway, who had helped her with her property move. But she was finding life tedious. 'In a slump. Need a change of scene desperately – or else,' she wrote on 24 November 2000. Two years later, she told Hazzard: 'This week Manoly was ninety. I sent him flowers and wrote to him. He's very well taken care of, with the housekeeper who really loves him, and "carers" twenty-four hours a day. His memory isn't good.' She was adamant now that her writing days had passed. When Geoffrey Lehmann and Sally McInerney's daughter Lucy published a novel in 2002, Elizabeth told her: 'I won't write any more, it's very hard and painful when you make yourself go back into the world of writing a novel and it takes over your life.'

Yet the little girl who had remained optimistic in spite of a disrupted childhood was alive in the adult: Elizabeth loved big events, and in 2000 she was swept up in the Sydney Olympic Games:

for years, months and weeks we were bored and intimidated
by the gloom and cynicism of all radio and television and

newspaper reports of what would happen when it all started … Many friends flew off to America, Japan, Canada, France. Those of us who were left in the about-to-be-destroyed city said that we'd just buy enough food to survive the siege and stay in … Sydney was unveiled, looking wonderful. Overnight, a sort of celestial radiance descended on the mood, organisation, public transport, population and weather of the whole city. We were all, mysteriously, like people who drank champagne night and day with no ill-effects and all the joy. Something happened to us … Crime disappeared. People were wonderfully friendly, kind and helpful to each other … Those who escaped have now come back to the realisation that they missed something rare.[9]

A few years later, in 2004, with Australia involved in the war in Iraq, Harrower was desolate at the likely return of the Coalition at the next election. 'Daily they lie, ignore revelations, destroy those brave enough to speak out, patronise all of us and take part in exercises that result in the accumulation of dead bodies in the world … It's not that we think our side – Labor – is made up of saints, far from it, but they wouldn't have gone to war, they wouldn't have kowtowed to Bush, and they wouldn't be destroying the public school system (money flooding into rich private schools) and the Medicare public health system.' In October she told Hazzard: 'Our election takes place next Saturday, and the almost certain return of the Howard government is depressing absolutely everyone I know.'

In June 2005 Hazzard again travelled to Sydney for a NSW State Library dinner, but the interactions between the two women were prickly. Elizabeth wrote in a note to herself: 'S took the opportunity

11 years after the Italian holiday to complain (as far as I could make out) about my not going to NY. It was a noisy restaurant … I thought the whole thing was strange … Miles Franklin dinner 23rd, afternoon tea at Intercontinental 24th … went by taxi to see Margaret then back for dinner till 11.15. … It was so noisy, boisterous crowd, that I heard – literally – almost nothing. And didn't even try. I knew S. could talk on and on and had no intention to stop.' (Elizabeth had her dates mixed; it was twenty-one years, not eleven years since the distressing holiday on Capri.)

Harrower's work had not been forgotten. Early in 2006, the academic and critic Susan Sheridan wrote asking for access to her papers for a project, 'Lost Generation: Women Writers and Post War Modernity'. It was to be a group biography of the professional lives of Australian women writers in 1945–65. Sheridan wrote: 'Although Judith Wright's poetry and your own and Thea Astley's fiction gained recognition at the time and subsequently, there were many other women whose writing was neglected, or failed even to reach print, in the post war years.' It had been a high point for local publishing enterprises, yet women figured little in this lively literary scene, Sheridan told Harrower, and their careers had been:

distorted (like Harwood's), interrupted (like Hewett's) or completely stalled (like Jolley's). Other fiction writers whose outstanding work would not see the light of day until the 1970s and '80s were Amy Witting, Olga Masters and Jessica Anderson. From the late 1940s onwards Kylie Tennant, Ruth Park, Nancy Keesing and Nancy Cato gained popular success writing historical fiction, children's stories, radio plays, but the growing separation of literary from popular writing meant that they lacked serious critical attention (Margaret Dick's study of Tennant being the obvious exception). Talented poets who had made a strong start in the 1940s, like Hewett, Rosemary Dobson and Dorothy Auchterlonie (Green), published little, or irregularly, as the 1950s went on.

Sheridan's point was that Harrower did not fit this pattern. She had published 'well-received' novels between 1957 and 1966. Sheridan wanted to include Harrower as 'an exception that might prove the rule', but the author was not interested. She denied access to her papers and granted Sheridan an interview only to say no. Sheridan visited Harrower in Cremorne and recalled: 'She was very charming and very determined that she wasn't going to do it and she was quite clear that I wouldn't be able to include her.'[10]

Elizabeth had kept diaries since she was a child but now the entries were brief, recording names of people seen or telephoned. Each year as she began a new journal, she listed key dates – her parents' birthday and death dates; the dates when she met friends like Patrick White and Judah Waten. She recorded the people who sent her birthday cards, and the gifts exchanged with friends. The detailed diaries may have been a memory device. 'I'm older and older than I ever expected to be,' she wrote to Clare Golson. 'It doesn't worry me unduly as long as I feel all right. I don't think your mind has an age attached to it although that could be wrong. No, it isn't wrong.' She was still typing letters, filled now with details of her health and that of friends; her dentist and doctor appointments; and meals and films shared with Andrew and Clem, Gavin Souter and others. Her diaries were filled with mundane details.

She agonised over hair loss, for example. She was taking Fosamax, a medication to ward off osteoporosis, which can lead to hair loss in some patients. Friends were fading. On 18 May 2007, she took a phone call from Helene Nolte; Ferdi had suffered a stroke and was severely disabled. On Christmas Day 2008, Elizabeth had lunch with Margaret Dick in her nursing home. Margaret was ninety-two and blind. The cousins played Scottish folk songs on a cassette player and Elizabeth later confided in her diary: 'M liked. I cried silently. She is drifting away.'

Elizabeth's correspondence with Hazzard was now intermittent. Hazzard's memory and concentration were failing, although in 2005 she was still able to 'manage social events and conversations and to take pleasure', according to biographer Olubas. Friends noticed Hazzard's physical fragility and in early January 2008 she had a serious fall in Rome which required surgery. Later that year, Elizabeth took a call she 'couldn't understand' from Hazzard, who she knew had had an accident and who sounded 'very unlike herself. Left a message, staying in bed, leg hurts, and things like that. I was mystified. Can't remember if I rang, but know I sent a card wondering what was happening. Didn't hear and didn't do anything else, since there were more than enough happenings in my own life.'[11]

In her Christmas card to Hazzard that year Harrower said: 'I think of you and Francis, of YM (somewhat differently), the prodigious letters/thoughts exchanged, the girl in your story who often comes to mind, hoping to see things less clearly.' Hazzard's last public appearance was in September 2012, after which, as her dementia worsened and she became bedridden, she did not leave her apartment until her death on 12 December 2016.[12]

Her decades of correspondence with Hazzard had given Elizabeth an entrée to a world she could not replicate in Australia, a world she had been attracted to since staying with the Nolans in London. The Steegs and the Nolans had enjoyed the security of external status and domestic stability. At times over the years, Elizabeth had seemed resentful of the support that Shirley received from her marriage. Elizabeth had been supported by Kylie Tennant, but that relationship was unacknowledged and never accorded the status of coupledom.

As early as 1987, as the Steegs headed back to New York from their annual sojourn in Italy, Elizabeth had written to Hazzard: 'This room where I am typing is hideous with papers overflowing from filing cabinets. Those not destroyed will go to a library soon. When there is only one of you these things seem tedious, not to say mountainous, but must be done … You'll be arriving home with work completed, proofs on the way, good events all over the place.' Hazzard had it all – marriage and success as a writer. Over forty years of correspondence, Harrower heaped praise on yet another Hazzard novel or essay or interview, but these comments suggest she nursed disappointment and confusion over her less stellar career.

In her early eighties, with her papers and past filed away in the National Library, Elizabeth was no longer recognised as A Writer. Many friends knew little or nothing of her writing life and her years at the centre of a lively literary circle. And, like her, they could not imagine what lay ahead.

# 19

## Second Act: *The Watch Tower*

Elizabeth Harrower was eighty-three in 2011, living quietly in her apartment in Cremorne when, one rainy afternoon, she received a letter that would transform the last decade of her life. The Melbourne-based publishing house Text Publishing, which had embarked on a program of discovering and republishing Australian classics, wanted to publish *The Watch Tower*.

A month later, Text principals Michael Heyward and Penny Hueston travelled from Melbourne to Sydney. Harrower caught the bus into the city and over afternoon tea at the Menzies Hotel, one of her favourite spots, the trio bonded. It was the beginning of a strong friendship and 'a joyous publishing experience'.[1] First cab off the rank was *The Watch Tower*, regarded by some as her masterpiece. It was forty-five years old and little known other than by academics and devotees of mid-century Australian literature.

One of Harrower's long-term fans, the novelist Joan London, had read the novel as an undergraduate at the University of Western Australia in 1970 and suggested it could be part of the Text Classics series. Text editor David Winter was also aware of Harrower's work and pushed for it to be included. London was tasked with writing the introduction.

Harrower was caught up in the excitement. She had spent decades in the shadows. 'I was mesmerised,' she recalled later. 'The whole experience has been dreamlike. Perhaps it's not too much to say that there has been a fairy tale feeling to it, coming at this late stage in my life.'[2] But she was a little 'exasperated' by the long wait for *The Watch Tower*'s release and wrote in her diary: 'Had a sad night thinking about my books + their fate.' In the heat of an Australian summer, she slept badly and resorted to pills.

Her age could not be denied. In February 2012 she tripped in the street and staggered home for a brandy; in March she was tired after visiting Margaret Dick, who was now in care. But on 21 April, when Gay Alcorn, a senior writer and editor at *The Age*, flew from Melbourne to interview her, Harrower was in good form. This was her first newspaper interview for many decades, and Alcorn, who took her to a nearby restaurant for lunch, got a big tick from the author. 'Very congenial nice young woman,' Elizabeth wrote in her diary.

Alcorn's feature appeared in *The Age* and *The Sydney Morning Herald* on 6 May, to coincide with the novel's release. Harrower was a great story – the forgotten Australian writer, up there with Patrick White and Christina Stead, living an anonymous life in the suburbs after walking away from it all at the peak of her powers. It was the stuff of a movie script. At its centre was the mystery, the puzzle, of why Harrower had stopped writing in her forties.

'My friends thought I let other people waste my life,' she told Alcorn. 'They would try to pressure me to keep writing, which should have been encouraging, but I wasn't easy to save … Writing has to matter more than anything else, and other people don't like being abandoned. Other people have an interest in your not writing.' Harrower was referring to the pressure applied by White, but whom did she mean when she said other people had an interest in 'your not writing'? Kit Hazzard's demands had distracted her, but was Harrower also referring to her relationship with Kylie Tennant and the Rodds? What of the withdrawal of *In Certain Circles*? Harrower was unsure why she had lost faith in the novel. The reasons for shelving it 'are totally mysterious to me now', she told Alcorn. She noted it 'was well written because once you can write, you can write a good book but there are a lot of dead books out in the world that don't need to be written. The fact that you can start and write so many words does not make it a novel.' Harrower revealed the manuscript was buried in her archive in the National Library and suggested she was not even sure what it was called. She told Alcorn: 'I think it would have disappointed people. Patrick would have been disappointed. I was disappointed … It is just one of those dead books.'

Harrower was a good interviewee and the feature revealed her as intelligent, reflective, warm and vulnerable without being fragile. At eighty-four, she was consciously narrating her life but she was philosophical. 'We've arrived here, on a great holiday. There are beautiful places, and we have a long, complicated holiday. And, like any holiday, it comes to an end. You know you'll have to go home.'

The Text Classics edition of *The Watch Tower* included a superb introduction from Joan London, who invited readers to see Felix Shaw and his 'victims', the sisters Laura and Clare Vaizey, as part of a bigger story. 'Who … has not endured, or witnessed, or participated in the attempt of one human being to have power over another?' London asked. Reviewer Salley Vickers said she 'read this book twice. Once for sheer pleasure – if pleasure can be the correct term for an experience that is so distressing – and once for the purposes of this review … It left me with the strongest sense I have had for a very long time of the infinite preciousness of consciousness, at whatever cost, and of our terrifying human vulnerability.' Reading the novel, Vickers wrote, was like meeting 'a thrilling new love', discovering a writer who understands that human fate 'inevitably feels to the fated "like a fantastic misunderstanding"'.[3]

There were other positive reviews and Text announced it would republish all her books. Harrower was now at the centre of a minor celebrity bubble; *The Watch Tower* delivered a level of fame she had never imagined. She sat back and let it wash over her, but she was astonished: 'The past is still alive in fiction. I thought nobody would be interested, but there are readers everywhere, and they're tremendously interested in finding out about the past, because the world won't always be as it is.'[4]

Harrower had won the trifecta: she was much more interesting now, given her age; she had been rescued from obscurity; and the books were appreciated as artefacts which yet seemed contemporary. It was a unique event in Australian publishing. Plenty of books were republished in the twenty-first century, but not many of their authors were still alive and so alert.

Harrower was feted as an extraordinary octogenarian, but it was not easy being old. She was using an iPad for emails rather than typing letters, but sometimes the technology let her down, adding to the sense of isolation that easily crept upon her: 'iPad not working … No one ringing. Not feeling great. No calls from anyone for ages. What goes on? It's not nice!' she told her diary on 4 June 2012. The next day, she was still annoyed: 'Must get iPad fixed and then go town. Can't stay in with no calls for days/weeks.' On 8 June she was desperate: 'No plans for whole week! Awful.' These entries are hard to read; despite her composure, and genuine joy in her literary renaissance, Elizabeth struggled with aspects of her life, from technology to her reduced physical strength, even as she maintained a dignified demeanour.

*The Watch Tower* had been written in a different era but in 2012 it resonated with contemporary debates about gender and power. It was somehow timeless. Harrower described a modern world before the advent of mass tourism, before the rise of second-wave feminism, before neoliberalism, and before the Whitlam government's concerted boost to Australia's literary infrastructure. In her fiction, critics said, 'we see the seismic cracks appearing in that mid-century world. Her characters move between torpor and passivity, and towards the shock of awakening.'[5] Harrower was claimed by feminists, but the novel is free of ideology or theory. We hear and see the coercion executed by Felix Shaw on his wife and sister-in-law, but there is no analysis of the domestic violence in their home. The power of the story comes in the realistic rendering of psychological manipulation within a marriage. Writer Fiona McGregor told me: 'There is an enduring truth to her work because it looks at power, its abuse and inequity, which starts in the home, in interpersonal relations.'

Harrower had always been reticent about analysing her work. In 1982, when postgraduate student Nola Adams had written to her asking about several references in *The Watch Tower*, Elizabeth had demurred, telling Adams that her mention of the opera *Manon* had no great meaning. She'd put it in the book simply because, 'In the midst of wars and human tragedies apple trees keep growing and the ABC plays opera. Something like that. Women comb their hair and apply make-up when loved ones are dying. Even obsessed people (if sane) will take an interest in things other than the obsession from time to time.'[6] In 2012 Harrower was still dismissive of textual deconstruction. Gay Alcorn reported that Harrower had 'discovered dusty academic articles about her work' but felt that it 'was interesting and not interesting [to read them], a bit like pulling wings off a butterfly'.

Like Christina Stead, Harrower did not want to be labelled a feminist writer. 'I am just a woman, a human being,' she would later tell the Adelaide Festival Writers' Week: 'I obviously believe in justice for everybody …' She told Alcorn in 2012: 'It doesn't suit me, this feeling of grievance.' Still, *The Watch Tower* was a prescient critique of misogyny. Throw in the question of whether Harrower would have won the Miles Franklin back in 1967 if her name had been Eric, not Elizabeth, and the author was readily claimed for feminism in the twenty-first century.

The new edition of the novel prompted a wave of critical analysis within the academy. American Nicholas Birns, a specialist in Australian literature and a former editor of the US-based *Antipodes*, 'a global journal of Australian/NZ literature', saw Harrower's male characters, like Felix Shaw, as complex. The 'Harrower man' was a domineering megalomaniac who sought to control others but could not exercise self-control, but he was also vulnerable and feared his own inadequacy. They were lower-middle-class or working-class men who felt the world conspired against them. Birns noted the change in women's power since the novel was written, saying it was difficult for a twenty-first-century reader to understand why 1940s women would attach themselves to a man like Felix. They had done so, Birns argued, because they had been looking for an escape from the 'stasis' of their restricted lives in those decades.[7] The reference to lower-middle-class or working-class men identified another theme in Harrower's work that was more obvious in a twenty-first century reading. Two of her most fallible male characters, Felix Shaw and Stan Peterson, were self-made men who married up and created havoc in the process – using women to cut through class barriers yet at the same time subjugating them.

There was also a closer analysis of Harrower's critique of consumption, a theme spelt out at a Sydney symposium by novelist Michelle de Kretser, who argued that the toxic forces that drove Felix in wartime Australia signalled the dangers of war or, in peace time, a 'grab-all materialism'.[8] De Kretser said she had been struck by the 'sheer quantity of objects mentioned' in the novel. There were cars, neon signs, clothing, jewellery, household objects, patent drinks, shop window displays. Felix had presented his new bride with a quantity of silverware. 'Judas's thirty pieces of silver come irresistibly to mind,' de Kretser said. 'Harrower's evocation of objects appears incidental in a novel predominantly concerned with the psychological, yet … *The Watch Tower* suggests that the rise of consumerism leaves its imprint on consciousness, normalising the fetishisation of objects and its corollary, a deadening of affect in human relations.'[9]

In 1966 critics and reviewers had focused on the themes of *The Watch Tower* rather than the life of its author. Some might have wondered where she had met such a venal character as Felix Shaw, but Harrower seemed neatly middle-class and there was nothing in her bio to suggest childhood trauma. In 2012, Harrower was at a different stage of her life. She was still guarded about her family but now labelled herself a 'divorced child' and as she revealed more about her childhood it was easier to track the autobiographical elements in her 'coming-of-age' novel, *The Long Prospect*. Some critics could draw the links between the monstrous grandmother Lilian and the sociopathic Felix Shaw in *The Watch Tower* but still Harrower revealed nothing of the links between Felix Shaw and her stepfather Richard Kempley, whose dodgy business dealings were well hidden in newspaper archives. My research has shown how much Harrower drew on her stepfather for *The Watch Tower* – from his business dealings in confectionery and liquor to his physical appearance as a 'swarthy, nuggety man of 44'.[10] There is little doubt that Kempley, whom Harrower claimed was an alcoholic and possibly mentally ill, was the model for Felix Shaw.[11] But even in the last stages of her long life, when she had learnt so many 'fundamental' lessons, Elizabeth Harrower was not about to unlock the painful memories that had shaped so much of her fiction.

20

# Remembering Newcastle:
## *The Long Prospect*

CHRISTINA STEAD HAD NO DOUBT THAT *THE LONG Prospect* was Elizabeth Harrower's best work. In 1976, commissioned by *The National Times* to write a survey of Australian fiction, she called the novel, published twenty years earlier, 'Harrower's masterpiece'. It was, she wrote, 'subtle and straightforward. Withheld and passionate, so honest and sympathetic in its story of the first affections of a very young girl, almost adolescent, that it has no equal in our writing; and abroad.' If it had been published in France, Stead suggested, the novel would have attracted 'persistent acclaim for its restrained compassion; this book is of a quality not elsewhere met here'.[1] Perhaps it was not surprising Stead had such a warm reaction: some critics have noted the similarities to her own masterpiece, *The Man Who Loved Children.*

*The Long Prospect* always felt autobiographical to readers, but when Text republished it in October 2012 and Elizabeth revealed more of her own childhood living with her grandmother in Newcastle, it was clearer still she had written a version of her own story. This time, *The Weekend Australian* was offered the exclusive interview to promote the book, and I spoke to Harrower for a feature. Meticulous as ever, Harrower recorded my visit in her diary: 'Friday 14 September 10.00 Helen Trinca. Helen nice. Italian parents'

234

and 'Sept 20 Call from Helen Trinca'. We had indeed spoken about Italian, a language Elizabeth studied for some years, and at some length about my mother who, just seven years older than Harrower, was an equally keen reader.

At Text, David Winter was handling the reprint, having taken over the Classics list from Caro Cooper, and he exchanged many friendly emails with Harrower. She told him the book design was 'terrific' and that W.H. Chong, Text's art director, had 'such insight, intuition. When the cover appeared – mysterious, thought-provoking – it gave me a shock.' Fiona McGregor was to write the introduction. She had first read Harrower's books in the late 1980s and met the author as she prepared the piece. The women talked over sandwiches and tea at the Menzies Hotel. 'She struck me as a person of acute intelligence, somewhat guarded, yet curious,' McGregor told me. In her introduction, she wrote:

Harrower's writing is devastating. The prose is exact, spiky, a chiaroscuro of dread pace and bright voice. You laugh and cringe at the same time. The psychological precision is relentless. It's like watching keyhole surgery; Harrower's gaze is so penetrating you can feel her looking through the pages, down the years at us … Harrower moves through the terrain of prepubescent love unencumbered by prurience and sentimentality. Her formal studies in psychology are evident; she is an expert in human behaviour, and her analysis of it underpins everything. Yet the writing is aflame with emotion arising from the characters' quests and ordeals. And we are always aware of the author's service to her craft. Harrower is, as the cliché has it, a writer's writer.

*The Long Prospect*, unlike *The Watch Tower*, *Down in the City* and *The Catherine Wheel*, had a vicious and dangerous woman – rather than a man – at its centre, and McGregor noted: 'I've read critiques of Harrower's work as an exposé of misogyny, but that is reductive, if not defensive. Her women can be as sadistic as her men, her men as dignified as her women. What she exposes is the will to power. Its politics, its battles, its terrible atrocities rage within the domestic realm – and the world remains indifferent.'

In our conversation ahead of publication, Harrower was friendly yet guarded. Tall and upright at eighty-four, her white hair was well cut, her clothes low-key but appropriate. Seated in an armchair in her nondescript flat, she was nonetheless somewhat intimidating. There was a presence not easily captured by words. We relaxed as Elizabeth talked about the past and her friendship with Patrick White and she mentioned how many of the people who had been central to her life were dead. She batted away questions about whether *The Long Prospect* was her own story and defaulted to her role as interrogator.

'As lively as a cricket', in her own words, Harrower told me she was surprised to be the age she was: 'You can remember yourself in the midst of great world events and experiencing them. When you are old – and it happens overnight, believe me – you have this long, lived experience. It's excellent as long as you are still in it ...' In a follow-up interview, Harrower admitted regret at not writing more novels. In earlier interviews she had suggested she had stopped writing, in part, at least, because she had nothing more to say. Now she said: 'I should have put down more. I knew more interesting things; I knew more exciting things. I feel guilty because this is something I can do and the fact that no one was all that interested certainly doesn't excuse you … I would love to have written more books. People say: did you have nothing else to say? Well, that's not true. I have always had things to say. I am full of observations and opinions and not only that – characters. In my own mind I have lived dangerously, dangerously in the sense of finding out more and more about human nature … I am not quite sure who exactly I was punishing but I was punishing somebody by not writing … At this age you are aware of some very contrary and dangerous things you have done with your life as if you were going to be immortal. This is the irritating thing, now it is dawning on me that I am not immortal.'

Harrower said she was not sure what to make of the characters in *The Long Prospect*: 'I suspect that if I read some of them now, I would think they were incredibly high-minded, which I think would irritate me now – except that you should never patronise your younger self. I really couldn't do any of those books now … [Yet] I think in each of the books there's something in them about human nature that I thought were mine.' Harrower made this point several times in various interviews – her conviction that she knew things 'that I would never let anyone contradict'. She told me that day: 'I have understood more than I want to understand sometimes and this is why not everyone is going to like the books because sometimes they tell you things you don't want to know.'

She was precise about the damage done to her. One of the first things she said to me that day was that she was a 'divorced child'. Not a child of divorced parents, or a child whose parents had divorced, but a 'divorced child'. This strange choice of words revealed the depth of her hurt. Seventy years after her parents' divorce, Harrower was like a child being taunted in the playground. Her words confirmed the parallels with *The Long Prospect*'s Emily Lawrence, whose parents, while not divorced, were distant, neglectful figures. It was clear that the path from devastated child to composed elder had been a difficult journey for Harrower. She had grown into herself with age, but even at eighty-four she dodged questions about the autobiographical elements in the book. That day, I was struck by Harrower's mixture of ego and humility. She was practised at balancing intimacy and distance, a stance that US critic James Wood would later describe as her 'wounded wisdom'.[2]

She linked the end of her writing career with missing out on the Miles Franklin in 1967, saying: 'I thought, if they don't want me, I don't want them.' She wasn't necessarily proud of the reaction she'd had at that time, but she offered it as a reason for her writer's block. Being overlooked by her peers had, over the decades, been integrated into Harrower's narrative of herself as the literary outsider. Missing out on the big prize amplified her image as the neglected, abandoned child, misunderstood and unappreciated by those around her. Harrower had not stopped writing after she missed out on the Miles Franklin, but in retrospect it became a reason to be offered up when journalists asked about her writer's block. In my interview with her in 2012, she mentioned her mother's death but made no mention of Kylie Tennant and the emotional pressures she had faced when writing *In Certain Circles*. Nor did she say much about Shirley Hazzard, the woman with whom she had shared a vast correspondence and whose mother she had spent so much time assisting.

Harrower was reluctant to talk about her biological father and made no mention at all of her stepfather, Richard Kempley, leaving me with the impression that she and her mother had confronted the world alone after her parents' divorce. She mentioned living at times with her grandmother Helen, but she did not offer any connection to Lilian, the careless grandmother in *The Long Prospect*. Yet Helen was surely a model for Lilian. More proof of this lies in a 1976 short story, 'The Retrospective Grandmother'. Told in the first person and comparing two grandmothers – the maternal and paternal – the story was published in the Melbourne *Herald* but never in a collected volume. The maternal grandmother is also called Helen and is a force of nature who 'held men in general in contempt, this was as nothing compared with her feelings about women … Child of the Calvinist north as she was, and undisputed star of her circle, she obliged women to act in her presence a role towards men that she herself adopted only spasmodically and dropped at whim – the scurrying serving maid. Dictatorial! Intimidating!' The narrator recalls the grandmother, 'my wild Helen of Troy', with 'her erratic pronouncements, open-handedness, wrong-headedness, violence. Oh, she was entertaining and self-centred. Her egotism was fascinating. She made me laugh and cry … she could out-shout and out-pose Bette Davis. She sounds terrible. And yet she was prodigiously generous … And she made everybody laugh and feel more alive. She never sulked or moped. She was in a hot Australian town at a time when few saw the world. A small part of her glamour was that she had come from afar and could tell her audiences of the world's existence … She was so used to bullying and getting her way that it must have seemed inconceivable that she should never ever be able to force circumstances to yield what she needed.'

An event in the story references the plot of *The Long Prospect*, in which Emily's non-sexual relationship with the boarder, Max, is derailed by Lilian. In the short story, the narrator says: 'Someone loved me – a stranger, for no reason except that I was myself – and I loved him. My grandmother sent him away, in an unusual, even unique, excess of common sense or propriety. It was dreadful. I was put on a train to another city, to return to my mother, and I said in my head, and possibly, though I can't be certain, out loud to her: I'll never forgive you.' The repetition of this story adds to the possibility that Harrower is drawing on a similar incident from her childhood.

The paternal grandmother in the story is easily read as Elizabeth's grandmother Catherine Harrower: 'The other one, the proper Grandma, figured less, disappeared sooner, and was, like the rest of the human race, misunderstood. At least, by me. That is, I accepted what I heard – that my Australian-grown, Victorian-seeming, very correct Grandma was the baddy. My father's mother. She had springy lawns that I liked to walk on. Everything else had weeds and asphalt, so her cushiony grass, those crisp bright edges of cut grass bordering garden paths, was noticeable. She had roses, fig trees, rows of vegetables, hens' eggs … There were puddings at her table … Even to me, she seemed conventional and pious … When my parents had parted, I heard that Grandma had made life deeply miserable for my young mother from the day of her marriage. I loved my mother. So I listened and drew up my accounts … She took me to the church down the hill from her house. It was very boring …' In the short story, this 'proper' grandmother organises piano lessons and has dresses made for the young narrator, who is wary of her father's family: 'A certain truth is that although I was sure of my welcome as a grandchild of the house, I also felt myself to be in alien territory. They were nice to me, but what about my gentle mother?'

In 2015, Harrower described the short story as 'probably' a mixture of fact and fiction about 'warring families in a confined space, almost within sight of each other'.[3] The facts tell us much about Harrower's early days in Newcastle, where she moved between various relatives after her parents separated. The story states: 'My two grandmothers lived less than half a mile apart, yet never once in my presence met or spoke … I can remember periods when I not only abandoned the house near the church but actually rushed into doorways to avoid Grandma if I saw anyone like her anywhere in town. Perhaps the divorce was going on. I heard things. My mother and father were absent forever, it seemed, living and working in different cities.' Other details suggest Harrower was writing about her own life. The short story says: 'when I had spots, Grandma was the one who noticed and took me a long way by train to a skin specialist', recalling Harrower's own acne treatment.

The Text publication of *The Long Prospect* in 2012 opened the way for Harrower to speak more openly about her childhood but she did not find it easy to talk about herself. She was initially happy with my feature in *The Weekend Australian*. When she saw it in print on Saturday, 27 October, she wrote in her diary: 'Good piece but everything is stressful.' By Tuesday she was upset: 'No sleep. Stressed with terrible piece in *Australian* at weekend. So negative.'

Reading this in her diary a decade later, I was reminded of what a dramatic change Elizabeth was dealing with at that stage of her life. She was fit and able, her mind was sharp, her presence powerful, but the republication of her books was proving an emotional challenge as well as a joy.

**21**

# Remembering Sydney:
## *Down in the City*

HE FRESH PUBLICATION OF *THE WATCH TOWER* AND *THE Long Prospect* had transformed Elizabeth Harrower's world. She was thrilled by the attention her work was receiving, but life was not perfect for someone approaching her eighty-fifth birthday. She looked strong and healthy, and she was curious and engaged, but in early 2013 she was out of sorts as she wrote in her diary: 'Don't feel great – eyes, ear, teeth, skin, balance (energy – not there). Just too tired.'

The media focus had reminded her, too, of the need to get her house in order. *Down in the City*, her first novel, was to be published again – a cause for joy. But Elizabeth was now preoccupied with protecting her privacy after her death. She set about tearing up her past. She had deposited papers in the National Library, but there were stories and letters and journals in filing cabinets in her Sydney flat. The material included correspondence with her mother in the eight years Elizabeth spent in the UK in the 1950s. They were sometimes tough years in which Elizabeth appears to have had a couple of romantic relationships. What might those letters have revealed about the young woman's adventures and emotions?

On 9 July, she sent an email to David Winter, who was finalising the introduction by writer Delia Falconer to *Down in the City*. 'Dear David,' Elizabeth wrote. 'Thanks for your letter. Yesterday I made a big decision to destroy more than 400 foolscap typed pages of literary thoughts – part journal, part stories, eye-witness accounts, secrets and so on. This means that I am not up to any more decisions for the moment, and I am happy to leave the final version of the introduction to you and Delia.'

Winter was horrified: 'I suppose it is no use my saying that I hope you might rethink your big decision? It is yours alone to make, but I groaned involuntarily when I read your email yesterday. Must those papers disappear – I would not be alone in thinking that at least some of them could find a good home at the National Library.' Elizabeth wrote back the next day saying she had had second thoughts, but it was too late: 'I'm afraid I had torn up the 400 plus foolscap pages before I wrote to you about the Introduction. Having made a not very good decision, I thought it best not to have any more opinions for a while. Now it seems clear that I should have read all those pages and perhaps torn up half. It would have taken energy which, at that moment, I didn't have. A pity, but not the end of the world! Life goes on.'

Earlier in her life, Elizabeth had hated the thought that people would see letters after she was dead, in part because she was keenly aware that her adult persona had been carefully shaped over the years. She could not control access to hundreds of letters she had written to friends, but she could control the exchanges with her mother. Her control extended to her novels. She told Giulia Giuffrè in 1985 that she tore up drafts because 'I don't see that there's any value in people going over early drafts'.

*Down in the City*, which had been the 'dry run' for her more important later books, reminded twenty-first-century readers of the often-painful issues of her life that she had been willing to explore, albeit through her fiction. First published in 1957, its rendition of class and coercion, of male insecurity turning into domination, and of the woman, Esther Prescott, who could not escape, who indeed did not really wish to escape, this world of male power, resonated with contemporary issues of gender. In her introduction, Falconer noted that the novel 'glows with a sense of place and with layers of significance that remain tantalisingly elusive … Esther Prescott is a Sleeping Beauty … Her mother died when she was small, and her father, for inscrutable reasons of Waspishness and wealth, has kept her hidden from the world. When we first see her, she is comfortable in the tree-lined citadel of their Rose Bay mansion but untutored in ambition or feeling. Thus, "she was shackled from childhood with completest freedom. All guidance was determinedly withheld."'[1]

As a child, Elizabeth had been neglected, but at twenty-three she was arguably overprotected when she was chaperoned by her parents on her first trip to Europe. She was unworldly, prone to crushes on older women and as 'untutored' in feeling as Esther Prescott. Falconer described Esther as a 'bourgeois woman' who was attracted to Stan's aggression as a 'call to life' and noted the writer's preoccupation with class in a story about 'a self-made man stripping a woman of privilege until she is his slave'. Falconer noted too that 'the worse crime in Harrower's claustrophobic fictional universe is parental neglect … Esther is so "irrevocably" damaged that she can't imagine her life differently; orphanage-raised Stan has no idea how to treat her. They are trapped in a folie à deux.'

Falconer resisted the effort of other critics to shoehorn the 1950s novel into a feminist framework but noted Harrower's interest in different genres and ideas. 'It would be convenient to read this jangle of fairytale, psychological thriller, social comedy and intense evocation of place as symptoms of a young writer's wonder at all the possibilities of fiction,' Falconer wrote. 'But it is precisely these layers, each brushing uneasily against the other that gives this book its unusual and lasting power. In the end, *Down in the City* is only so interested in its main storyline. It wants to throw bigger patterns of dark and light.' It was a fascinating exegesis but, in the end, Falconer found the book to be unsettled: for all its 'bright poise and brilliant light' it flickered 'constantly between the trivial and the sublime'.

By the time *Down in the City* was published in October, Harrower had developed something of a fan club among readers. Everyone wondered why such a great writer pulled out of the game in the 1970s. Susan Sheridan suggested Harrower may have felt it was time to go: 'Perhaps by the age of forty she had completed all the novels that needed to be written, springing from what she described as her "turbulent" childhood and youth.'[2]

In her media interviews, Elizabeth was confident, almost arrogant, about her ability to understand human behaviour. She suggested intuition rather than any study of psychology had led to her insights into human nature. In fact, Elizabeth assiduously gathered material from her conversations with friends. She had a talent for vacuuming up detail. She listened with intent. She may not have lived every experience she wrote about, but Harrower was skilled in creating the push and pull of sexual attraction and emotional dependency.

She described her first novel as a 'love letter' to Sydney but the true terrain of *Down in the City* is psychological, and it resonated well with a 21st-century audience. Stan's coercive control of Esther and her capacity for self-sabotage were eerily contemporary at a time when psychological violence had begun to dominate debate about gender and power. Given the secrecy about domestic violence in the 1940s and 1950s, it was remarkable that Harrower had captured Esther's complex journey of desire and dismay. She had witnessed arguments and manipulation as her grandmother dealt with her alcoholic grandfather, but it was her stepfather who possibly provided more nuanced material. Elizabeth's diaries suggested Richard Kempley generated anxiety and fear. He ruled through mood swings and unpredictability rather than physical violence, and Elizabeth and her mother tiptoed around this patriarch just as the fictional Esther navigated Stan's drunkenness and moods.

David Winter and Harrower emailed often in 2013 as she grew more accustomed to her fame. Winter found her 'quite giggly, almost giddy' but also needy. If he didn't email for a while, Harrower would send an email proclaiming mock unhappiness. 'She liked to feel special,' Winter recalled. Their emails were often mundane – the weather, a walk to the shops – but Winter enjoyed them and felt that as a child himself of divorced parents, he and Elizabeth shared a bond. He considered Harrower a natural psychologist but one who had also read all the available psychological texts when young. Her love of the great Russian novelists refined her sensibility and gave her a great sense of dramatic scope, he told me.

Long after the books were republished, Elizabeth maintained contact with Winter: her iPad was a lifeline, and she was delighted about the 'second life' she had been given, even as she grew tired. In May that year, a Spanish artist based in New York emailed me asking for Elizabeth's contact details, but she asked me to blow him off: 'I don't want this passing interest in the books to kill me, and

I am so tired. My life is mostly very pleasant, and I can enjoy it – even days like this one: four banks, three buses, bad coffee, good friend, optometrist – but extra things are wearing.'

She was thrilled that her novels had been rediscovered by a new generation of readers but there was one story she was still not prepared to reveal.

22

—

# The Lost Novel:
## *In Certain Circles*

I N A WORLD WHERE EVERYONE CAN PUBLISH ALMOST any fragment of text online and find readers and sometimes fame, it is hard to believe Elizabeth Harrower was prepared to consign a fully formed novel to the archives and leave it there for almost fifty years. She might have regretted dumping *In Certain Circles* in 1971, having spent three years writing and rewriting it, but she never resiled from the decision she made at the age of forty-three. Until she did.

Sometime in 2013, after Text boss Michael Heyward gave up trying to convince her to give him permission to read the draft, Harrower raised the 'lost manuscript' with him: 'Why has it taken so long for you to read that novel? I know that when I am dead, you're going to publish it so I might as well be around to see what happens when it comes out.'[1] It was a cute way of admitting she was keen to see it in print. Harrower would never have used the word, but in many ways she wanted the book published for 'closure'. Her unexpected fame had revived childhood memories. The media interviews had not been easy; she had not been able to escape questions, yet for Harrower that early sadness was resolved by this exhumation of her past. The final, failed novel was unfinished business.

Given the green light, Heyward travelled to the National Library in Canberra and sorted through the versions of *In Certain Circles*

248

to find the final proof, the one sent to Macmillan publisher Alan Maclean in the late summer of 1971. It would be April 2014 before the book was published, but it was clear from the start that it would be gold for Harrower's career and for Australian publishing. The romance of a work buried for decades was a marketer's dream, especially when the author was alive to see it in print and had a brilliant backlist to boot. For fans, it was an unexpected bonus, and for academics and critics a chance to see the author's development after *The Watch Tower* – and wonder what might have been if Harrower had continued to write. Supporters hoped too that *In Certain Circles* would earn Elizabeth the awards that had eluded her in the past. Would she finally win the Miles Franklin?

Journalists sought interviews, but Harrower told Text publicist Jane Novak that she was tired and preferred not to speak to the media. Instead, Novak circulated her comments, which noted that while fashions change, 'people eternally struggle with their lives as they always have. I'm sure these characters are walking the streets now.' Elizabeth commented, too, on her failure to publish after the 1970s: 'When I stopped writing, also for reasons mysterious now, I metaphorically put the books in a cellar and regarded them as buried treasure.'[2]

Harrower told David Winter she would not reread the book: 'Thank you very much for the bound proof of ICC. I've put it in a cupboard with a few old hardcovers of the other four to mature. Better really if I don't read it … Better that I don't berate myself for an arbitrary decision when I was 41/2.' A month later when copies arrived, she wrote to him: 'It's definitely exciting for me to open up the packing to see *In Certain Circles*. I've now read for the first time that it's an intense psychological drama – that certainly sounds like me. Addicted to human nature.' She repeated a statement she had made many times about her motivation to write fiction – essentially that she knew things that must be said: 'Novelists, like scientists, must pass on their discoveries, and there are some in this book.'

The 'discoveries' in the novel emerge through the four central characters whose lives span about twenty years from just after World War II. Brother and sister Russell and Zoe Howard are the children of wealthy medical and academic parents growing up, indulged and educated, but not necessarily wise, in a comfortable mansion on the north side of the harbour. Their adult lives run in parallel with another brother and sister, Stephen and Anna Quayle, orphans from the other side of the city. Harrower's themes are once again class, power and materialism, but there is less horror and more heartbreak in this novel which departs from the almost claustrophobic, restricted mood of the earlier works. Zoe marries Stephen in what becomes a destructive emotional relationship not unlike that of Clemency and Christian in *The Catherine Wheel*, while Russell and Anna attempt to put integrity and honour ahead of pleasure.

As Elizabeth waited for the release of the novel, she was busy caring for Margaret Dick and for her own health. In March 2014, she emailed me: 'The last two days have contained everything but books. Yesterday a kind neighbour drove me to the GP and North Shore Private for X-rays for a damaged right wrist. No more broken bones. Then a tiny drama about my unoccupied car space. Today I was called early to the nursing home by the roommate of my 98-year-old cousin.' Margaret, who had been in an aged-care facility then a nursing home at Kirribilli for several years, was dying and on Sunday, 23 March, Elizabeth wrote in her diary 'everyone kind … God knows what tomorrow holds.' The next day, she wrote 'Margaret DIED.' Then with a purple pen: 'MARGARET DIED, THIS MORNING.' The women had known each other for more than sixty years, and two days later Elizabeth wept as she sorted through photographs of her cousin. In her eulogy, Elizabeth wrote that her cousin was never bored and 'loved life, thought our existence a miracle'. She 'laughed easily and had a sense of the ridiculous, yet there was always a sense that reading and thinking came more naturally to her than anything else … She put up with the great calamity of loss of sight from macular degeneration in the last years with patience but did say she sometimes swore when she was alone.'

It was a tough time for Elizabeth but soon there was the excitement of the fifth novel. Five days after its release, Elizabeth wrote to Winter: 'Yes, I am in a whirl and can't sleep. Old popular songs come into my head and (luckily) go. Friends all react differently which is interesting and noticeable. All that time ago … I think I said to Susan Wyndham that I'd never have stopped writing if I'd had a fraction of the encouragement that's come my way since October 2011.'

The novel received excellent reviews, was longlisted for the Miles Franklin and the Kibble Literary Award and shortlisted for the NSW Premier's, WA Premier's and Prime Minister's literary awards, and the Colin Roderick Literary Award. Elizabeth won the $5000 Voss Literary Prize, awarded by the heads of English departments at universities. But the real prize was the international recognition. In October 2014, *The New Yorker*'s literary critic James Wood published a glowing essay. Her writing, he suggested, was 'witty, desolate, truth-seeking and completely polished'. Her sentences had an 'unsettling candour'. Her themes were repeated but her prose had endless variety: 'She can be bracingly satirical … She is generally tart; she can be savagely metaphorical … her wit often teeters on the edge of pain.' Wood was one of the most influential literary critics of the age and his endorsement announced Harrower to a global audience, positioning her as one of the most significant modern writers in English. Harrower's interest, Wood wrote, was in 'how easily we submit to cruelty and coercion, the relations between men and women in a frankly misogynist era … Harrower's five novels have an almost relentless thematic consistency and a strikingly similar darkness of vision … the women enter apparently freely into those relations and help to sustain and excuse their own abuse.'[3]

Wood noted the novel's structural difficulties but said this was a minor quibble compared to Harrower's sensibility, her 'wounded wisdom, the elegance and strictness and perilous poise of her sentences, the humane understanding, and ceaseless incisions of her intelligence'. Harrower emailed Fiona McGregor to say she was pleased with the reviews: 'I can see I made a very strange decision when I stopped writing. It was the thing I could do, and had worked hard to do, and wanted to do, so … No idea now what I was thinking. But I certainly didn't think it would all disappear.'

Harrower, perhaps mindful of critics and friends who had urged her to move away from the toxic males and oppressed women of earlier novels, had attempted in *In Certain Circles* to write a more overtly psychological analysis of relationships, leaving behind the sometimes-simplistic portraits of anti-hero and victim present in her other work. Harrower often said that there were some good 'things' in the novel. She was right; there are brilliant patches of commentary on life and psychological insights that demonstrate her rigorous moral and intellectual framework. *In Certain Circles* has a more ambitious structure than her earlier books and the story is less obviously autobiographical. She was experimenting with a more imagined space filled with a moneyed, educated, worldly class of Australians and she aimed for nuance in her depiction of class, power and love. Her fifth novel brings together tribes separated by money rather than pedigree. Brother and sister, Stephen and Anna, are poor, but they are equal to the Howard siblings in talent, awareness and character. Harrower was writing twenty-five years after the end of World War II at a time when immigration and prosperity were breaking down the old class divides in Australia. The conservatives' grip on government was weakening and Gough Whitlam led a Labor Party that envisaged a more equal nation that was very much part of the world. It was a country in transition and Harrower, too, was attempting a different style.

Her canvas here is much bigger than in her earlier work and David Winter considered the novel thus had less psychological intensity than *The Watch Tower*. It was 'more manufactured' than her earlier work and there was 'slightly more labour evident in the writing' yet it was a work that could have been published at that time, he said. Harrower was more modern and more conversational than Patrick White; and crisper than Christina Stead, who typically wrote longer, 'baggier' books. Winter believed that if Elizabeth had continued writing, *In Certain Circles* could well have been seen as the 'transitional' novel – uneven, yes, but preparing the ground for more complex characterisations and ideas.

The novel is more clearly feminist and explicit in its portrayal of the 'ideological tension' between men and women but also more hopeful of the capacity of women to exercise independence. 'What I do understand,' says Zoe, 'is that at any point in a woman's life she may come across something like a cement pyramid in the middle of the road. Another person. People. She's capable of sitting there, convinced that it would be impossible to forsake her position, till it becomes a private Thermopylae. This sort of block was probably designed for the survival of our species, but the cost's high. What makes men superior is that they don't – *on the whole* – stop functioning forever because of another person. They lack this built-in handicap, and are they lucky!'

*In Certain Circles* contains far less of Harrower's life story than her other novels, yet it is deeply personal. Harrower is in this book – not so much in the events and characters as in the aspirations and reflections of its protagonists. The reader does not need direct autobiographical proof to see the adult author in these pages; her intensity, her preoccupation with the motives of those around her, and her constant self-analysis are all here in the four main characters who grow up and grow wiser over the decades. Given how much it reveals of Harrower's deepest feelings, it's interesting to consider whether she withdrew the novel from publication because she felt too exposed by it.

There was more excitement for Elizabeth later in 2014 when *The Catherine Wheel*, her third novel and the only one set outside Australia, was republished by Text, with an introduction by broadcaster Ramona Koval. There was limited media coverage but the book, with its surprisingly contemporary tone, added to the author's 'second act'. With its London setting, the rerelease of the book must have prompted nostalgia for Elizabeth, especially given Margaret's recent death: the cousins had shared lodgings in the years when Elizabeth wrote the book at a special table in a mansion flat in Clapham.

We know little of Elizabeth Harrower's London life – whether she had lovers or friends – but Clemency's emotions are so well rendered in *The Catherine Wheel* that they seem based on at least some personal experience. There are some common factors: Clem and Elizabeth were both Australians abroad, studying and working part-time, and there was something of the outsider in each of them, a steely resolve undercut by great vulnerability. Once again, details in the novel converged with real life: in *The Catherine Wheel*, Clemency's choice of overcoat establishes her aspiration to fit into London: 'this uniform reserved for genuine socialists; this for hereditary shoppers in Harrods and so on … What were the legitimate trappings for an Australian, aged twenty-five, living alone in a bed-sitting room, and studying for the bar by correspondence?' Here we see the reflection of the expensive winter coat Harrower splurged on in London in the 1950s.

Above all, *The Catherine Wheel* is a study in psychology, a novel in which Harrower is attempting to understand the complex lies we tell ourselves and others. Clemency's interior monologues may at times seem childish and repetitive, but Harrower was intrigued by the connections between personality and mental illness. She had read widely in psychology and had also experienced somewhat unhinged behaviour from her stepfather.

She had told Ramona Koval in their 2013 interview: 'There's a friend I have who talks about the charisma that is sometimes part of mental disturbance; that it has a sort of exceptional charm, exceptional attraction, magic, something quite special … People live dangerously to discover it. Sometimes it's a high price to pay.'

*Elizabeth, aged eighty-four, at her home in Cremorne.*

To have lived dangerously was a badge of honour for Elizabeth; she referred often to a life in which, in her terms, she had taken risks – and paid a price. And as she approached her nineties, it seemed the risks of fifty years ago had all paid off.

23

# The Short Stories: *A Few Days in the Country*

THE PUBLICATION OF *IN CERTAIN CIRCLES* AFTER A DEC-ades-long delay capped Elizabeth Harrower's renaissance as one of Australia's great twentieth-century writers. Then came the icing on the cake, through Text – a collection of her short stories which were out of print or had never been published. It was the first time her stories were printed in a stand-alone collection. Harrower had always been somewhat dismissive of her short stories and Winter told me: 'She almost looked at them as something that might have been written by another person.' Harrower told me the stories were 'a mystery' to her and that she had reread only two of those published in the new collection. She preferred the longer medium of the novel, yet she mastered the shorter form beautifully and often used them as dry runs for her books, experimenting with incidents which later popped up in her novels.

In March 2015, Elizabeth was as busy as ever with friends, catching the bus in Military Road near her flat to go into the Queen Victoria Building for coffee, and to lunch at the Peppercorn in Cremorne. She was 'worn, because things keep happening, mostly very good'. One good thing was the decision by *The New Yorker* to print a short story called 'Alice', written in the 1970s but never published. Harrower told me it was 'the first and only piece of my own stuff that I've read in decades'. She agreed to record the story for *The*

*New Yorker*'s website; it was remarkable to hear the author return to words she had written half a century earlier.

'Alice' proved a hit with *New Yorker* readers and listeners. Written in the 1970s, it crystallises the key themes in Harrower's work. There are references to her family: Alice is likely an amalgam of Elizabeth's mother Margaret and Elizabeth herself. As a child Alice is ignored, overlooked and neglected, then finds herself in an unhappy marriage in an increasingly subservient role. One day, however, she is truly 'seen' by another, finally recognised. 'After this,' Harrower writes, 'she looked the same, and her circumstance didn't alter, but she was a different person altogether.' 'Alice' is a remarkably hopeful slice of life and suits this condensed form. It is also filled with semi-autobiographical references to Harrower's Newcastle family, reminiscent of *The Long Prospect* and the 1976 short story 'The Retrospective Grandmother'. Harrower was surely thinking of relatives when she wrote: 'Her [Alice's] mother was Scottish born and bred – irrational, raucous, bony, quick-tempered, and noisy. She was bright, like anything burning: a match, a firecracker, a tree.' This mother (surely Elizabeth's grandmother) has two sons (surely Elizabeth's uncles) as well as Alice (possibly Elizabeth's mother). Just like her uncles, one son plays a mouth organ, the other trains at the local gym with a group of amateur boxers. Alice marries Eric (surely Elizabeth's father Frank) who is 'almost as young as she was and knew no more about the world. In fact, he knew less, because this was his birthplace. He had no snowy memories, no castles, no wild cherry trees, no sound stone houses with polished brass and roaring fires … Poor Eric had only this empty place where no one belonged.' Eric goes to the country to work, sends money home and is unfaithful: 'Eric had slept with a girl.' They reunite and Eric goes back to the country and sleeps with another girl, and this time there is a divorce. The story continues: 'It didn't really matter, though, because the mother had found another man for Alice, a man who might make more money. He was much older than she was and very different from Eric – demanding, critical, sarcastic, powerful, brutal.' (Surely this is Richard Kempley.)

*The New Yorker*'s publication of 'Alice' created a global audience for Harrower and generated more interest in the short stories, published in October 2015 as *A Few Days in the Country and Other Stories*. The volume comprised twelve short stories, including the 1977 work which gave the collection its name. Only five had been published around the time they were written, the latest being 'A Few Days in the Country', in *Overland*. A few were published when Text began rereleasing her novels; and two were published for the first time in this collection. Harrower was pleased, and emailed Winter: 'Your letter and attachments came at just the right time. Looking at Chong's designs and reading the lists, I'm persuading myself that I haven't entirely wasted my life. There should have been more, but there is something, and you have to believe that it's had meaning for a few people. There are so many books, so many motives for writing. It looks elegant and beautiful, David. Thank you for all the hard work.'

The stories revealed more of Elizabeth's life but also how she constantly reworked her themes and character. One story, called 'Margaret', concerns the sudden grief of a husband for a wife whom he has 'bullied into the grave'. It's difficult to separate the characters in this story from Margaret and Richard Kempley. Margaret predeceased Richard by about four months. Did Harrower imagine him consumed with grief once Margaret died? Another story, 'The Beautiful Climate', has the middle-class menace of *The Watch Tower* and a central aggressive character called Hector Shaw. 'The Fun of the Fair', never before published, takes as its key figure the neglected and misunderstood child. The portrait resonated with that of Emily in *The Long Prospect*. 'A Few Days in the Country' can be seen, according to academic Bernadette Brennan, as a companion piece to *In Certain Circles*. In both works, a single, intense woman goes to the edge of suicide before recognising she can continue with life. In *Australian Book Review*, Brennan argued that Harrower was exploring loneliness, bereavement, cruelty and depression but that a key point of the collection was 'the need to be seen', to be recognised and 'valued'.[1] In *The Australian* John Freeman wrote that Harrower was a 'radical' writer: 'This is not someone who is happy with humanity, or remotely cheered by the social order. Her stories are shaped by the refining fires of rage and grief. One needn't match them up to her life to feel the heat of expensively acquired knowledge.'[2]

The final two months of 2015 proved busy for Elizabeth. She gave an ABC interview, appeared on stage for the first time in an author event, accepted the Voss prize for *In Certain Circles* and celebrated that book's shortlisting for the Prime Minister's prize for fiction. As well, there was a major symposium on her work held at the University of NSW. On the ABC on 5 November, arts broadcaster Michael Cathcart was warm and enthusiastic as he invited his morning listeners to celebrate Harrower's work. It was a meeting of minds, although at times, Elizabeth seemed to lose her thread. She reprised a comment she had used often in the past: 'I always had an alarming and dangerous interest in human nature. And so recently, I think I was answering some questions, and I said that I felt that I had urgent messages to deliver. I wanted to tell people things.'

Later that day, Elizabeth went to the Mosman Library. She wore a terrific black pants suit and simple necklace. Her face was lined but she looked a decade younger than her eighty-seven years. She was the star of a literary event, relaxed because Michael Heyward was interviewing her. She talked about her love of reading and read aloud from *The Long Prospect*. She described her decision to stop writing as 'a total severing, as if someone had gone off to war and never returned'. It had been a terrible mistake and a self-destructive impulse, she told the audience. In an internet post later, the writer Charlotte Wood who was at the event, said Harrower had an 'incredibly straight spine' and had been 'clear-eyed, alive' during the event. Wood asked Jane Novak if Elizabeth was getting tired and Novak responded: 'I think she's having the time of her life.' When it was over, Elizabeth went to dinner with friends and journalists, including me, at a nearby restaurant, although she struggled to hear above the noise.

On 25 November, she was at the University of Sydney's Woolley Building to receive the Voss Literary Prize, dedicated to the memory of historian Vivian Robert de Vaux Voss and judged by the heads of university English departments. It was a small gathering but an emotional one for Elizabeth, who had not attended university but was on this night surrounded by admirers. David Winter accompanied her to the event and the next day she emailed him to say: 'For me, it was a totally unique evening. You can hardly imagine how amazing it was for me to meet all those young academics who had been reading and teaching and enjoying my writing for years. It was lovely and astonishing, as I say. As a non-prize-winner (and prizes were few) with very good scattered reviews, but isolated reactions through literary journals, I was writing into a void. So I was bedazzled and pleased.'[3]

The judges noted a novel which was both 'in and out of its own time' and praised it for its portrait of the 'fragility and tenuousness of human interconnection', for its 'incisive and stately prose' and for its 'subtle interweaving of perspectives in the drawing of its circles of sociability and seduction'.[4]

Elizabeth was enjoying herself, but the pace took a toll – she told her diary on 28 and 29 November that she was 'knocked out' and had trouble hearing people: 'So not able to understand anyone. Awful.' She had a similar reaction at the crowded Prime Minister's Literary Awards at Carriageworks. Elizabeth had told me the previous year that she no longer worried about winning awards: 'The time for prizes is long gone. I am not sure I should give anyone the chance to reject me, I refuse to be rejected.' But she had hoped *In Certain Circles* would be selected by the PM's judges and was disappointed when it lost out to Joan London's novel *The Golden Age.*

As the year ended, Elizabeth told Tom Carment: 'Age is interesting Tom, not tragic – apart from loss of close friends – which of course matters greatly. But you keep learning + thinking – though you understand it can't go on forever.' She made new friends, even as many of her contemporaries died. Fiona McGregor was among the writers and journalists who moved from a professional to a slightly more personal relationship with Harrower. McGregor recalled: 'She was always so well-dressed, so well-mannered.' Harrower had been curious but 'nonplussed' by McGregor's writing on queer culture. McGregor told me: 'I thought that Elizabeth would not be an easy person to get to know. The reserve was very typical of a middle-class Anglo woman; a touch of wariness, maybe born of a lifetime of not being given equal dues. I think she was thrilled at the revival of interest in her work, but maybe a bit sceptical of it, and never quite able to relinquish that part of herself that hadn't the confidence to continue.'

Harrower told me in 2015 that the past four years 'would have been quite lonely, with all the best friends having flown one by one, [but instead] have been interesting and happy'.

# 24

# Fame and Acclaim

BETTY HARROWER HAD FELT IGNORED AS A CHILD and unsure as a teenager. As she transformed into Elizabeth and published books under that name, she was critically acclaimed but scarcely noticed by readers. In her thirties and forties she had the attention of older writers and was part of a lively intellectual group in Sydney. But she had gradually slipped into the role of 'former writer' and eventually into suburban anonymity. Now in her eighties, against the odds, she was flavour of the month among the crowd she really valued – the readers and writers, the producers and consumers of culture. Her fame was global, thanks in part to coverage in *The New Yorker*. In 2015, British actor Ben Whishaw delighted her by recommending *The Watch Tower* in an article in *The Guardian*: 'I am telling everybody about an Australian writer in her 80s: Elizabeth Harrower … I found her books incredibly moving and feel an affinity with her. She seems hyper-aware of currents under the surface of human relationships, the conflict between having to keep up a certain social normality and the burning emotions underneath.'[1] In March 2016, Harrower told me by email that her connection with Text had been phenomenal: 'Like a good fable. At 88, you're definitely older, but hanging in!'

A couple of months later she was at the Sydney Writers' Festival, where once again she was interviewed by Michael Heyward.

She wrote in her diary: 'Huge event … venue v crowded M gives me confidence …' Harrower had been shortlisted for the Kibble Literary Award but told David Winter by email that she was unlikely to get to the awards lunch in July: 'I'm fading fast, not up to outings and crowds and people talking.' She was invited to the Melbourne Writers' Festival in August/September but was not sure: 'Since my ears have given up hearing properly, the last thing I need is to confront a great many writers I don't or even do know. And I know very few. Mostly I just see friends one at a time and remind then to speak up if they want a conversation.'[2] She told Tom Carment: 'These days I just tend to catch buses locally, up and down Military Road, then to meet friends who live far afield in the city for coffee I catch a red bus into town. That's an effort, however, since I'm extremely reluctant to trip over in the city and break more bones.' She needed to take care: she had recently broken a finger in a cutlery drawer.

In the end she flew to Melbourne with Jane Novak and Jane's partner, David Pearson, and told the festival audience that 'at eighty-eight and a half, I don't need to say things I don't mean'. It was a successful hour, once again with Michael Heyward interviewing. The director of the Adelaide Festival Writers' Week, Laura Kroetsch, was in the audience and she 'immediately decided that Harrower should not only be a guest at her festival but that it should be dedicated to her'.[3] Elizabeth had been at one of the first events in 1962. She had gone by car, driven, along with others, by Olaf Ruhen, the poet. They had enjoyed the road trip, singing all the way.[4] Now she was keen to go to Adelaide again but was too nervous to fly. In typical Elizabeth style, she began a campaign to be driven across the country. Every time she saw Novak and Pearson she raised the festival invitation. 'Every time we went, she said the same thing,' said Novak. 'She said, if only there was some kind person willing to drive me now. It dawned on me that she meant me.'

The trio drove for fourteen hours, reprising the trip Elizabeth had made almost sixty years earlier, stopping at Hay in far western New South Wales overnight. Harrower sang all the way, often the Redgum classic 'I Was Only 19'. She wrote to Carment:

We were heading for Hay. Eventually there was no-one, and it was heaven. I loved the emptiness, the huge skies, the road, the occasional signs telling us to look after ourselves. Then I loved Hay. It was empty, swept, radiant, spread out so neatly, all the doors closed. Up early and off the next morning to the Hay plain. Again, the light, the air, and the wonderful flatness of the plain (unique in the world apparently) had the three of us mesmerised. At times along the way, all this is to tell you that you are some-one I thought of when I saw particular isolated trees or shadows or tiny human establishments in the middle of nowhere. What brought this human in the distance to this remote little place? What would Tom think? ... So, Tom, all of this is to let you know you were thought of, and that I really loved the outback.

Elizabeth's diary recorded the 'clean, lovely air on the way to Hay' and the 'tired but triumphant' arrival in Adelaide, followed by a sleepless night. Now she was convinced she had been persuaded to do the trip against her better judgement. She noted in her diary that while it might be 'an adventure for Jane and David ... it is life threatening for me. Look awful.' But then, there was the stage and 2000 people, and her great friend and publisher

Heyward asking the questions. Elizabeth was a polished performer now, and Heyward scarcely got a word in. Jane Novak recalled, 'She was right into it; she had really evolved into the full public author and she was absolutely amazing.' Once again Harrower answered questions about why she had stopped writing: 'I can recognise something in myself. If I lock the door on somebody or something, I really lock the door … I put those books in the cellar [but] I had no thought in the world that they wouldn't be revived. I had terrific confidence in them … In other areas I might not have been confident, but about writing, and the books – yes. I knew they wouldn't just expire.'

Elizabeth spent an hour signing books and then joined the Text crew for a celebratory dinner. Up early on Sunday for the trip back, Jane and David were exhausted, but their passenger was high on adrenaline. After decades of obscurity, Elizabeth Harrower had been seen. In photographs from the trip, she looks years younger. It is as if the late-life acclaim stripped away the disappointment of the past and turned back time. As she headed to her ninetieth birthday she still watched her weight and cared about clothes. Ulrik was doing a great job with her hair. Jane Novak recalled: 'She was terribly proud and vain in that way women are about their looks. She would eat like a bird because she was worried about getting fat. Clem and Andrew were always dropping around food, and she would just put it in the freezer.' The freezer was doubtless full but when Elizabeth got back to Cremorne from the Adelaide event, she felt flat and lay low: 'Mostly in bed. No one to talk to,' she told her diary.

The past couple of years had been splendid and now, with no more books to republish and no more events on the calendar, she began to rely increasingly on the people she had met at Text. Michael Heyward and Penny Hueston were friends, and David Winter maintained an email correspondence with Elizabeth. She didn't dwell on the ruptures of the past, but she liked to mention Patrick White and his efforts to make her write another novel. Winter recalled that she delighted in the knowledge that White had expended so much energy on her and had been very fond of her.

In 2014, when Elizabeth was in the midst of her late-life renaissance, she sent me an email: 'Why did no-one impress on me much sooner … I must have thought I was immortal: that I could waste my life and still have it.' She told Fiona McGregor that writing was natural, instinctive, and that 'Stopping wasn't ever anything I anticipated doing. It was the only thing I could do, and the only way I intended to spend my life.' Three decades earlier, she had told Giulia Giuffrè she didn't believe in God: 'I tend to think that humanism is a fairly sterile philosophy, but I'm not attached to any orthodox church or religion. I think I have a religious view of life without believing in God, or without believing in anything other than …'

The past few years had brought new friends, acquaintances from the media and deeper relationships with the children of friends. It was Jane Novak, living in Sydney but no longer working at Text, who organised the ninetieth birthday party in Elizabeth's flat. It was a happy event and for some of Elizabeth's friends almost the only time they met each other. She had appointed Linda Nolte and Laurel Laurent – the daughters of friends – to look after her affairs but had not bothered to introduce them to each other. Nor had she told them of the arrangements made with her lawyers. She had, however, done the paperwork to give Laurel her power of attorney and appoint her as the co-executor (with a lawyer) of her will, and Laurel and Linda as co-guardians.

There were no siblings or family members to call on in these final years. She had not developed a relationship with Francis, David and Yvonne Harrower, her half-siblings. She had contact with her cousins Thurza and Verity in Newcastle, but she was on her own when it came to organising her will and property and her care. She had made many friends over her long life, although she had fallen out with some, including the devoted Barry Willoughby. Some of her oldest friends were now dead or in need of support themselves. Elizabeth's decline was obvious to those who saw her regularly. Brian Galway recognised the signs of dementia, and Ulrik and Andrew and Clem noticed her anxiety verging on paranoia and her fear of living alone in her apartment. One wet winter in Sydney, as the rain lashed her balcony windows and seeped into her living room, Elizabeth felt very alone. Her iPad was now a key connection with the outside world but the woman who had loved words all her life was finding it harder to string them together. Emails were shorter and Winter often found them difficult to understand. She talked to Brian Galway about whom she should leave her money to, who most needed help, and changed her will in May 2018. Diary entries in August 2018 reveal she was anxious about handing over power of attorney over her affairs. Linda Nolte recalled: 'She needed a lot of care in 2018. My mother [Helene] was in a home up in the Blue Mountains and I was living in the Blue Mountains at that point as well. Elizabeth needed more and more care and people were kind of dropping out because she was becoming a little bit more needy.' There was confusion about who was legally responsible for Elizabeth as she slipped into dementia. Jane Novak ran chores, organised cleaners and took Elizabeth to medical appointments after she fell and broke a wrist in 2019. 'The next thing I knew she was in hospital with a urinary tract infection,' Jane recalled. Elizabeth had told Brian Galway she wanted him as her guardian but eventually her lawyers contacted Laurel to explain the joint guardianship she had with Linda. The women organised 24-hour care in the Cremorne flat, but Linda often had to travel across town to manage a crisis.

*Elizabeth with Barney Wilson, Linda Nolte and their daughter, Kasavere, Elizabeth's goddaughter, in Sydney, 1990.*

After Helene Nolte died, Linda became more involved, especially after Elizabeth was released from hospital into her care in

2019 with a formal diagnosis of Alzheimer's. 'Practically every day I would have to go there and instruct the carers,' Linda told me. 'She gave them a very hard time. She would go off and wander and I would get a call from Ulrik, 'she's just sitting here, she won't go home', or one of the neighbours would ring. So at least three or four times a week I would have to go over there.' Soon it was unsustainable for Elizabeth to remain in her flat and she moved to the Scalabrini Nursing Home in Rozelle. An email chain kept friends informed of her condition. Elizabeth asked to see cousins Thurza and Verity and they visited several times, as did Brian Galway and Tom Carment and Andrew and Clem, with visits strictly monitored by Linda and staff after doctors advised that Elizabeth was agitated by too many visitors.

Elizabeth was desperate at times. On 28 March 2019, while still in her flat, she emailed David Winter: 'Dear David, Looking for a village. Not happy here. Need company badly. Strange environment. Young girls look after. Me. Supposedly. Strange atmosphere. One girl at a time looks after me. Can't sleep at night. Long nights. Hope to see you soon. Hope Michael comes soon. Nervous about falling. Have a pusher. This building very unbuilt. Love to all Elizabeth Xxxxxxxxx.' A week later, on 4 April, she sent him an email headed 'Trouble is I am lonely and not used to it'. It read: 'Dear David trouble is I am lonely. And I am miserable. I had Margaret and I am lonely. I can't get used to it. Help if you can. Love. Elizabeth.' Winter wrote back: 'I know, and I am so sorry to hear it. It is an affliction. We are all putting our minds to the problem. Sending you love.'

Then in March 2020, as Covid-19 hit, Scalabrini went into lockdown, like nursing homes across the country, and no visitors were allowed. Elizabeth's messages now were heatbreaking. She was suffering from dementia but felt trapped and pleaded with friends to get her out.

Soon, doctors advised her guardians to confiscate her iPad because it was causing such distress. Linda recalled: 'She was in a delirium. She was in psychosis and the iPad really set her off. She was under the care of a gerontologist, and we were very careful about doing everything absolutely properly and with the right guidance and making decisions for the benefit only of Elizabeth … to maintain her dignity and her reputation, which she was busy destroying by behaving in the manner in which she was behaving.'

In July, as she lay dying, Linda was at Elizabeth's bedside: 'I held her hand when she died, nobody else was there. They wouldn't give her morphine. I had to hassle them, and she was in pain, she was not comfortable. When they gave it to her, she looked at me and she said, "That's wonderful. Thank you."' The end came on 7 July. Elizabeth had specified she did not want a funeral, but friends were shocked when they read of her death in a brief notice, inserted by undertakers, in *The Sydney Morning Herald*: 'Harrower, Elizabeth 8.02.1928 – 7.07.2020; The writer passed away peacefully on Tuesday, Rest In Peace, Private cremation, no funeral service.'

Harrower had once considered making the writer Christine Williams her literary executor. They had met and hit it off when Williams was researching Christina Stead's biography. Elizabeth told Nancy Phelan in 1989 that Williams might be her literary executor and could also receive royalties and benefits from her works. Around that time, too, Elizabeth gave Williams a necklace which Stead had gifted her. But in her 2018 will Elizabeth appointed her friend and publisher Michael Heyward as her literary executor and gave the rights to her works to Heyward and Penny Hueston.

Elizabeth felt that the couple, whom she had met in 2011, had transformed her life and literary reputation in her final years. Elizabeth had earned next to nothing from her writing over the years and had not been in paid employment after the 1970s. In the 1980s, while asset-rich thanks to her big home in Mosman, she had worried about her cashflow, but by the time she died, her friends considered her comfortable, if not wealthy.

Linda Nolte collected Elizabeth's ashes from the undertaker. 'I kept them for a little while, but I eventually let her ashes go off Govetts Leap [in the Blue Mountains] where I had let my father's ashes go, and [Linda's husband] Barney's ashes go. That's how she wanted it. She didn't want a great big funeral and everybody blathering on about things that they really don't know about.'

In 1985 when Elizabeth was fifty-seven, Giulia Giuffrè had asked if she was afraid of death. 'I don't think so, but then I don't know,' she replied. 'Really, I don't think I'd be very good at having a long-drawn-out illness, but nobody wants that. When people say they don't want to be old – no one wants to be old – the choice is between being old and being dead.'

Three decades later, Elizabeth told me how wonderful it was to have had such 'long, lived experience'. In her 2012 interviews she said: 'You have come to terms with all the things that you should not have done or would not have done, and you are not unhappy. The world is so beautiful, so interesting that you don't want to leave it. It's a shame because you feel you have just grown up ready for anything.'

# Conclusion

Elizabeth Harrower did not have a good death in the orthodox sense of that term; she had dementia and was confused as she lay in her bed at the nursing home. But she had had a good life. Not in the conventional sense of marriage, romance, children and grandchildren perhaps, but in a more profound sense. From her earliest, complicated and often unhappy years, Harrower sensed the real meaning of life was the search for that meaning. She had suffered emotional turmoil, but her struggle was with what lay beneath the here and now. Throughout her life, the big question that excited her, personally and professionally, was not how or what or where, but why? She asked it of herself and of others. She sat, as she once told Margaret Dick, for a very long time, trying to understand motive and behaviour.

Harrower had always had an acute sense of the reality of the human experience. She saw clearly that 'certain sufferings and sorrows are absolutely unavoidable'. In her fifties she told Giulia Giuffrè: 'I have friends who know people who go through life from beginning to end and apart from expiring at the end have nothing bad ever happen to them. And the people they told me about have never grown up, and they do nothing but buy clothes and have their kitchen done again or something. In a way whether you suffer or not, it's only by knowing about the adverse and terrible visions that you can value life.'

Elizabeth Harrower was not averse to the pleasures of eating and drinking and other frivolous pastimes, which she referred to as 'shopping for clothes'. But the pursuits that so defined Western societies after World War II were never the main game for her. Harrower worked a different canvas. She looked for happiness – as fleeting as it might be – in understanding people. The little girl from Newcastle, who always believed her duty was to pass on messages about the world, became the writer who did just that in her small but perfectly formed bundle of novels and short stories.

# Author's Note

I FIRST MET ELIZABETH HARROWER IN 2012 WHEN I INTER-viewed her for *The Weekend Australian*. Her second book, *The Long Prospect*, written in the 1950s, was to be republished and the interest in this 'rediscovered' writer, who just might have become another Patrick White, was high. The material from that meeting and notes from other phone conversations, plus several emails over the next few years, form a part of the research for this book. I visited Elizabeth two or three times for morning or afternoon tea in her Cremorne apartment and those personal visits also informed my understanding of this friendly but guarded woman. I wanted to ask her permission to write her biography but held back. I liked her immensely and enjoyed our chats and was reluctant to threaten that with a professional request. Elizabeth mentioned several times that she did not want a biography. I'm not sure that was true, but she certainly tried to control the record of her life; she tore up many letters written and received over the years. Luckily, she was such a prolific correspondent over her long life that her archive – and the archives of others – contain many letters rich in material about her domestic and professional life.

This book draws on Elizabeth's papers in the National Library of Australia as well as those of Shirley Hazzard (State Library of NSW); Kylie Tennant (NLA); Judah Waten (NLA), Nancy Phelan (State Library of NSW); Margaret Dick (NLA) and John and

Audrey Blake (State Library of NSW). I tracked down other letters to Clare Golson and Tom Carment and I thank the Golson family and Tom for their assistance. I have also drawn on several diaries and other papers courtesy of Elizabeth's literary executor, publisher and friend, Michael Heyward. These papers include an unpublished 'memoir' on Patrick White; brief notes on her friendship with Shirley Hazzard; and a lengthy eulogy for her second cousin and great friend, Margaret Dick. Many of her early diaries did not survive Elizabeth's efforts to cull her past, but those that did reveal much about how she lived her long life.

Many of Elizabeth's contemporaries are no longer alive but there was no shortage of friends of all ages willing to share memories of her. Thanks to Linda Nolte, Laurel Laurent, David Winter, Andrew Robertson, Clem Yap, Stephanie Claire, Salvatore Zofrea, Vivian Smith, David Malouf, Geoffrey Lehmann, Tom Carment, Sally McInerney, Benison Rodd, Jane Novak, David Parsons, Fiona McGregor, Jinx Nolan, Ulrik Funch and Brian Galway.

Elizabeth's cousins Thurza Snelson and Verity Matzoll and her half-siblings, Yvonne, David and Francis Harrower, were also kind enough to share their memories and rare early photographs of 'Betty'. My thanks, as well, to Yvonne and Thurza for assistance with childhood photographs of Elizabeth.

This book also draws on divorce and probate papers, newspaper stories, court reports, interviews and reviews dating back to the 1920s. Oral history recordings, and taped interviews with Hazel de Berg, Jim Davidson, Christine Williams and Giulia Giuffrè, revealed Elizabeth's thoughts in her early and middle life; while later ABC radio interviews with Ramona Koval and Michael Cathcart captured her at the height of her 'second act', after the republication of her books by Text Publishing. Elizabeth was older but no less charming and incisive in her conversations with Michael Heyward at writers' events and literary festivals in Sydney, Melbourne and Adelaide. Thanks also to film maker Catherine Hunter, who bothered to search for an interview she had with Elizabeth for her 2009 documentary on Sid Nolan; and to Robert Bolton for accessing essays and research material. I returned often to *The Australian Dictionary of Biography*, run by the National Centre of Biography at the Australian National University – an invaluable source on the lives of the nation's writers.

My thanks go to Emeritus Professor Susan Sheridan for her expert reading of the manuscript and advice on Australian fiction; and to publisher Tom Thompson for help sorting the publication details of Elizabeth's novels in the 1970s and 1980s.

I am indebted to Michael Heyward and Penny Hueston at Text for their support in the early stages of this project and to Michael as literary executor for permission to quote from Elizabeth's letters. Thanks to the estates of Kylie Tennant, Christina Stead, Judah Waten, Nancy Phelan and Max Harris for copyright permissions for their letters. Direct quotes from Elizabeth and others have been footnoted only when precise dates are important in the narrative.

I'm grateful to my siblings, Jenny McPhee, Robin Trinca and Mathew Trinca, for their support and for reading early drafts. Thanks also to Bruce Wood for reading the final. Bruce and his friend, family historian Jason Eden, who lives in England, spent countless hours researching Harrower's stepfather, Richard Kempley, and his UK wife and family. Thank you to writer and publisher Geordie Williamson and my agent, Fiona Inglis, at Curtis Brown, for their advice; and to Chris Feik and everyone at Black Inc.

and La Trobe University Press for embracing this project. Special thanks to editors Jo Rosenberg and Kirstie Innes-Will for their help in shaping the final product.

My friends and extended family displayed their usual fierce loyalty, patience and support throughout, and I thank them all. This book is for my late mother, Jo Trinca, who, like Elizabeth Harrower, liked nothing more than to bury herself in a book.

Sydney, February 2025

# Image Credits

**pp. 9, 15 and 17**: Photographs courtesy of Yvonne Harrower.

**p. 50**: Photograph courtesy of *The Australian*, copyright holder unknown.

**p. 53**: Photograph by Martin Webby, 1984, courtesy of Australian Broadcasting Corporation Library Sales.

**pp. 72 and 99**: Photographs courtesy of *Sydney Morning Herald*.

**p. 139**: Photograph by Grant Peterson, 1967, courtesy of *Sydney Morning Herald*.

**p. 175**: Photograph by Ferdinand H. Nolte, 1974, courtesy of Linda Nolte.

**p. 186**: Photograph by William Yang, 1978, courtesy of the National Library of Australia.

**p. 256**: Photograph by Sam Mooy, 2014, courtesy of *The Australian*.

**p. 270**: Photograph by Ferdinand H. Nolte, 1990, courtesy of Linda Nolte.

# Notes

**1. A DIVORCED CHILD**

1   Elizabeth's first passport, issued in December 1950, shows her as Betty Harrower. A new birth certificate in the name of Elizabeth Harrower was issued in 2012.

2   Elizabeth Harrower [EH] interview with author, 14 September 2012.

3   EH interview with Giulia Giuffrè, in Giulia Giuffrè, *A Writing Life: Interviews with Australian Women Writers*, Sydney: Allen & Unwin, 1985.

4   EH note in her National Library of Australia archive MS 8237, MS Acc06.016, MS Acc06.142 [It was prepared in the 1980s ahead of the republication of her novels by Angus & Robertson.]

5   EH interview with author, 2012.

6   Ibid.

7   Ibid.

8   NSW Supreme Court documents of divorce proceedings between Robert Hughes and Helen Burns Hughes.

9   Andrew Robertson interview with author, 3 August 2023.

10  EH note in NLA archive.

11  EH to Penny Hueston, 15 February 2090 (but EH had the wrong date – it was probably early 2012).

12  Ibid.

13  EH interview with Hazel de Berg, National Library of Australia, Oral History and Folklore Collection ORAL TRC 1/299, 18 October 1967.

14  EH interview with Jim Davidson, *Meanjin*, vol. 39. no. 2, 12 July 1980 (interview conducted 5 May 1980).

15  EH interview with Ramona Koval, ABC Radio National, October 2013.

16  EH 'memoir' on Patrick White, 1991–92, files of Michael Heyward, literary executor.

17  According to UK public records, Richard Herbert Kempley was born on 3 June 1892. He entered the Greenwich Naval Academy in

1906 at the age of thirteen and served as a 'writer', responsible for administrative and payroll support. He appears to have deserted in 1911 at the age of nineteen, then married and migrated to Australia, where he and his wife had two children. His wife and sons were back in the UK by 1921. By September 1922, Kempley was the lessee of the Golden Fleece Hotel in Surry Hills. Three years later, he was involved in civil litigation with his former employer at the Liberty Confectionery College. By 1931, he was a commercial traveller in the Hunter Valley and was in trouble for carrying illicit liquor in his car and possession of an illicit still. His problem with alcohol was apparent; in July 1932 he was charged with drunken driving at Scone.

18   Court reports show a Richard Herbert Kempley involved in civil cases in the 1920s. In 1925, a Sydney judge described him as a man of shady character and suggested he might have committed bigamy with a woman in Darlinghurst. By the 1930s, Kempley was a commercial traveller in regional NSW. My research suggests this man was Harrower's stepfather.

## 2. SYDNEY: THE WAR YEARS

1   Helen Hughes to Margaret Dick, 5 January 1970.

2   EH email to David Winter, 31 August 2018.

3   EH interview with Koval, 2013

4   There are multiple reports in daily newspapers in 1944 detailing the blackmarket conspiracy case against Richard Herbert Kempley, an accountant, and three other men, and their unsuccessful appeal against their three-year jail sentence. Kempley's prison file has details matching Harrower's stepfather's history and there is evidence, including date of birth, height and colouring, that they are the same man. However, in the absence of a direct verification, it is possible, if unlikely, that the jailed Kempley was not Harrower's stepfather.

5   Margaret Kempley to EH, 15 July 1965.

6   Malcolm Abbott and Chris Doucouliagos, *The Changing Structure of Higher Education in Australia 1949–2003*, Working Papers Series, Melbourne: School of Accounting, Economics and Finance, Deakin University, 2003.

7   EH interview with Koval, 2013.

8   EH interview with author, 2012.

9   EH interview with de Berg, 1967.

10   EH interview with author, 2012.

11   EH diaries, files of Michael Heyward, literary executor.

12   EH note, NLA.


**3.  SCOTLAND: A NEW WORLD**

1   EH to Shirley Hazzard, 21 November 1984. Shirley Hazzard correspondence and other papers, 1966–circa 2005, State Library of NSW, MLMSS 10249/Box 1, MLMSS 10249/Box 2X.

2   EH to Judah Waten, 10 June 1980.

3   Margaret Dick to Hazel de Berg, National Library of Australia, Hazel de Berg Collection DeB391, 22 August 1969.

4   Letter from the personnel officer Miss M.B. Rankin at T. Wall & Sons, The Creameries, Craigmillar, Edinburgh, 11 October 1952.

5   EH interview with de Berg, 1967.

6   Ibid.

7   EH interview with Michael Cathcart, Radio National, 5 November 2015.

8   EH interview with de Berg, 1967.


**4.  THE LONDON YEARS**

1   EH interview with author, 2012.

2   EH to Christina Stead, 10 February 1976.

3   EH interview with Koval, 2013

4   EH interview with Davidson, 1980.

5   Ibid.

6   *The Sunday Times*, 11 November 1956.

7   EH interview with Davidson, 1980.

8   Giuffrè, *A Writing Life*, 1985.

9   Adele Oliveira, 'Late American bloomer', *Kirkus Reviews*, 4 May 2013.

10   EH to Margaret Dick, 18 May 1972.

11   EH interview with Davidson, 1980.

12   EH interview with de Berg, 1967.

13   Giuffrè, *A Writing Life*, 1985.

14   Elizabeth Webby, 'Sydney in the Fiction of Elizabeth Harrower', in Elizabeth McMahon and Brigitta Olubas (eds), *Elizabeth Harrower: Critical Essays*, Camperdown: Sydney University Press, 2017.

15   Geordie Williamson, *The Burning Library: Our Great Novelists Lost and Found*, Melbourne: Text Publishing, 2012.

16  D.R. Burns, *The Directions of Australian Fiction 1920– 1974*,
Melbourne: Cassell Australia, 1975.

17  Ray Mathew, 'City charms', *The Sydney Morning Herald*, 19 October 1957.

18  Susan Sheridan, 'Bright and wicked', *Australian Book Review*,
No. 358, February 2014.


## 5.  A WRITING LIFE

1  EH interview with Davidson, 1980.

2  Ivor Indyk, 'A really long prospect: Elizabeth Harrower's fallen world',
in McMahon and Olubas, *Elizabeth Harrower*, 2017.

3  Nicholas Birns, 'A wrong way of being right: The tormented force of
the Harrower Man' in McMahon and Olubas, *Elizabeth Harrower*, 2017.

4  EH to Shirley Hazzard, 22 October 1982.

5  Letters between EH and agent Paul Scott at Pearn, Pollinger &
Higham, May 1957.

6  EH 'memoir' on Patrick White, 1991–92.

7  Sidney Baker, 'Tender Australian tale of a lonely child', *The Sydney
Morning Herald*, 28 April 1958.

8  Suzanne Falkiner, *Mick: A Life of Randolph Stow*, UWA Publishing,
2016, p.248.

9  Nola Margaret Adams, 'A dark realism: The fiction of Elizabeth
Harrower', Master of Arts, University of Western Australia,
December 1982.

10  EH note, NLA

11  EH interview with Cathcart, 2015.


## 6.  HOME AGAIN

1  *The Bulletin*, vol. 80, no. 4142, 1 July 1959.

2  EH interview with Koval, 2013.

3  'Cousins write novels', *The Sydney Morning Herald*, 5 July 1959.

4  'A literary line up', *The Sydney Morning Herald*, 9 November 1967.

5  EH interview with de Berg, 1967.

6  EH note, NLA.

7  EH to David Winter, 19 January 2015.

8  Reference from the librarian of City of Sydney Library, 28 October 1959.

9  'Spoiled beauties', *The Times Literary Supplement*, 28 October 1960.

10  Barbara Jefferis, 'Wisdom from the well of anguish', *The Sydney
Morning Herald*, 31 December 1960.

11  Nancy Keesing, 'Australians in London: *The Catherine Wheel*', *The Bulletin*, vol. 81, no. 4218, 14 December 1960, p. 58.

12  EH interview with author, 2012.

13  EH interview with de Berg, 1967.

14  John Hetherington, 'Elizabeth Harrower: The student suddenly began writing novels', *The West Australian*, 6 May 1961, and *The Age*, 29 April 1961.

15  Lonnie Coleman to EH's New York agent Irma Weitzman, 9 March 1962.

16  To Irma Weitzman, Willis Kingsley Wing, from C.M. Newman, *The New Yorker*, 8/2/1962.

17  EH to Willis Kingsley Wing, 27 June 1962.

18  EH to Max Harris, 8 August 1962.

19  EH interview with author, 2012.

20  EH to Max Harris, 14 July 1961.

21  Max Harris to EH (undated but in 1961).

22  [Unsigned but accepted as the work of Max Harris], 'The novels of Elizabeth Harrower', *Australian Letters*, vol. 4, no. 2, December 1961.

23  Diana-Gabriela Lupu, 'The innocent American girl in Henry James's international novel', *Gender Studies*, vol. 11, no. 1, 2012.

24  EH to Shirley Hazzard, 10 May 1978.

## 7. THE KYLIE QUESTION

1  Nancy Phelan, *Writing Round the Edges: A Selective Memoir*, St Lucia: University of Queensland Press, 2003, p. 115.

2  Kylie Tennant, *The Missing Heir: The Autobiography of Kylie Tennant*, South Melbourne: Macmillan, 1986, p. 144.

3  Kylie Tennant diary fragment, National Library of Australia MS 7574, box 14, folder 86. Quoted in Jane Grant, *Kylie Tennant: A Life*, Canberra: National Library of Australia, 2006, p. 93

4  Margaret Kempley to EH, 30 November 1964.

5  Grant, *Kylie Tennant*, 2006, p. 105.

6  Tennant, *The Missing Heir*, 1986, p. 156

7  EH to Margaret Dick, 30 March 1972.

8  EH interview with author, 2012.

9  EH interview with Davidson, 1980.

10  EH interview with de Berg, 1967.

11  Ibid.

12  Grant, *Kylie Tennant*, 2006.

13  Kylie Tennant to Mavis Cribb, 27 September 1968 [NLA MS 7574, box 4, folder 23].

14  Kylie Tennant interview in *Hemisphere*, vol. 25, no. 3, Nov–Dec 1980.

15  EH 'memoir' on Patrick White, 1991–92.

16  Gavin Souter, 'Data', *The Sydney Morning Herald*, 25 October 1966.

17  Gavin Souter, 'Data', *The Sydney Morning Herald*, 11 July 1966.

18  H.G. Kippax, 'Of good and evil in Neutral Bay', *The Sydney Morning Herald*, 19 November 1966.

19  Geoffrey Lehmann, 'Portrait in black', *The Bulletin*, 12 November 1966.

20  Williamson, *The Burning Library*, 2012.

21  EH interview with Davidson, 1980.

22  EH to Judah Waten, 23 July 1978.

23  R.G. Geering, *Recent Fiction (Australian Writers and Their Work)*, Melbourne: Oxford University Press, 1974.

24  Giuffrè, *A Writing Life*, 1985.

25  Ibid.

26  EH to Judah Waten, 1 June 1971.

27  Hilary McPhee, 'A woman writer has no protection', *The Sydney Morning Herald*, 19 January 1982 (review of *Exiles at Home: Australian Women Writers 1925–1945* by Drusilla Modjeska).

28  Giuffrè, *A Writing Life*, 1985.

29  EH interview with author, 2012.

## 8.  THE HAZZARDS: KIT AND SHIRLEY

1  EH to Shirley Hazzard, 13 December 1967.

2  Biographical details of Kit and Reginald Hazzard's lives are drawn from Brigitta Olubas, *Shirley Hazzard: A Writing Life*, Virago, London, 2022.

3  Shirley Hazzard to EH, (undated), October 1973.

4  Shirley Hazzard to EH, 23 February 1975.

5  Brigitta Olubas, *Shirley Hazzard: A Writing Life*, London: Virago, 2022.

6  Shirley Hazzard to EH, 29 August 1974.

7  EH to Shirley Hazzard, 25 March 1974.

8  EH to Shirley Hazzard, 14 July 1974

9  EH private note on Shirley Hazzard, files of Michael Heyward.

**9. THE MILES FRANKLIN AFFAIR**

1   The Miles Franklin Award for books published in 1966 was judged and announced in 1967

2   David Marr, *Patrick White: A Life*, Milsons Point: Random House, 1991.

3   Peter Pierce, 'Sunshine and shambles: The Peter Mathers papers', *The La Trobe Journal*, No. 83, May 2009.

4   *The Sydney Morning Herald*, 21 May 1966.

5   Marr, *Patrick White*, 1991.

6   Margaret Dick to *Australian Book Review*, 22 April 1967 (published in *ABR*, vol. 6, no. 7, May 1967, p. 113).

7   Judah Waten to Margaret Dick, 15 May 1967.

8   EH interview with de Berg, 1967.

9   Elizabeth Harrower, 'Australia', *The Kenyon Review*, vol. 31, no. 4, 1969, pp. 479–85.

**10. CRISIS OF CONFIDENCE**

1   EH interview with author, 2012.

2   'Goodbye to the rent and Diamond Head' includes written comments by Elizabeth Harrower in Helen Frizell, 'Data', *The Sydney Morning Herald* 31 October 1968.

3   EH to Gay Alcorn, 'Other people have an interest in your not writing…', *The Age*, 6 May 2012.

4   EH interview with Davidson, 1980.

**11. LOVERS AND FRIENDS**

1   EH to Margaret Dick, 9 August 1972.

2   Grant, *Kylie Tennant*, pp. 44, 128.

3   Ibid.

4   Kylie Tennant used the phrase a 'domestic tyrant' in her 1986 memoir, *The Missing Heir*, p. 144.

5   Susan Wyndham, 'Elizabeth Harrower: Nearly 90 and still dangerous', *The Australian*, 3 February 2018.

6   EH to Margaret Dick, 9 August 1972.

7   Margaret Dick to EH, 14 July 1972.

**12. LIVING WITH THE NOLANS**

1   EH to Shirley Hazzard, 13 December 1967.

2 EH 'memoir' on Patrick White, 1991–92.

3 Ibid.

4 EH to Margaret Dick, 13 February 1972.

5 EH to Margaret Dick, 15 February 1972.

6 EH to Margaret Dick, 7 May 1972.

7 EH to Shirley Hazzard, 1974 (possibly 26 August).

8 Pre-production interview with EH for the documentary *Mask and Memory: Sidney Nolan*, directed by Catherine Hunter, produced by the Art Gallery of NSW and Catherine Hunter Productions, 4 June 2009.

9 EH to Tom Carment, 26 April 1999.

10 EH to Shirley Hazzard, 26 April 1972.


**13. HUNTERS HILL: MOVING ON**

1 EH interview with author, 2012.

2 Lewis Rodd to Mavis Cribb, 24 March 1973.

3 EH to Shirley Hazzard, 20 March 1973.

4 EH to Shirley Hazzard, 22 July 1973.

5 Geoffrey Lehmann interview with author, 2024.


**14. GOUGH AND ELIZABETH**

1 Gavin Souter, 'Data', *The Sydney Morning Herald*, 25 October 1966.

2 Giuffrè, *A Writing Life*, 1985.

3 Ibid.

4 Alcorn, 'Other people have an interest', 2012.

5 EH 'memoir' on Patrick White, 1991–92.

6 Patrick White, *Flaws in the Glass: A Self-Portrait*, London: Jonathan Cape, 1981.

7 EH to Shirley Hazzard, 12 September 1984.


**15. OTHER PEOPLE'S LIVES**

1 Tennant, *The Missing Heir*, p. 163.

2 Kylie Tennant, 'Murder Mountain' (unfinished), quoted in Grant, *Kylie Tennant*, 2006, Chapter 4, p. 115.

3 EH to Shirley Hazzard, 10 June 1976.

4 EH to Shirley Hazzard, 12 July 1976.

5 Giuffrè, *A Writing Life*, 1985.

6   EH report on Alexander Mackie residency, 1978.

7   Frances McInherney's essay on *The Watch Tower* is regarded as an important and influential analysis. It was originally published in the feminist journal *Hecate* in 1983 and again in editor Carole Ferrier's *Gender Politics and Fiction* (UQP, 1985).

8   Nola Margaret Adams, 'A Dark Realism: The fiction of Elizabeth Harrower', Master of Arts, UWA, December 1982.

9   EH to the Steegs, 16 April 1984.

10  'Life for murder of man killed in fall', *The Sydney Morning Herald*, 21 December 1978.

11  Tennant, *The Missing Heir*, 1986, p. 162.

12  Patricia Rolfe, 'Kylie tells all and heads for a hollow log', *The Sun Herald*, 6 April 1986.

13  EH to Shirley Hazzard, 15 March 1983.

14  Dorothy Green 'Review of *The Novels of Kylie Tennant* by Margaret Dick,' *Australian Literary Studies*, vol. 2, no. 4, 1966.


## 16. PATRICK WHITE: THE GOOD, THE BAD AND THE UGLY

1   Marr, *Patrick White*, 1991.

2   EH interview with Susan Wyndham, 'Ahead of her time but rewards flow 30 years after last novel', *The Sydney Morning Herald*, 9 November 1996.

3   EH 'memoir' on Patrick White, 1991–92.

4   EH to Alcorn, 'Other people have an interest'.

5   EH 'memoir' on Patrick White, 1991–92.

6   Ibid.

7   EH to Shirley Hazzard, 20 May 1981.

8   EH to Shirley Hazzard, 29 September 1976.

9   EH 'memoir' on Patrick White, 1991–92.

10  EH email to David Winter, 19 January 2015.

11  David Marr (ed.), *Patrick White: Letters*, Milsons Point: Random House, 1994.

12  EH to Shirley Hazzard, 10 October 1990.


## 17. LIFE AT THE EDGES

1   Don Anderson, 'Out of print, out of mind…', *The Sydney Morning Herald,* 2 December 1988.

2   EH private note on Shirley Hazzard.

3   EH to Bill Cantwell, 26 November 1984.

4   EH private note on Shirley Hazzard.

5   EH 'memoir' on Patrick White, 1991–92.

6   EH to Audrey Blake, 19 February 1989.

7   Angela Bennie, 'A friend of words and writers', *The Sydney Morning Herald*, 16 January 2008.

8   Phelan, *Writing Round the Edges*, 2003.

9   EH to Judah Waten, 25 August 1981.


**18.  COPING IN CREMORNE**

1   Introduction to Cynthia Nolan, *Outback and Beyond,* Angus & Robertson, 1994.

2   EH to Tom Carment, 1 January 1994.

3   EH to Audrey Blake, 17 October 1994.

4   Wyndham, 'Ahead of her time', 1996.

5   EH to Shirley Hazzard, 30 November 1997.

6   EH to Shirley Hazzard 20 August 1995.

7   EH to Shirley Hazzard, 12 December 1999.

8   EH to Tom Carment, 11 October 2000.

9   EH to Shirley Hazzard, 31 October 2000.

10  Susan Sheridan completed her project and in 2011 published *Nine Lives: Women Writers Making Their Mark*, St Lucia: University of Queensland Press, documenting the rise of the women writers who were part of the literary renaissance between the mid-1940s and the 1970s. But Harrower, whose brilliance was never in doubt, had ruled herself out of Sheridan's revision of the traditional view of a male-dominated literary scene in these decades.

11  EH private note on Shirley Hazzard.

12  Olubas, *Shirley Hazzard*, 2022.


**19.  SECOND ACT: *THE WATCH TOWER***

1   Michael Heyward, obituary for EH, *The Australian*, 18 July 2020.

2   EH comments on *In Certain Circles*, March 2014, issued by Text publicist Jane Novak.

3   Salley Vickers, 'Vanity fare', *The Sydney Morning Herald*, 30 June 2012, review of *In Certain Circles* (Text Classics, 2012).

4 EH interview with Adele Oliveira, May 2013.

5 Brigid Rooney and Fiona Morrison, 'Discovering the long prospect', *Southerly* blog, 1 December 2015.

6 EH to Nola Adams, 6 September 1982.

7 Birns, 'A wrong way of being right', 2017.

8 Michelle de Kretser, 'Harrower's things: Objects in *The Watch Tower*' in McMahon and Olubas, *Elizabeth Harrower*.

9 Ibid.

10 In the 1920s, Richard Herbert Kempley had been involved in the well-known Liberty Confectionery College, a scheme under which people made sweets in their homes which were then purchased and sold through a central 'college'. In *The Watch Tower*, Felix Shaw sells his 'factory-produced, homemade chocolates' through a specialty shop in city. Kempley was involved in hotels and liquor; in *The Watch Tower*, Felix Shaw buys an interest in a hotel.

11 Brigitta Olubas and Susan Wyndham, 'Introduction', *Hazzard and Harrower: The Letters*, Sydney: NewSouth Publishing, 2024.

**20. REMEMBERING NEWCASTLE: *THE LONG PROSPECT***

1 Christina Stead, 'A view of Australian fiction', *The National Times*, 18–23 October 1976.

2 James Wood, 'No time for lies', *The New Yorker*, 13 October 2014.

3 'An exclusive story by Elizabeth Harrower', Text website, www.textpublishing.com.au/blog/an-exclusive-story-by-elizabeth-harrower, 9 October 2015.

**21. REMEMBERING SYDNEY: *DOWN IN THE CITY***

1 Delia Falconer, 'Introduction', EH, *Down in the City*, Melbourne: Text Publishing, 2013.

2 Sheridan, 'Bright and wicked', 2014.

**22. THE LOST NOVEL: *IN CERTAIN CIRCLES***

1 EH at Adelaide Festival Writers' Week.

2 EH comments on *In Certain Circles*, March 2014, issued by Text publicist Jane Novak.

3 Wood, 'No time for lies', 2014.

**23.  THE SHORT STORIES: *A FEW DAYS IN THE COUNTRY***

1   Bernadette Brennan, 'Fiction: *A Few Days in the Country and Other Stories* by Elizabeth Harrower', *Australian Book Review*, no. 377, December 2015.

2   John Freeman, 'Elizabeth Harrower in miniature', *The Weekend Australian*, 31 October 2015.

3   EH email to David Winter, 26 November 2015.

4   Press release, 'Voss Literary Prize Winner 2015', issued by the Australian University Heads of English, November 2015.


**24.  FAME AND ACCLAIM**

1   Kate Kellaway, 'On my radar: Ben Whishaw's cultural highlights', *The Guardian*, 8 November 2015.

2   EH to Tom Carment, 27 August 2016.

3   Jason Steger, 'Driving Ms Harrower to Adelaide', *The Age / The Sydney Morning Herald*, 17 July 2020.

4   The publicity for the 2017 Adelaide Festival Writers' Week dedicated to Harrower claimed she was at the first writers' week in 1960. This is incorrect: based on her correspondence with Max Harris, she attended the 1962 event.

# Index

www.ingramcontent.com/pod-product-compliance
Lightning Source LLC
Chambersburg PA
CBHW051437050726
47593CB00005B/1815